3/13

THE MEDIATION DILEMMA

A volume in the series
Cornell Studies in Security Affairs
edited by Robert J. Art, Robert Jervis, and Stephen M. Walt

A list of titles in this series is available at
www.cornellpress.cornell.edu.

The Mediation Dilemma

Kyle Beardsley

CORNELL UNIVERSITY PRESS   ITHACA AND LONDON

Cornell University Press gratefully acknowledges receipt of a subvention from the Emory College of Arts and Sciences and the Laney Graduate School at Emory University, which assisted in the publication of this book.

First published 2011 by Cornell University Press
Printed in the United States of America 35.01

Library of Congress Cataloging-in-Publication Data

Beardsley, Kyle, 1979–
   The mediation dilemma / Kyle Beardsley.
     p. cm. — (Cornell studies in security affairs)
   Includes bibliographical references and index.
   ISBN 978-0-8014-5003-7 (cloth : alk. paper)
   1. Mediation, International.   2. Conflict management.   3. Peace-building.   4. Diplomatic negotiations in international disputes.   5. Pacific settlement of international disputes.   I. Title.   II. Series: Cornell studies in security affairs.
   JZ6045.B43 2011
   327.1'7—dc23   2011021224

To Jessica, my peacemaker

It is as if there had never existed either Voltaire, or Montaigne, or Pascal, or Swift, or Kant, or Spinoza, or hundreds of other writers who have exposed, with great force, the madness and futility of war, and have described its cruelty, immorality and savagery; and, above all, it is as if there had never existed Jesus and his teaching of human brotherhood and love of God and of men. One recalls all this to mind and looks around on what is now taking place, and one experiences horror less at the abominations of war than at that which is the most horrible of all horrors, the consciousness of the impotency of human reason.

Leo Tolstoy, *Letter on the Russo-Japanese War*, 1904

Contents

Acknowledgments

I am grateful for the instutional support provided by the Department of Political Science, the Emory College of Arts and Sciences, and the Laney Graduate School at Emory University. The availability of graduate research assistance, access to library resources, and offer of adequate research leave were instrumental in the completion of this research. Elizabeth Gallu, in the Author Development Program at Emory University, provided especially important feedback on an earlier draft. Nigel Lo provided extensive assistance with data collection and aggregation. The Emory College of Arts and Sciences and the Laney Graduate School generously provided matching subvention funds to offset the costs of publication.

It would not have been possible to complete this book without the feedback and guidance of so many of my colleagues and friends. I am especially indebted to Dan Reiter, Michael Greig, Paul Hensel, Idean Salehyan, Cullen Hendrix, Tobias Böhmelt, Nathan Danneman, Nigel Lo, and Allan Stam for carefully reading earlier versions and suggesting important insights on how to improve the exposition. Holger Schmidt, Kristian Gleditsch, David Lake, Scott Gartner, Jonathan Wilkenfeld, Victor Asal, Sara Mitchell, Isak Svensson, Robert Rauchhaus, Paul Diehl, Cliff Carrubba, Jeff Staton, Eric Reinhardt, David Davis, Drew Linzer, Justin Esarey, and Jeffrey Gersh all served as invaluable sounding boards and sources of guidance on the project. I am also greatly appreciative of the feedback provided at various conferences, invited talks, and workshop presentations by Duncan Snidal, Charles Lipson, Andrew Enterline, Michael Tierney, David Dessler, Birger Heldt, Michael Lund, Stephen Gent, Megan Shannon, David Cunningham, Michael Gilligan, Molly Melin, David Quinn, Bernd Beber, Ambassador Ahmed Maher, Ambassador Aly Maher El Sayed, and Ambassador Michael Sahlin.

I thank Roger Haydon, Karen Laun, Susan Barnett, Julie Nemer, Mahinder Kingra, and the editors of the Cornell Series in Security Affairs for their poignant comments and for their assistance at each stage in the manuscrupt development process. I am grateful for Judith Kip's indexing work.

Finally, I am fortunate to have had boundless support and encouragement from my wife Jessica, parents Robert and Katherine, parents-in-law Conway and Weilie, and siblings-in-law Jonathan, Julie, Jennifer, and Dominic.

I take personal responsibility for any errors or ommisions in the research. Alas, I cannot take responsibility for the state of peace or conflict in our world.

THE MEDIATION
DILEMMA

THE DILEMMA

**Since one of the most promising approaches to the peaceful settle-
ment of disputes is skilful third-party mediation, we, the United
Nations, have a responsibility to "we the peoples" to professionalize
our efforts to resolve conflicts constructively rather than destruc-
tively and to "save succeeding generations from the scourge of war."**

—Ban Ki-moon, Report of the Secretary-General on Enhancing Mediation
and Its Supporting Activities, April 8, 2009

On August 11, 2006, after a month of fighting between Israel and Hizbullah,
the UN Security Council, with the approval of the Israeli and Lebanese leadership, formalized cease-fire arrangements by adopting Resolution 1701. Two days
later, the Israeli ground offensive came to a halt. The cease-fire resulted after
frantic, and frequently competing, U.S. and French mediation efforts. Not even
two weeks earlier, the United States had supported the Israeli use of force and
resisted imposing a cease-fire; meanwhile, most of the rest of the world pushed
for peace. The civilian toll from the hostilities and the loss of confidence in the
ability of Israel to prosecute the war eventually turned the U.S. position and
led this Israeli ally to endorse an end to the fighting. Immediately following the
cease-fire agreement, the United Nations Interim Force in Lebanon (UNIFIL)
and Lebanese troops deployed and maintained a semblance of peace while Israeli
forces withdrew. In the more than four years since the war, the cease-fire has held,
if only tenuously.

Was the rush by the international community to impose a cease-fire between
Israel and Hizbullah in the name of increasing peace in the region worthwhile?
The answer is not straightforward, in that we see the potential for significant
trade-offs. On the one hand, the international pressure did eventually help compel Israel to agree to the cease-fire, even in the middle of a ground offensive. As
a result, the merciless killing and displacement of noncombatants by Hizbullah
rocket attacks and errant Israeli air strikes did end sooner than they otherwise
would have. On the other hand, the peace that exists is perhaps more fragile than
might have been achieved had Israel continued fighting because Hizbullah has

rearmed—becoming much stronger than it was before the war and nearly draw-ing Lebanon into full-scale civil war in 2008—and many in Israel expect a second round with Hizbullah to occur sooner rather than later.[1]

We can imagine one possible scenario that might have transpired without the international pressure for a cease-fire—a clear military stalemate would eventu-ally have emerged after Hizbullah had depleted its rocket caches and its support from the local Lebanese population and after Israel had exhausted its domestic resolve to fight. The immediate negative humanitarian implications of such a course of events are clear. But future peaceful benefits could also have resulted if Israel had lost even more resolve for making further incursions into Leba-non and yet had pushed deep enough into Lebanon to more severely disrupt the ability for Hizbullah to deploy its arsenal of Katyusha rockets within striking distance of northern Israel. Although it is doubtful that such a scenario would have produced a permanent solution, it is likely that it would have significantly lengthened the time until it became feasible to renew the conflict. That the medi-ated cease-fire produced an outcome potentially more tenuous than this stale-mate scenario—as well as other possible outcomes that it also precluded, such as an Israeli victory, a Hizbullah victory, or a bilateral settlement—demonstrates the trade-off between short-term peace and long-term stability that combatants and the international community frequently face when considering external assistance in pressing for peaceful settlement. As in the 2006 Lebanon War, out-side involvement often increases the prospects for a short-term agreement and answers the humanitarian imperative that the international community should not stand idle while senseless killing rages unabated. But also, as in the Lebanon War, outside involvement can encourage temporary fixes and make the prospects for long-term peace less certain.

The Wisdom of Solomon or the Folly of Paris?

Peace tends to be fleeting and fragile in many parts of the world. At any given point in the past three decades, there have been at least twenty armed conflicts going on at the same time in the international system.[2] Conflict remains a perva-sive element of international politics in large part because most of the militarized contests that we presently observe have been going on for multiple years and have

---

1. See Hirst (2010, 382–93, 426); Harel and Issacharoff (2008, 261).
2. The definition of *armed conflict* comes from the Uppsala Conflict Data Program (UCDP)/ Peace Research Institute Oslo (PRIO) data and entails at least twenty-five battlefield fatalities in the year of observation (Gleditsch et al. 2002).

a history of relapse (Hewitt 2009). That is, once begun, armed conflicts tend to endure, and once ended, they tend to recur.

Conflict also does not occur in isolation. The outbreak, and even the potential outbreak, of violence affects much more than the disputing parties. Outside actors with interests in the conflict—security, economic, or moral—often become involved and shape the trajectories of the conflict and peace processes. One of the most common means of third-party involvement is mediation, which is the consensual, nonviolent, and nonbinding involvement of a third party in conflict management and resolution processes.[3] When actors cannot resolve an issue through direct negotiations, they often consult a mediator. Half of all interstate wars and one-third of all international crises since World War I have involved mediation.[4]

The frequent adoption of mediation in international conflict is presumably predicated on the notion that mediation tends to improve the prospects for peace.[5] Is such an expectation justified? If armed conflicts really tend to endure and recur, then the task of third-party peacemakers is twofold. First, the third parties must help the belligerents abandon the status quo of armed hostilities. Second, they must foster a new relationship between the combatants that precludes the return to violence. Achieving these two objectives simultaneously is the fundamental problem of peacemaking. As I demonstrate throughout this book, mediation in international conflict, especially when the third parties use leverage, excels in providing short-term peaceful dividends; however, these often come at the expense of the second objective, producing more fragile long-term arrangements than might have been achieved bilaterally. When combatants rely more on a third party to produce a hasty settlement, they become less capable of maintaining the peace by themselves over time. Mediation can decrease the incentives, at least temporarily, for belligerents to make the tough decisions necessary to fully resolve their conflicts. Instead of durable resolutions that could result from more challenging bargaining processes, intermediaries are prone to push for what is more easily attainable and to promote incomplete and watered-down peace terms that put off the most difficult choices to the future.

---

3. A widely cited definition of *mediation* is "a reactive process of conflict management whereby parties seek the assistance of, or accept an offer of help from, an individual, group, or organization to change their behavior, settle their conflict, or resolve their problem without resorting to physical force or invoking the authority of the law" (Bercovitch and Houston 1996, 13). In chapter 2, I present a more detailed discussion of what mediation entails.

4. These figures are based on the International Crisis Behavior (ICB) data set described in chapter 3.

5. Even when actors participate in a mediated peace process merely for show, as discussed later, they are mimicking the behavior of others who expect this to be an effective form of peacemaking.

A quick analysis (expanded on later) of all international crises since 1918 indicates there is a trade-off between the short-term and long-term effects of mediation. In the short run, we see that nearly half of all mediated crises ended with some sort of formal agreement, an indicator of successful conflict management, whereas only 15 percent of unmediated crises ended in a formal agreement. But the effect of mediation in the long run is not so grand—52 percent of mediated crises recurred and 50 percent of unmediated crises recurred. We get an even stronger indication that mediation actually makes peace less stable in the long run when we examine former combatants that had experienced peace for at least ten years. When mediation had previously occurred in this subset, 34 percent of such combatants ended up relapsing, whereas only 21 percent of them relapsed when mediation did not occur in their previous crisis.

The Rwandan genocide demonstrates the alarming potential for mediators to increase the fragility of post-conflict peace. The Rwandan Civil War resulted in a mediated power-sharing agreement known as the Arusha Accords after substantial cajoling from international actors who promised a level of enforcement that could not be fulfilled. The accords were never implemented and, instead, gave way to genocide. It is easy to lament the abandonment by the international community of the post-Arusha peace and its neglect during the bloodshed. Although *inaction* certainly characterizes the international involvement during the genocide, we must not forget that it was the *action* of the international community, in the form of heavy-handed mediation and unsustainable commitments, that was in no small part culpable for the fragility of the accords in the first place. We return to the failure of the Arusha process in greater detail in chapter 6; the point here is simply that the stakes involved as third parties struggle to set implementation on the right course can be quite high.

Despite the potential for mediation to struggle in securing a robust long-term peace, the onset of conflict in the international system is frequently accompanied by state leaders and diplomats offering their services to broker a deal before hostilities escalate further. At worst, they hope, their mediation initiatives will buy a brief interlude of peace; at best, their services could provide the key ingredient that resolves the conflict permanently and perhaps even be worthy of a Nobel Peace Prize. Yet this cavalier attitude toward mediation belies its double-edged nature of both substantial benefits and substantial risks.

Indeed, practitioners sometimes disagree on the appropriate level of third-party involvement, indicating that a systematic study of mediation trade-offs is worthwhile. A central argument explored here is that mediators employing substantial leverage on the combatants will struggle the most to achieve long-term peace. Some practitioners therefore urge caution in the use of third-party leverage, which might actually disrupt the ability of stakeholders to reach a sustainable settlement. For example, Martti Ahtisaari, in his Nobel Lecture on December 10, 2008, states, "[T]here tends to be too much focus on the mediators. With that we are disempowering the parties to the conflict and creating the wrong impression that peace comes from the outside. The only people that can make peace are the parties to the conflict, and just as they are responsible for the conflict and its consequences, so should they be given responsibility and recognition for the peace."

Yet the community of diplomats on the front lines of the peacemaking processes is not of one mind about the risks of heavy-handed mediation. Many practitioners stress the importance of strong third-party involvement and are comfortable blurring the line between mediation and humanitarian intervention while imposing peace. Such practitioners affirm Frederick the Great's maxim that "diplomacy without force is like an orchestra without a score." At the end of his memoirs on the successful conclusion of the Dayton Accords that ended the war in Bosnia, Richard Holbrooke calls for strong U.S. involvement to play an important role in pushing for peace:

> *There will be other Bosnias in our lives*—areas where early outside involvement can be decisive, and American leadership will be required. The world's richest nation, one that presumes to great moral authority, cannot simply make worthy appeals to conscience and call on others to carry the burden. The world will look to Washington for more than rhetoric the next time we face a challenge to peace. (1998, 369; emphasis in the original)

Many practitioners also rely on the heavy-handed use of positive inducements, as seen in November 2010 when the United States offered Israel, to no avail, twenty F-35 aircraft and greater support in the UN Security Council in return for a ninety-day settlement-construction moratorium during which peace talks could reconvene with the Palestinians.

For those who see little downside to heavy-handed third-party peacemaking, the mediator resembles a benevolent arbitrator, not unlike King Solomon standing in judgment of the two prostitutes, with the potential to forcefully find a permanent resolution that the parties could not reach on their own. The reality is that too often mediation resembles the Judgment of Paris, in which the prince of Troy successfully mediated among Aphrodite, Athena, and Hera in their dispute over who was fairest. But in so doing, choosing Aphrodite and her bribe of having the most beautiful woman in the world love him, Paris started a sequence of events that increased strife among both gods and humans. Instead of settling the competition among the goddesses, Paris's decision provoked Athena and Hera to unite against Aphrodite in their support for the Greeks in the Trojan War, with his taking of Helen providing the catalyst for that conflict. This story provides an admonition about the unintended consequences of third-party involvement that I explore at length in this book. Somewhat unrelated to the role of mediation in this story, the imagery of Paris accepting Aphrodite's bribe also drives home an additional warning about mediation—that actors will often trade utility in the future for utility in the present. Paris struck a deal whose consequences were quite similar to the deal made by Dr. Faustus with the devil, in which he would enjoy twenty-four years of unlimited power—and incidentally the ability to conjure up Helen of Troy herself—in exchange for an eternity in hell. By analogy, if mediation does trade some potential for long-term stability in return for short-term peace, is it something of a Faustian bargain?

To be sure, even though mediation typically involves a trade-off, this trade-off, from the perspectives of both the adversaries and the concerned observer, often is still worth accepting when the alternatives are considered. For example, even with the lingering dysfunctions in Bosnian politics, Richard Holbrooke did relatively well with his heavy-handed approach at Dayton; nevertheless, we would be mistaken to universally adopt this as a model for peacemaking. Belligerents and third parties alike must recognize the trade-off inherent in mediation so that their conflict management choices can be made prudently, unlike the deals struck by the hapless Paris and Faustus. Mediation is thus something that peace advocates should neither always adopt nor always avoid. It should be applied carefully with the eyes of the involved parties wide open to all its potential consequences, both good and ill.

The Argument

Careful consideration of the potential effects of mediation suggests an important dilemma. Most starkly, reliance on mediation risks the relapse of conflict after a brief interlude of peace, whereas avoidance of mediation risks imminent brutality as the scourge of war runs its course. If mediation occurs, the international community can play an active and often necessary role in pushing for the cessation of hostilities, but this itself frequently exacerbates long-term instability. Third-party conflict management, especially when the mediator employs substantial leverage, can be inimical to enduring peace. The alternative to mediation, however, is not strictly a better way to reach peace. Outside actors can remain aloof in hopes the combatants will be able to reach a sustainable accord on their own; meanwhile, people perish and resources are destroyed. Agreements that are reached without assistance will be more likely to be self-enforcing—when the interests of the principal disputants alone are enough to sustain a commitment to the terms—but the physical, political, and economic costs of getting there can be enormous.

Third-party involvement through mediation can shape the prospects for peaceful bargains for the better in the short run and for the worse in the long run. In the short run, mediators can provide incentives that expand the set of mutually acceptable alternatives, pledge post-conflict security guarantees, help the combatants to recognize appropriate offers, and give leaders political cover for concessions. But in the long run, the involvement of an intermediary can introduce artificial incentives for peace that do not persist, interfere with the ability for the actors to fully understand the bargaining environment, and enable the belligerents to stall in hopes of gaining an advantage during the peace process. The inclusion of an external peacemaker is thus often a necessary ingredient for short-term progress, but intermediaries can also make future renegotiation more likely and more difficult. So, although disputants typically seek mediation as a means of reducing their immediate barriers to successful bargaining, they do so at the risk of decreasing the durability of any peaceful arrangements that are reached.

The dilemma is not simply a matter of whether mediation should be employed at all but also a matter of how much involvement third parties should have when they do mediate. Third-party leverage exaggerates the trade-off because such intrusive involvement is best able to shape the short-term incentives for peace and least able to facilitate durable self-enforcing settlements. In the midst of substantial leverage, especially when the leverage creates a false sense of security or is used to level the playing field and create an artificial stalemate, the disputants' degree of satisfaction with their terms of peace will be even more prone to falter as third parties disengage themselves from the peace processes over time. In addition, heavy-handed third parties are more likely to interrupt the ability for the actors to learn from the dispute environment and to learn how best to engage one another directly. As one example, Shibley Telhami describes the trade-off that Henry Kissinger contributed to in his manipulation of the bargaining environment in the wake of the 1973 October (Egyptian-Israeli) War: "But while Kissinger's shuttle diplomacy succeeded in separating the forces in a fashion that reduced the risk of a new surprise war, it also contributed to the eventual stalemate of the negotiations. By defusing the crisis situation through a partial and technical agreement, a historical moment of opportunity for a more lasting settlement may have been lost" (1990, 68).

Without leverage, third parties will be less able to move things forward in the short run, but when they do, the peace will be relatively more likely to endure. Indeed, as we see in chapter 5, the expected probability of a crisis recurring one year after it ended decreases by 68 percent when heavy-handed mediation occurs during the crisis and by only 37 percent when the role of the mediator is limited to lighter forms of facilitation and formulation. In contrast, in the long run we see that the expected probability of a crisis recurring at ten years after it ended is nearly four times greater when leverage is used; there is no statistically significant increase when lighter forms of mediation are used. That is, unlike heavy-handed mediation, lighter mediation does not lead to a stark pacifying effect in the short run, but it also does not contribute to much of an increase in conflict relapse in the long run.

Patience and coordination are two additional factors that can condition the trade-off between short-term peace and long-term stability. Patience refers to the ideal situation in which the combatants do not feel rushed to make a decision that might not be self-enforcing, as when the leadership is stable and the costs of conflict are not unbearable. When actors have the ability to carefully deliberate and find resolutions that are likely to endure, mediation can result in long-term peace. For example, the Camp David Accords and subsequent Egyptian-Israeli peace treaty, which have been followed by stable interstate relations between Israel and Egypt, were reached after five years of relative peace between the two actors and not during a period of acute crisis in which decisions had to be made in haste.

Coordination comes into play because third-party influence will be less likely to fade prematurely if it is clear who is responsible for maintaining the needed incentives for a durable settlement. Single mediators with simple decision-making structures will thus do best in fostering long-term peace arrangements. Multiple mediators and mediators with competing decision-making nodes will struggle the most to provide a lasting and coherent commitment and to otherwise foster terms of settlement that are self-enforcing. For example, the abundance of and competition among various mediators—including most prominently Russia, Turkey, Iran, and the Organization for Security and Co-operation in Europe (OSCE)—has contributed to the difficulty of moving the Nagorno-Karabakh conflict between Azerbaijan and Armenia beyond a stalemated cease-fire and toward a more permanent resolution.[6]

Note that the dilemma at hand emerges most strongly from the perspectives of peace advocates in the broader international community. Such advocates normatively hope for peace in general, and the trade-off between short-term bargaining success and long-term stability becomes a dilemma as they make their choices on which course of action is best in a particular conflict. The actual mediation participants could find the dilemma less pronounced from their perspectives.

---

6. Wendy Betts (1999) makes this point directly.

As we will see, both disputant and third-party interests vary and may or may not have much concern for long-term stability. To the extent that the durability of peace does enter into their decision calculus, they must consider the difficult choice between smoother short-term conflict management and more precarious long-term conflict resolution.

Motivation in Context

We must understand conflict recurrence if we are to explain clearly the contentious politics in the world today. The relapse of conflict between former belligerents is a substantial source of international instability; actors with a lengthy history of conflict with one another are more likely to fight again. In fact, almost all the onsets of armed conflict in the past few years have been conflict recurrences (Hewitt 2009).[7] Yet recurrence is not solely a function of the post-conflict environment; the process by which a previous conflict episode ends can greatly affect the proclivity for its recurrence. More precisely, how peace is made informs whether peace can be kept.

Implications for Other Forms of Third-Party Involvement

Although other forms of third-party involvement can also give rise to this dilemma between action and inaction, my focus in this book is on mediation because its permissive and nonbinding nature makes it an interesting tool to explore in terms of how it can have a meaningful impact on conflict processes. It is more readily evident why nonconsensual and binding third-party involvements might affect the prospects for peace. Is it possible that a process that relies on permissive diplomacy can also shape both the short-term and long-term potentials for resolution? And if mediation can ultimately make peace more fragile, why would parties willingly enter into the process?

Nonetheless, the mediation dilemma is relevant to the broader discussion about whether there is an optimal level of intervention, writ large. Generally speaking, would a greater involvement of the international community in disputes increase global peace and security? Those who answer in the affirmative frequently decry the lack of international response to the abject brutality in many of the world's conflicts. To them, peace, stability, and the security of noncombatants are public goods that should be pursued and defended by a more active interna-

---

7. On this point of conflict history, a rich literature exists on enduring rivalries in interstate conflict (Diehl and Goertz 2000).

tional community, bolstered by a stronger United Nations or some other form of global governance. Without some sort of third-party push for peace, many conflicts ostensibly will continue to destroy and only cease when one side has completely defeated the other. Even if an assisted peace is unsuccessful or leads to only a brief pause in violence, this camp argues that it is still worth continually trying in the hope that the natural course of the conflict can be shortened or softened.

On the other side, some argue that it is generally better to let actors "fight it out" than to intervene. Edward Luttwak is the most vituperative critic of third-party intervention in international conflicts. He argues, "absent compelling reasons, wars should not be interrupted by outsiders, blocking their process of transformation" (Luttwak 2001, 265).[8] From this perspective, intervention is inadvisable because outside involvement and the artificial incentives it introduces can impede the combatants from finding an arrangement that can be maintained in the absence of third-party pressure. Intervention expends resources and effort on something that tends to make things worse. Richard Betts presents a more specific critique of *impartial* intervention, which "blocks peace by doing enough to keep either belligerent from defeating the other, but not enough to make them stop trying" (1994, 21). Greg Mills and Terence McNamee, in lamenting the state of peacebuilding in the UN system, similarly write, "our approach to peacebuilding must be sensitive to the oft-neglected fact that sometimes getting involved only makes matters worse" (2009, 59). It is also worth noting that international law tends to protect state sovereignty, except in rather extreme situations, which is another popular justification for third parties to holster their interventionalism.

The mediation dilemma considered here also has some parallels to the potential perverse incentives that humanitarian intervention can create—by promising support to one side as a means to deter hostility by the other side, an outside actor might actually enable the protected group to be more aggressive and move the conflict away from peace.[9] Robert Rauchhaus (2009), echoing Glenn Snyder's (1984) earlier work, has recently explored such incentives in humanitarian intervention in the context of what he calls the commitment dilemma. When the third parties are strong in their commitments, they risk encouraging misbehavior by those being assisted; when the third parties attempt to hedge their commitments, they risk failing to deter major hostilities by the dominant actor. This tension facing the would-be humanitarian intervener is similar to that of the would-be mediator considered in this book—no or weak involvement risks allowing con-

---

8. See also Luttwak (1999, 21).

9. Alan Kuperman (2008) and Peter Uvin (1998) warn against the potential for humanitarian intervention and development assistance to make conflict situations worse through increased moral hazard. Robert Rauchhaus (2009) argues that the problem of humanitarian intervention is more one of adverse selection than moral hazard.

flict to continue unabated, whereas heavy-handed involvement risks unsettling the conditions that are needed for the combatants to reach a sustainable peace.

At the heart of the debate is a tension between a duty to aid immediately the afflicted and a desire to avoid hasty action that could jeopardize more permanent international stability. Interventions are often obligatory in the former and only sparingly justified in the latter. This is the nature of the dilemma. The international community, especially under the UN system, frequently has the obligation to defend human security using diplomatic resources to push for peace, but in doing so the outside involvement can make long-term peace less stable and potentially even more violent.

We might see this dilemma as a catch-22 in which the international community can do no right. It can either intervene and contribute to long-term instability or not intervene and be complicit in whatever brutality follows. But this book is not a call for general pessimism regarding third-party assistance in conflict management. Instead, I contend that, even when the trade-off is unavoidable, intervention can still be worthwhile because the short-term benefits can outweigh the long-term costs. I also elucidate how, in specific cases, the dilemma can be more or less circumvented such that international involvement can both attenuate the immediate threats to human security and maintain the long-run prospects for peace. The key point is that external assistance in peacemaking is often a fundamental ingredient for international cooperation but such assistance must be carried out carefully and prudently.

Other Implications for Existing Scholarship

The dilemma between mediating and not mediating is not unlike the dilemma that the international community faces between encouraging some sort of settlement or stalemate and advocating total victory by one of the belligerents. Existing scholarship indicates that peace is often most stable after one side has achieved victory but is less stable otherwise.[10] Given that total victory often involves unacceptable amounts of bloodshed and the risk of genocide, potential interveners have the difficult choice of pursuing a course of action that is likely to breed further episodes of conflict or encouraging a course of action that can create a humanitarian disaster.[11] We can add an additional dimension to this discussion

---

10. With regard to interstate conflict, see Lo, Hashimoto, and Reiter (2008); Fortna (2004c); Werner (1999b); Werner and Yuen (2005). With regard to intrastate conflict, see Licklider (1995); Toft (2009); Walter (2002).

11. Note that Toft (2009) finds that negotiated settlements and cease-fires in civil wars tend to result in more fatalities than military victories. So the decision to intervene on humanitarian grounds is not clearcut.

by analyzing if and when third parties should consider avoiding mediation and letting the belligerents find their own way.

In this book, I also build on earlier studies of the shortcomings of assisted peacemaking. Jeffrey Rubin, for example, warns that "because of the disruptive effects of a third party's inclusion, that party may not only facilitate dispute resolution, but also may hinder it" because a third party "may have the effect of disrupting . . . productive momentum and slowing the pace of settlement" (1981, 7). As another example, Alan Kuperman (1996) faults mediation in creating the incentives in Rwanda that led to genocide. Suzanne Werner and Amy Yuen (2005) similarly demonstrate that agreements that follow substantial third-party pressure are less stable than agreements reached more "naturally." They note that third parties are primarily useful in keeping peace that the combatants have already achieved but that peacemaking attempts by third parties tend to destabilize relations.[12]

We get a sense, indirectly, of a trade-off between the short- and long-term effects of mediation when examining the extant empirical evidence of the consequences of mediation. Studies have found inconsistent results connecting mediation to peaceful outcomes.[13] The disparity in the findings is striking because it is not simply that there are some studies with statistically significant results and some without. Instead, we see that some studies observe that mediation has a statistically significant positive effect on conflict resolution, whereas other studies show a statistically significant negative effect. It is doubtful that such inconsistencies can be explained by variations in basic statistical procedures. There must be more systematic explanations.

These seemingly inconsistent results can be explained by differences in the definition of *success*. The studies that find a positive correlation between mediation and peaceful outcomes assess short-term peaceful measures such as cease-fires, formal agreements, and de-escalation. In contrast, many studies that do not find a positive correlation between mediation and peaceful outcomes define *success* as the absence of conflict following a cease-fire or settlement, a more long-

---

12. Other work has similarly considered how third parties can interfere with the combatants' incentives to fully resolve their conflicts. See, for example, Greig and Diehl (2005); Gurses, Rost, and McLeod (2008). Lo, Hashimoto, and Reiter (2008), however, show that Werner and Yuen's (2005) findings are not robust.

13. Studies using quantitative analyses that find mediation having a positive effect include Dixon (1996); Beardsley et al. (2006); Wilkenfeld et al. (2003, 2005); Frazier and Dixon (2006); Regan and Stam (2000); Regan and Aydin (2006); Walter (2002); Svensson (2007b); Rauchhaus (2006). Some studies using experimental research designs that find a positive effect are Carnevale and Pruitt (1992); Wilkenfeld et al. (2003, 2005). In contrast, studies that find that cease-fires after nonbinding third-party pressure are either no more durable or are actually shorter lived than uninterrupted conflict bargaining include Werner (1999b); Werner and Yuen (2005); Gartner and Bercovitch (2006); Mitchell and Hensel (2007); Lo, Hashimoto, and Reiter (2008).

term measure. That these two measures have different relationships with media-tion suggests that third-party conflict management influences the bargaining environment differently depending on the relevant time frame. The literature is thus generally consistent in demonstrating that what is true about mediation efficacy in the short run is not necessarily true in the long run.[14] The theoretical framework and analysis presented here better enable these existing studies to speak to one another.

Even though some of the existing literature has demonstrated the risks of outside involvement, we must not go too far in the negative assessment of the entire enterprise of third-party intervention. If we did, it would be difficult to explain why assisted peacemaking is such a common conflict management vehi-cle without some positive peaceful effects. The approach here highlights both the benefits and risks of outside involvement, lest we lose track of why it occurs at all. Intermediaries can enable leaders to make prudent concessions, along with other efficiency gains in their bargaining processes; these are some of the key benefits of third-party conflict management. Even though most of these gains tend to be temporary, they are often much more attractive than the alternative of total war, especially when the actors can pursue mediation again in the future should peace prove unstable. I thus analyze the negative as well as the positive consequences of third-party conflict management to fully understand its role in conflict bargaining.

Finally, this book is relevant to the growing literature on mediation styles and their outcomes.[15] In particular, the theoretical framework and findings I adduce call into question whether leverage is a tactic that should be universally applied whenever possible. Alastair Smith and Allan Stam (2003), in constructing a theo-retical model of mediation and peacekeeping, posit that altering the material costs and benefits of the combatants is the only means by which third parties can increase the prospects of a peaceful settlement. Timothy Sisk (2008) similarly argues that power mediation is often the only way for third parties to resolve civil wars. Likewise, William Zartman and Saadia Touval write, "Leverage is the ticket to mediation—third parties are only accepted as mediators if they are likely to produce an agreement or help the parties out of a predicament, and for this they usually need leverage" (1985, 40).[16] This view goes along with the supposition that third parties that devote more resources to conflict resolution are more likely to realize their peaceful goals.

---

14. See also Gartner and Melin (2009).

15. For empirical analyses of mediation styles, see Bercovitch, Anagnoson, and Wille (1991); Bercovitch and Houston (1996); Bercovitch (1986); Beardsley et al. (2006); Svensson (2007b); Quinn et al. (2006); Wilkenfeld et al. (2003, 2005); Rauchhaus (2006,2011); Schrodt and Gerner (2004).

16. Also see Touval (1994).

The presumed relationship between substantial leverage and peaceful out-comes, however, warrants some scrutiny. It is not clear that third parties will always enjoy positive returns from each additional unit of effort put into managing conflict. As Ban Ki-moon warns, "Evidence suggests that the ill-conceived or simplistic use of externally imposed leverage often causes resistance and backfires, especially when parties believe that conceding to such pressure threatens important values, such as their sense of identity, honor, or commitment to a goal, or creates a loss of face with constituents" (2009, 10).[17] Spanning these perspectives, I posit here that leverage does comparatively well in the short run but that its use also poses an even greater risk to long-term stability.

Project Scope

In what follows, I develop the theoretical basis for the mediation dilemma. The theoretical framework centers on a rational bargaining model of war and deduces the impact that mediation can have on information asymmetries and commitment problems. The framework also includes domestic political dynamics to consider the various pressures on foreign policymakers to resolve or continue their conflicts. From such a framework, we can form observable and testable implications of the effect of mediation on both the immediate and future prospects for peace. Perhaps most important, we can anticipate the situations in which the short-term benefits and long-term risks of mediation are minimized or maximized.

The theoretical discussion also recognizes the potential that mediation may be intended for ends other than peace. Participants may have sincere desires for conflict abatement as well as insincere incentives to use the peace process to stall or to garner international and domestic support. By considering the disparate short-term benefits of mediation, we are able to see both why mediation is an essential element in reducing conflict suffering when the disputants need assistance in reaching at least a temporary bargaining arrangement and why intermediaries must be cautious in their efforts when the disputants strive to manipulate the process for stronger bargaining positions.

Although the argument has many implications for conflict management practitioners, the approach here is firmly one of positive social science. The theory is deductive and speaks to existing scholarship in security and peace studies.

---

17. Robert Rauchhaus (2006, 2011) also finds that coercive intervention is not well suited to creating incentives for peace, whereas lighter forms of mediation are better able to reduce the levels of uncertainty that plague dispute resolution.

I take the arguments to their logical and testable conclusions as a means of confirming the underlying theoretical framework. In this way, the chapters present a number of observable implications from the theory that are then tested empirically. The quantitative portions of the book allow for the generalizability of the findings and the ability to both hold constant possible confounding variables and capture endogenous processes. Too often, however, quantitative approaches get lost in searching for statistical significance and unbiased inferences, paying scant attention to more substantive implications. To avoid this, I save the details of the regression analyses for the appendix. The presentation of the results in the chapters focuses on graphical depictions of the effects.

A number of illustrative case studies are discussed throughout the book to demonstrate how the arguments apply to historical examples. The case studies also provide more depth and detail of what mediation entails. Some readers might note that the bargaining framework used here excludes mediator skill as a factor driving peace processes. Although skill does indeed matter because mediators are actual people with varying abilities and positions, and are not perfectly interchangeable, I leave this factor for further analysis. So, even though the theory is unable to form predictions about precisely how the tangible and intangible characteristics of the individual people at the negotiating table matter, the case studies do provide a window to the on-the-ground efforts by some of the most noteworthy peacemakers.

The purpose of the case studies is not just to show that mediation, especially when leverage is used, struggles to foster long-term peace. The outcomes of the cases vary so that we might better understand under which circumstances the dilemma is minimized. For example, when Theodore Roosevelt mediated the termination of the Russo-Japanese War at Portsmouth in 1905, the agreement was relatively successful in both the short and long terms. Roosevelt's reluctance to be intrusive during the negotiations demonstrates, in part, how peace has a better chance of being self-enforcing when third parties target their use of leverage selectively and carefully.

A second example of long-term success, the step-by-step mediation by Henry Kissinger that produced the disengagement agreements following the 1973 October War and Jimmy Carter's efforts in 1978 and 1979 that produced the Camp David Accords and Egyptian-Israeli peace treaty, illustrates that substantial leverage can produce a durable peace if the third parties sustain the pressure over time. But the Kissinger and Carter mediation successes regarding the Egyptian-Israeli bilateral relations stand in contrast to their progress on a more comprehensive peace. Both attempts involved substantial leverage, but the leverage was sustained only in the former. Although an important framework was established at Camp David regarding the settlement of the more complex issues of the Palestinian question and the permanent status of the occupied territories, this framework was mostly abandoned, in part because political realities prevented the United States from sustaining its push for progress. The U.S. mediation in the Middle East from 1973 to 1979 thus demonstrates that leverage can foster long-term peace if it is maintained but can lead to less stable relations when the leverage quickly attenuates after the agreement. It turns out that the sustained U.S. involvement with regard to the Israel-Egypt peace is fairly exceptional but that the weak follow-through on the comprehensive peace is more typical of third-party engagement in difficult peace processes.

The final major illustrative case considered is Jimmy Carter's mediation as a private citizen between the Democratic People's Republic of Korea (DPRK or North Korea) and the United States in 1994. This case demonstrates the trade-off well because Carter's mediation helped produce the Agreed Framework, which froze the DPRK plutonium program for eight years but failed after the United States discovered that the DPRK had begun a covert uranium-enrichment program. The incentives for the 1994 agreement, skillfully manipulated by Carter, were simply too far removed from the incentives in 2002. Moreover, this case demonstrates the role of insincere motives in contributing to the short-term and long-term trade-off, in that it appears that the DPRK had intended to use the Agreed Framework only as an opportunity to stall.

In addition to being prominent examples of Nobel Peace Prize laureates at work, these illustrative cases were chosen because of their similarities in involving interstate crises, the occurrence of mediation, and the achievement of short-term success. The variation in long-term outcomes allows us to observe some of the factors that maximize or minimize the trade-off. In this way, the case of Roosevelt's mediation in the Russo-Japanese War demonstrates that the absence of substantial leverage, when more is not needed for immediate progress, can foster sustainable peace; the case of U.S. involvement in attaining the Egyptian-Israeli peace treaty demonstrates that continuous involvement over time can yield long-term stability; the case of U.S. involvement in pushing for a more comprehensive peace in the Middle East, in contrast, demonstrates that leverage without follow-through can hinder implementation; and the case of Carter's mediation in North Korea demonstrates the important role of insincere motives in driving the trade-off.

The trade-off at the heart of the mediation dilemma can play out in intrastate conflicts as well; I take this up in chapter 6 with additional illustrative case studies. Intrastate conflicts may be even more prone to the trade-off because implementation is particularly precarious—combatants need to become vulnerable if they are to truly resolve the conflict and share common borders, the security apparatus, and the means of distributing public resources. Third parties can also interfere with the social contract between the rulers and the ruled. In addition, actors have a greater incentive to use mediation for ends other than peace in intrastate disputes. Finally, the involvement of a mediator can complicate problems related to spoiler groups and the competition for legitimacy. I illustrate these dynamics with the cases of Rwanda, the U.S. involvement in Haiti in 1994, Norwegian mediation in Sri Lanka, and the Oslo peace process in the Middle East. The importance of these factors can also be seen through the peacemaking role of the Crisis Management Initiative (CMI) in Aceh, Indonesia, which has experienced a high degree of success in generating a sustainable peace precisely because it was able, by both skill and fortune, to avoid these issues.

In addition to the main arguments of the book, I also provide policy-relevant recommendations that follow from the theory and evidence. The analysis reveals the darker side of third-party conflict management, but my intent is not to encourage a sense of futility concerning third-party involvement in peace processes. Although the trade-off between short-term peace and long-term stability is often unavoidable, the actors involved need to know when those long-term risks are worth taking. In many situations, actors will accept the possibility of future renewed hostilities, especially when those hostilities can be reasonably contained, if they are able to achieve progress on more immediate aims. In other situations, mediation is not mutually net-beneficial to the actors involved because it creates serious vulnerabilities in the post-conflict environment that can lead to massive violence and other severe losses in utility for at least one of the sides. Being able to identify such situations is crucial to improving the practice of third-party conflict management.

NEGOTIATING MEDIATION

> The task of the mediator is to help the parties to open difficult issues and nudge them forward in the peace process. The mediator's role combines those of a ship's pilot, consulting medical doctor, midwife and teacher.

—Martti Ahtisaari, Nobel Lecture, December 10, 2008

What Is Mediation?

There are three necessary components of mediation in a conflict: (1) the mutually permitted involvement of a third party, (2) third-party reliance on nonviolent tactics, and (3) an absence of authority for the third party to make a binding resolution. It is worth noting that some scholars and practitioners draw a distinction between mediation and facilitation or conciliation.[1] Because facilitation meets these criteria and because it is often difficult to distinguish facilitation from other mediation activities, my approach here, like many other notable studies, includes it as a specific style of mediation.[2] At various points, the theory and analysis later will consider the different effects of mediation with leverage and mediation without leverage, which can be thought of as a distinction between pure facilitation and more heavy-handed mediation. At the other end of the spectrum, some instances of mediation blur the criterion of nonviolent tactics. For example, both Richard Holbrooke's mediation of the Dayton Accords and the U.S.-led mediation of Jean-Bertrand Aristide's return to Haiti in 1994 involved a combination of traditional diplomacy and military action. Such situations, in which there are both mutual consent and a credible threat of violent military action, are relatively rare. Any expectations pertaining to the use of leverage in mediation, as developed here, should be maximized in such cases, which fall somewhere between mediation and humanitarian intervention.

---

1. For instance, see Touval (1982); Egeland (1999).
2. See, for example, Bercovitch (1997); Beardsley et al. (2006).

The three criteria help to distinguish mediation from other third-party conflict management techniques. Arbitration and adjudication, which involve legally binding third-party conflict resolution, are rarer than mediation, especially when high-value issues are at stake. Third-party consultations constitute another means by which outside actors attempt to manage disputes and are characterized by third parties' holding talks with only one side of the dispute to push for a solution. Without the participation of all parties to the dispute, such activity remains distinct from mediation. Humanitarian intervention involves violent coercion by third parties to push for peace and does not involve the consent of at least some of the combatants. Finally, peacekeeping relies on military or observer forces typically deployed after negotiation has produced an agreement or cease-fire.

The Demand and Supply of Mediation

To what ends are mediators typically employed? In building expectations about the effect of mediation on conflict outcomes, we must first have a sense of what the involved actors are trying to achieve through it. Mediation is consensual, which means that both the users (the disputants) and the providers (the third parties) must believe that it will provide some net benefit.

Incentives of the Disputants

Armed conflict is part of a bargaining process. If actors want a policy on some issue or good to be at their ideal point and all actors do not have the same ideal point, then the actors will have to bargain over what the arrangement should be. Bargaining power is determined in part by each actor's best alternative to negotiated agreement (BATNA)—actors that would not be inconvenienced much by the absence of settlement have substantial leverage over bargaining partners that are more desperate for agreement.[3] To maximize their shares of the bargains, actors will often threaten to use force and thereby try to decrease the perceived attractiveness to their opponents of alternatives to making concessions. Because there is no monopoly on the use of force in the international system, and even in many domestic systems, bargaining often occurs in the shadow of potential violent conflict.

Mediation occurs within this context. Disputants form their preference for mediation based on their expectation of its ability to improve their prospects

---

3. Fisher and Ury (1981) provide some of the seminal work on this concept.

relative to its chief alternatives of bilateral diplomacy and armed conflict. When potential mediators are well suited to producing more attractive settlements and to smoothing the peace process compared to bilateral talks and conflict, the disputants will have a high demand for their services.

If the primary intended goal of mediation is an improved bargained settlement, this means that peace itself is not the desired end. When mutually satisfactory agreements are reached, peace tends to result, but that should not be conflated with the ultimate goal. In some cases, prolonged peace might actually be inconsistent with the demand-side incentives for mediation. For instance, actors may pursue mediation as a stalling tactic.[4] During the peace process, such actors might regroup and recruit so that they can then take the battlefield from a stronger position and ultimately end up with a better agreement. In such situations, mediation is still being used to improve the stalling actors' bargained settlements, but it is actually enabling belligerence. As one example of this stalling dynamic, Saadia Touval (1982, 129) notes that one of the reasons that Robert Anderson was unsuccessful in brokering an agreement between Israel and Egypt in 1955 and 1956 is that the Israelis suspected that Nasser was merely biding his time until he could get more Soviet armaments.[5] As another example, Jimmy Carter successfully mediated a cease-fire in Bosnia in December 1994, but Bosnian President Alija Izetbegovic told Richard Holbrooke that the parties accepted the cease-fire only because of the difficulty of fighting during the winter and that they planned to resume fighting before the end of the agreed-on four months (Holbrooke 1998, 61–62).

In addition to being a stalling tactic, mediation might also be used insincerely to gain recognition or to provide a veneer of cooperation that might be rewarded by various audiences. When disputants depend on support from domestic or international actors that desire de-escalation, they might have an incentive to go along with a mediated peace process with no intention of conceding, in the hope that they might eventually return to combat while blaming their opponent for the lack of progress. This is especially an issue in civil wars, as when the Liberation Tigers of Tamil Eelam (LTTE) in Sri Lanka used the 2002 cease-fire agreement to establish its legitimacy as the sole representative of the Tamil people, to win greater support from the Tamil diaspora, and to increase aid-donor pressure on the government to grant concessions (see chap. 6). Although the use of medi-

---

4. Richmond (1998) has provided an extensive discussion of such motives for mediation and calls these "devious objectives." Greig (2001) finds some empirical confirmation that this phenomenon exists. Toft (2009) also argues that third-party guarantees are limited in preventing conflict recurrence because they typically fail to address the problem of stalling tactics.

5. Aaron David Miller similarly notes that "Playing for time in the hope of getting out of a tight spot has always been an effective Arab and Israeli response to ideas they don't like" (2008, 70).

ated peace processes for insincere motives is certainly prevalent, there are also plenty of sincere attempts to reach a peaceful settlement, otherwise mediation would never occur because of fears by third parties and combatants alike that one side was definitely stalling.

In addition to the potential devious uses of mediation, in order to explain fully why disputants sometimes choose alternative conflict management approaches, we must consider its costs to the disputants. Coordinating to find a mutually acceptable third party, negotiating the terms of its role as an intermediary, and actually engaging the mediator are likely to be costly to the combatants in both tangible resources and time. Less tangible but equally important, the extent to which third parties constrain the flexibility and autonomy of the disputants also affects the perceived costliness of third-party assistance in conflict management.

One way to think about the possibility of reducing autonomy is to consider the degree to which actors become susceptible to coercion. When actors that are able to threaten strong punishments are brought in to mediate, the combatants risk a higher chance of being coerced into certain patterns of behavior. Bringing in a mediator does not necessarily entail giving up any residual rights of control and establishing a hierarchical relationship.[6] But it does give the intermediary a legitimate seat at the negotiation table, where it can better observe which disputant is responsible for the bargaining failure and can more credibly threaten actions against the intransigent party. By gaining inside information on the bargaining dynamics, mediators are better able to determine against which actors to use sticks in hopes of moving the negotiations forward. In addition, third-party threats to punish obstinate actors become more credible when that third party has a vested interest in being effective in its role as mediator. So, combatants risk a greater chance of third-party coercion by giving a mediator better access to the bargaining dynamics and a greater incentive to press for an agreement.

For example, prior to Carter's Camp David efforts to mediate between Menachem Begin and Anwar Sadat, Israel was hesitant to include an intermediary and for a time preferred bilateral talks. Israel had much to risk by allowing the United States to mediate.[7] Specifically, Israel risked having its failure to reach an agreement alienate the United States, which might have led to some withdrawal of U.S. support to Israel in the face of Soviet interests in the region and stronger U.S.-Egyptian ties. By keeping the United States on the sidelines of any negotiations, Israel would have avoided such risks because it would not have put the

---

6. See Lake (2009) for what hierarchy can look like in international politics.
7. Princen (1992) makes a similar point.

United States in the position of having to succeed in what Carter saw as a last-ditch effort at achieving Arab-Israeli peace.[8]

Mediation can also reduce the flexibility of a combatant in negotiations. Third parties generally have a preference about the outcome of the conflicts in which they are involved. Either the broker is biased to have the outcome favor one of the actors, or it is biased toward a quick peace over any outcome that might lead to prolonged disagreement.[9] Regardless of what the preference is, the mere existence of a third-party preference about the outcome entails that mediator involvement can limit the availability of certain outcomes. Actors that want to have as many options to choose from as possible may therefore be unwilling to bring in a mediator that will narrow the range of options to not only what is acceptable to an opponent but also to what is acceptable to the third party. Similarly, mediators will often make side bargains as a means to a negotiated settlement.[10] These side bargains can constrict the set of options that are unanimously agreed on, similar to a veto-player logic.[11]

Incentives of the Third Parties

On the supply side, as previously mentioned, third parties have their own distinct preferences about mediation. The provision of mediation should be considered similar to the provision of other impure public goods, which provide both public benefits and private benefits to the producers.[12] In terms of public goods, the collective benefits of successful mediation include a more stable international system, decreases in negative externalities and risks of conflict in neighboring states, and benefits related to humanitarian affinities. Because mediation can provide benefits that are not directly consumed by the third party, private benefits typically must also be present for mediation to be worth the costs of provision.

The costs to the third party of providing mediation can be considerable because the diplomatic resources of the third party are often quite limited in terms of staffing and high-level negotiations often require substantial attention. For example, U.S. Secretary of State James Baker conducted four rounds of shuttle diplomacy in the Middle East in 1991 just to get the actors to the Madrid Confer-

---

8. The incentives for mediation in this case are considered more fully in the next chapter.

9. For a thorough treatment of these biases, see Kydd (2006); Rauchhaus (2006).

10. See Young (1967); Princen (1992).

11. Chester A. Crocker, Fen Osler Hampson, and Pamela Aall (1999, 27) consider a related issue in which flexibility is lost because the inclusion of third parties can greatly complicate the path toward resolution.

12. For an overview of impure public goods applied to security, see Sandler (1977); Bobrow and Boyer (1997). For an earlier discussion of collective security and public goods, see Olson and Zeckhauser (1966).

ence, which ultimately produced little tangible output (Baker 1999). Moreover, while prenegotiation and actual mediation can be resource consuming in terms of person-hours, many mediation attempts also involve paying the physical costs of material benefits or sanctions. As one example, the Bill Clinton administration was remarkably ambivalent about its success or failure in reaching the Dayton Accords, which it was mediating through Richard Holbrooke, because success would mean having to fulfill its commitment to send thousands of U.S. troops as peacekeepers at a time when doing so was unpopular at home (Holbrooke 1998, 307). There are also risks to the reputation of the third party of initiating a peace process and then looking incompetent if the situation does not improve or even gets worse.[13] To the extent that a third party is concerned about how others at home or in the international system perceive its leadership abilities—although, to be sure, some third parties might not care at all—it will sometimes prefer inaction over mediation to escape the attribution of blame. On this, Henry Kissinger writes, "A reputation for success tends to be self-fulfilling. Equally, failure feeds on itself: A Secretary of State who undertakes too many journeys that lead nowhere depreciates his coin" (1982, 803). Similarly, mediators could face domestic political costs for encouraging a settlement that is unpopular at home. As I explore later, U.S. mediators have come up against this constraint in their handling of the Arab-Israeli conflict.[14]

Because of the costs associated with mediation provision and the public benefits that can result, the supply of mediation faces a free-rider problem—third parties will hesitate to contribute to an optimal provision of mediation, preferring to reap the benefits produced from the efforts of others. There will be a greater supply of mediation when there are more selective incentives, or private benefits that give the third parties extra motivation to pay the costs of involvement.

We might consider three types of private benefits that affect third-party mediation decisions. First, third-party states directly benefit from mediating and contributing to conflict resolution when they can reduce any spillover costs from the outbreak of violence (e.g., refugee concerns and trade disruptions) that they must bear. It is well known that conflicts frequently breed other conflicts,[15] so potentially affected actors have an incentive to contain the contagion of conflict. Second, some actors value the humanitarian benefits of peacemaking more

---

13. See Bercovitch and Schneider (2000).

14. For a thorough discussion of how domestic politics has shaped U.S. policy in the Middle East, see Mearsheimer and Walt (2007); Miller (2008).

15. For example, see Buhaug and Gleditsch (2008); Gleditsch (2002, 2007); Gleditsch, Salehyan, and Schultz (2008); Gleditsch and Ward (2000); Kathman (2010); Most and Starr (1980); Siverson and Starr (1990, 1991); Starr and Most (1983); Ward and Gleditsch (2002).

than others. Intergovernmental organizations (IGOs) and nongovernmental organizations (NGOs) are especially likely to value peace and stability as ends in themselves, especially because promoting these ends is often in their charters and statements of purpose.

Third, actors of all types receive substantial benefits from mediating conflicts in which they have much at stake. Conflicts present an opportunity for rules and norms to be restructured, and affected third parties will want to be part of the resolution process so that they can shape the international and regional orders in their favor. For example, the United States is one of the most frequent mediators, which is to be expected of a hegemon with so many global interests. Less obviously, even countries such as Norway and Switzerland frequently offer their mediation services because this gives them substantial relevance in global affairs when their lack of military and economic power and their abstention from the European Union otherwise limit their clout. In addition, when outside actors are biased toward one of the disputants, they will benefit from increasing the potential that the protégé's preferred agreement will be reached.[16] Note in this regard that the third parties themselves might be insincere in pushing for peace because they sometimes benefit from the actual extension of conflict if a settlement will be contrary to their interests. For example, U.S. Secretary of State Condoleezza Rice initially supported the Israeli foray into Lebanon in 2006 as a way to leverage Syria and actually used her involvement to prevent a hasty cease-fire.[17] She later helped push for the cease-fire only after the humanitarian toll became unacceptable, but even then she made sure that Israel had two more days after the cease-fire to complete its offensive campaign (Harel and Issacharoff 2008, 216–19).

It is worth reiterating that there are multiple reasons for third parties to find it worth their while to become involved as mediators, and we should not assume that they are acting altruistically. Even when the benefit that mediators receive is primarily related to humanitarian concerns this does not mean that the third party is acting with the best interests of the combatants in mind, in that the mediator is still shaping the outcome according to its own objectives. Many third parties often have a mixture of incentives to take part in a peace process. For example, the United States has a number of reasons for its frequent involvement in Middle East conflicts that include supporting important allies, stabilizing oil flows, competing with other great powers for influence, reining in the threat of

---

16. The existing literature differs in its assessment of whether being biased toward a particular *adversary* affords the mediator greater efficacy; however, a general consensus has emerged that being biased toward *peace* inhibits the third party from affecting the perspectives of the combatants (Kydd 2003, 2006; Rauchhaus 2006, 2011; Favretto 2009; Savun 2008; Smith and Stam 2003; Touval 1975).

17. See Harel and Issacharoff (2008, 105, 146–47); Hirst (2010, 361).

radical Islamist groups, and addressing humanitarian concerns.[18] As another example, the United States eventually assumed the central peacemaking role in the war in Bosnia because of both humanitarian concerns and a desire to demonstrate the continuing importance of U.S. leadership in Europe (Holbrooke 1998, 359–60).

That mediation is costly to administer, is provided by self-interested third parties, and has the properties of an impure public good suggests that it tends to be provided suboptimally from the standpoint of international peace and stability. In particular, third parties frequently withdraw their engagement in a peace process soon after they achieve their primary objectives, and they typically have little incentive to stay actively involved just to solidify the stability of whatever outcome had been achieved. Once the fighting stops, the threat of negative externalities has diminished, and the third parties have shaped the outcome in their favor, the third parties often divert their diplomatic resources to other issues on their radar. For example, the North Atlantic Treaty Organization (NATO) diverted many of its peacekeeping resources committed to the Yugoslav theater in the early 2000s because they were needed in Afghanistan.[19] Third parties might also fear creating perverse incentives if the combatants become overly reliant on outside involvement. The point is that the involvement of a third party as a mediator is typically temporary and often briefer than is needed to maximize the stability of peace.

Three Barriers to Conflict Bargaining

To grasp how mediation affects peace and conflict dynamics, we must first understand why disputants sometimes fail to resolve their contentions peacefully and resort to armed conflict.[20] From a rationalist perspective that sees armed conflicts as inefficient bargaining failures, the tragedy of war is that, for all its fury and devastation, the outcome is generally something that could have been achieved

---

18. Of these interests, James Baker writes, "The United States, of course, has always had its own interests in the Middle East. But as the world's leading body our interests are always complex and broad ranging enough that we, unlike countries that inhabit the region, have an overriding interest in a comprehensive regional peace that benefits all parties" (1999, 204).

19. See Ritscher (2005, 117).

20. The idea that war results when actors are unable to resolve their bargains via peaceful means has been well developed and has a long history. See, notably, Clausewitz (1832 [1968]); Iklé (1971 [2005]); Blainey (1973); Snyder and Diesing (1977); Pillar (1983). More recently, numerous formalizations of bargaining models of war have produced a foundation for explaining conflict onset, duration, termination, and recurrence. For seminal work, see Fearon (1995); Powell (1999). For reviews of how similar models have been used, see Reiter (2003); Lake (2003).

without a war actually taking place. The concessions could have been exchanged and the defeated could have submitted well before the first battle. War is thus a grand detour, inefficient and costly, to resolving a problem in the distribution of issues and goods.

This suggests that being able to use alternative means to realize the same ends as war will make war less relevant. This is where mediation enters the picture. Like war, the chief end of (sincere) mediation is to attain a bargained outcome. Like war, mediation occurs when the actors choose to pursue it as a conflict management strategy. It is thus useful to couch the role of mediation in terms of how it affects the bargaining environment and, specifically, how it addresses three primary sources of bargaining failure: uncertainty, political constraints, and commitment problems.

Uncertainty

The first factor that can plague the ability for actors to reach an agreement short of armed conflict is uncertainty. Actors often have asymmetric information—they know more about their own capabilities and capacity to absorb the costs of conflict than about those of their opponent—and a strategic incentive to misrepresent their own red lines, or minimally acceptable terms of agreement. Not only are there incentives for actors to *misrepresent* themselves, but there might also be cognitive or organizational barriers that cause actors to *misperceive* what an appropriate bargain looks like.[21] Either way, it may be difficult for the actors to identify what bargains an opponent would find acceptable. In the face of such uncertainty, parties may push for a settlement that is not mutually agreeable or may refuse to believe that a challenger is legitimately dissatisfied with the status quo, leading to bargaining failure. For example, in 1904 Russia underestimated the capability and resolve of Japan to effectively compete for influence in Northeast Asia, which, in part, led to the Japanese attack on Port Arthur and the beginning of the Russo-Japanese War (see chap. 3).

Political Constraints

A second source of bargaining failure involves the domestic audience, or political, costs of concessions. Leaders can become locked into a conflict because they will be sanctioned domestically for backing down. To stay in power, leaders require some level of consent from those with the ability to remove the leader

---

21. For an extensive discussion of the causes and consequences of misperception, see Jervis (1976).

from office—this is often termed the selectorate and typically includes such actors as the domestic public, military, or party elites, depending on the political system.[22] The political costs of concessions can arise because leaders are expected to advance the cause of the polity and retreating from the status quo can generate discontent among the selectorate. In such a situation, bargains may not be possible if the leaders' political costs of conceding offset the costs of fighting and create a null set of alternatives that are mutually preferable to conflict. The problem of being locked-in can especially arise when a leader has tied his or her hands by taking a hard-line stance in a conflict to deter an opponent.[23] The leader may make bold claims about the prospects of victory and about the worthiness of the cause to enhance his or her credibility, making it more likely that those with political power will punish the leader if concessions are made. If the hard-line stance fails as a deterrent to the combatants, the leader may find continued conflict more attractive than conceding because of the political costs. We might imagine, for example, the political embarrassment that the George W. Bush administration would have faced, after famously spending considerable effort making a case for toppling Saddam Hussein's regime, had it reconsidered the prudence of its decision to invade Iraq and decided instead to back down.

Domestic audiences can also derail a bargaining process when fighting brings political benefits that would be forgone if concessions had been made. Foreign policy leaders may be motivated to pursue a bellicose approach in a dispute if doing so is popular among their selectorate. For example, leaders may try to appease a strong autonomous military by causing conflicts that will bring resources and prestige to the military elite.[24] Or leaders may feel compelled to fight and not back down when a group of people is profoundly hated by the general public, for example, when there is a desire for retribution and revenge against the group responsible for past misdeeds. Having a selectorate that is thirsty for conflict and averse to concessions can improve the leaders' bargaining leverage because the other side knows that it has to give up more in order to avoid war.[25] Less benign, such domestic pressure can also lock in conflict when the leaders of disputing parties actually receive a net utility gain from conflict because of the political benefits.

---

22. Recent studies have explored the domestic constraints that leaders face and their logical implications to foreign policy behavior (Bueno de Mesquita et al. 2003; Chiozza and Goemans 2003, 2004a, 2004b; Gelpi and Grieco 2001; Goemans 2000, 2009; Lake 1992; Tarar 2006; Tarar and Leventoglu 2009; Wolford 2007).

23. Fearon (1994) has used this logic to explain why democracies are better able to avoid escalation to war.

24. Jack Snyder (1984) presents a variant of this argument applied to World War I.

25. See Putnam (1988); Tarar (2005).

Commitment Problems

The third source of bargaining failure is a difficulty in committing to an agreement credibly.[26] In this regard, the timing of the exchange of commitments can be a substantial barrier to peace. Actors typically are unwilling to be a first mover in making concessions because doing so risks the possibility that their opponent will exploit their cooperation.[27] Unless the mutual implementation of concessions can be guaranteed, combatants may prefer to be in conflict than become vulnerable to an opponent that reneges once it gets its desired outcome.

Similarly, when an actor is likely to want to change the terms of an agreement in the future, because of changing capabilities or other dynamics that shape the relative costs and benefits of conflict versus peace, the actor finds it difficult to convince its opponents that it will not defect from a settlement. This specific type of commitment problem is a time inconsistency problem; arrangements that are mutually preferable in the present cannot be sustained because of the changing desirability of peace over time. One stark example of such a time inconsistency problem is the rapid German rise in power in the 1930s that led it to repeatedly alter and eventually reject altogether the terms of peace reached at Versailles in 1919.

Time inconsistency problems help explain both the cessation of conflict at the point of bargaining and the recurrence of conflict once agreements have been reached. When the belligerents anticipate that their opponents will have incentives to renege and renegotiate the terms later, they will hesitate to settle. Instead, they may prefer to fight until they reach an arrangement, such as complete victory, that their opponent does not have the ability or incentive to challenge in the future.[28] If the disputants do not anticipate the future defection of the opponent, or when they discount the future sufficiently to not care about future renegotiations, time inconsistency problems can help explain why agreements that are reached eventually break down.[29]

Another type of commitment problem, separate from time inconsistency issues, can confound efficient bargaining as well. Negotiating parties sometimes cannot follow through on a promise because the promised action is not something within their control; this is common in many modern conflicts involving

---

26. For seminal studies of commitment problems as causes of bargaining failure, see North and Weingast (1989); Fearon (1995, 1998); Walter (2002); Powell (2004b, 2006).

27. Kydd (2005) similarly defines *mistrust* as the belief that an opponent prefers to exploit rather than reciprocate cooperation, and he shows mistrust to be an important component of conflict.

28. On the relevance of victory to commitment problems, see Toft (2009); Reiter (2009); Lo, Hashimoto, and Reiter (2008).

29. Werner (1999a) demonstrates that rapid shifts in power increase the potential for conflict recurrence.

nonstate actors or weak states. Actors at the negotiating table may not be able to police their constituent members or subsidiaries, which can make the negotiation and implementation of agreements quite difficult. For example, one of the difficulties impeding progress in the current round of Middle East peace talks is that Mahmoud Abbas and his Fatah party lack the ability to hold significant portions of the Palestinian population accountable to any agreements that are reached. This is the *spoiler* problem in which actors external to the bargaining table actively try to disrupt the implementation of a settlement to recruit people to their cause or delegitimize a party that was at the bargaining table.[30]

Conflict Onset, Duration, and Recurrence

Such barriers to bargaining directly explain both the onset and duration of armed conflict.[31] Militarized conflicts begin when there is an underlying bargaining problem delaying settlement, and they end when those underlying problems are resolved through pure diplomacy, coercive diplomacy, or brute force. When uncertainty is at the heart of conflict, the conflict will move toward termination when the actors have learned enough, on the battlefield or elsewhere, to reach a mutually acceptable agreement. To paraphrase Geoffrey Blainey (1973), wars begin when actors do not agree about what a suitable bargain should be, but they end when actors can agree. When political constraints are at the heart of conflict, leaders are more likely to reach a deal when the political costs of concessions become low enough compared to the costs of belligerence. When a commitment problem is at the heart of conflict, it is more likely to end when the actors can eventually trust that their opponents will actually implement an agreement.

These bargaining barriers echo the ripeness framework that is common in the conflict resolution literature. According to the ripeness framework, conflict proceeds in stages, some of which are more amenable to resolution than others. Work by I. William Zartman, Jacob Bercovitch, and other scholars has found that periods of conflict associated with a mutually hurting stalemate are especially amenable to, or ripe for, successful conflict management.[32] Although this

---

30. See Stedman (1997).

31. For an account of how a bargaining approach to war can explain conflict termination, see Reiter (2009).

32. See especially Zartman (1985); Bercovitch (1997); Bercovitch and Langley (1993); Haas (1991); Young (1967); Northedge and Donelan (1971); Ott (1972); Pruitt (1981a); Mooradian and Druckman (1999). For a provocative critique of the ripeness framework, see Kleiboer (1994). For more recent approaches, see Greig and Diehl (2006); Greig (2005); Bercovitch and Jackson (2001); Regan and Stam (2000).

framework predates much of the literature on the rational bargaining models of war, its implications are quite consistent with what we might expect from a bargaining perspective. For example, ripeness framework scholars often highlight the importance of recognizing a mutually hurting stalemate and the potential for reciprocation in order for de-escalation to be possible. This maps nicely to expectations in the conflict bargaining literature that actors tend to choose settlement over conflict when they come to recognize the true costs of conflict (as during a hurting stalemate) and have confidence that their cooperation will not be exploited (i.e., when there is potential for reciprocation).

The three barriers to efficient bargaining can also be used to explain conflict recurrence, which is crucial in understanding the effect of mediation on the long-term durability of peace.[33] As a heuristic device, it is worth considering how conflict renewal is really a function of two underlying conditions. The first is the propensity for actors that were previously in dispute to renegotiate the status quo that emerged from the conflict, whether that is the terms of a formal agreement, an implicit arrangement, or some form of stalemate. The second condition is the potential for those renegotiations to fail to reach a new bargain peacefully. In other words, factors that increase either the probability of dissatisfaction or the probability of that dissatisfaction resulting in bargaining failure increase the propensity for conflict relapse.

A direct link exists between the propensity for renegotiation failure and each of the three factors of uncertainty, commitment problems, and political constraints. A bargaining environment in which these factors are strong makes renegotiation difficult to achieve peacefully. The need for renegotiation in the first place, however, is mostly related to the commitment problems caused by time inconsistencies and spoilers. When the status quo achieved at the end of an episode of conflict is no longer acceptable to one of the antagonists, as a result of changes in military capabilities, economic capacities, or political leadership, that actor will push, while threatening hostilities, for a new arrangement. Renegotiation also becomes likely when the existing order is simply inadequate to deal with new challenges or when there are spoilers with interests in subverting that existing order. In such instances, the original belligerents may still be, in principle, satisfied with the existing arrangement but face the need to adopt new measures to deal with other actors or events that make the current order untenable.

---

33. For related discussions of how conflict relapse pertains to a bargaining-model perspective, see Smith and Stam (2003); Werner (1999b); Werner and Yuen (2005).

The Effects of Mediation on Bargaining

In considering how mediation can ameliorate the bargaining environment, it is useful to distinguish between mediation with and without leverage.[34] Mediation with leverage, or heavy mediation, tries to maximize the costs of nonagreement and thereby expand the set of mutually acceptable alternatives. The targets of such leverage are the opportunity costs of not reaching an agreement, so both positive inducements for agreement and negative inducements against fighting are forms of leverage.[35] Such tactics can affect the ability of combatants to find terms of settlement; in addition, mediators can use leverage to assuage implementation concerns. Toward the latter objective, intermediaries can use security guarantees or threats of future punishment to increase the expected costs of noncompliance with the agreement and thus reduce the incentives to renege later.[36] Some existing empirical evidence finds that heavy-handed mediation tactics fare best in resolving international disputes or in enabling formal agreements to be reached.[37]

Mediation without leverage, or light mediation, primarily involves enabling the actors to find an agreement within the existing set of alternatives that are mutually preferable to conflict.[38] The key is for the mediator to allow the actors to achieve some agreement without actually changing the incentives for compromise. The third party does not introduce external inducements for peace and, instead, focuses on bringing together and integrating the existing political incentives in play to reach a deal. Ban Ki-moon describes the purpose of such mediation: "The mediator's challenge is to transform this adversarial process into one of problem-solving. In our usual practice, the mediator becomes an interlocutor with each party to understand its core interests and concerns and to help it move away from entrenched positions to explore innovative options that might address its interests, as well as those of the other side" (2009, 9).

---

34. Following Rauchhaus (2006, 2011), these two types of mediation can be referred to as heavy and light mediation, respectively. Heavy mediation also closely corresponds to what Zartman and Touval (1985) term manipulation.

35. See Schrodt and Gerner (2004).

36. For discussion of this potential mediator role, see Susskind and Cruikshank (1987); Bercovitch (1997); Young (1972); Lake and Rothchild (1996); Touval and Zartman (1985); Zartman and Touval (1985).

37. For studies on the relationship between leverage and general conflict resolution, see Bercovitch, Anagnoson, and Wille (1991); Bercovitch and Houston (1996); Bercovitch (1986); Carnevale (1986); Schrodt and Gerner (2004). For similar analyses of formal agreements, see Svensson (2007b); Quinn et al. (2006); Wilkenfeld et al. (2003, 2005); Beardsley et al. (2006). Rauchhaus (2006, 2011) finds that heavy-handed involvement actually tends to be inferior to lighter mediation.

38. Carnevale (1986) and Kressel (1972) use *integration* to refer to the same type of third-party involvement.

TABLE 2.1 Mediation and bargaining problems

BARGAINING PROBLEM	MEANS OF INFLUENCE	MEDIATION STYLE
Uncertainty	Expand set of acceptable alternatives	Heavy
	Information exchange	Light
Political constraints	Political cover	Light
Commitment problem	Implementation assistance	Heavy

Short-Term Effects of Mediation

Turning to the specific mechanisms by which mediation interacts with the bargaining environment, we can begin to understand its potential short-term and long-term effects. Let us start with the short-term effects. Table 2.1 divides mediation into four roles and places them in the context of the three sources of bargaining failure we have considered. We next consider each of these four roles in turn, starting with the heavy mediation roles.

EXPANDING THE SET OF ACCEPTABLE ALTERNATIVES

Starting with the use of threats and promises—sticks and carrots—to increase the opportunity costs of conflict, the most intrusive mediators can expand the number of peaceful alternative outcomes that are mutually preferable to conflict so that the actors have a greater chance of reaching a bargain. Leverage is a function of mediation that is frequently highlighted as essential to what third parties do. This is especially popular when using a realist framework to understand conflict and peace processes. If actors are primarily motivated by power, then it is easy to understand why leverage might be important. Actors will reduce their demands and pursue a more peaceful tack when third parties use some sort of power of persuasion to deter further aggression and make more alternatives appear preferable to conflict. This mode of explanation has an appeal of being direct and tangible. Henry Kissinger's and Jimmy Carter's penchant for tying billions of dollars worth of aid to progress in the Egyptian-Israeli peace process, Hillary Clinton's offer of stealth aircraft in return for a ninety-day Israeli settlement freeze, and Richard Holbrooke's encouragement of NATO military action while he attempted to broker a peace in the Bosnian war are all extreme examples of the inducements that mediators might provide.

Incentives can involve tangible rewards and punishments such as promises of aid or threats of sanctions, but they also can involve intangibles such as the promise of improved relationships, legitimacy, moral persuasion, or threatened alienation. For example, the United States was able to establish leverage in southern Africa when mediating the independence of Namibia and the withdrawal of Cuban forces from Angola because South Africa, Angola, and even Cuba to some extent desired closer relationships with the United States (Crocker 1999). Another common, less tangible, source of leverage is the ability of the mediator to publicly blame parties for their intransigence. Mediators might signal to domestic and international audiences that a prudent arrangement, which should have been mutually acceptable to all parties, was not reached because of the obstinacy of one particular negotiator. To the extent, which varies greatly across actors and disputes, that the negotiators care about how constituents, political elites, or international partners perceive their willingness to cooperate, this provides the negotiators an incentive to be reasonably cooperative. Such a tactic can be said to increase the audience costs of pursuing a hard-line strategy. As an example, Jimmy Carter found this to be an especially important tactic in his peace initiatives; as he typically informed the participants that he reserved the right to go to the media and assign culpability for any negotiation breakdowns.[39] In his memoirs, Carter reflects on how this proved useful in his Middle East negotiations: "A real or implied threat that proposals will be made public sometimes helps to prevent the rejection of patently attractive or fair offers. We used this device in dealing with Prime Minister Begin, who was almost always the most recalcitrant member of the Israeli delegation" (1984, 18–19).

A critical assumption behind using leverage to facilitate actors' reaching a negotiated bargain is that the likelihood of their reaching an agreement increases with the number of alternatives that are preferable to conflict. With a larger bargaining space, there is a wider margin built in for misestimation and there is less chance that the disputants will actually be dissatisfied with the current arrangement, as when the status quo falls below an actor's red line.[40] The assumption makes most sense when we consider that, in practice, the division of an issue or good is often not perfectly continuous. For instance, as we see later, when Russia and Japan were negotiating about the division of Sakhalin Island in 1905, they considered only the focal points of (1) complete Japanese control, (2) a fifty-fifty split, or (3) complete Russian control. Any other division would have been awkward to justify. So bargaining may sometimes involve only a limited number of options, not the infinite number of alternatives that are presented in standard bargaining models. In such situations, expanding the set of mutually preferable alternatives could mean allowing just one of the limited options to become recognized as clearly reasonable.

---

39. I thank President Carter for offering this insight during a discussion at the Carter Center on November 12, 2008.

40. For a similar argument that a larger overlapping bargaining space is more conducive to identifying acceptable outcomes, see Hopmann (2001). This logic is not unchallenged; Wilkenfeld et al. (2005) find some experimental evidence that a larger bargaining space may decrease the ability of actors to improve their utility.

In short, third parties can use heavy-handed mediation to make peaceful alternatives look more attractive than ongoing conflict. The more leverage placed on the combatants, the more eager they will be to either settle on a new arrangement or to back down and abide by the status quo. That is, third parties can be useful in creating something like a mutually hurting stalemate, as suggested by Chester Crocker: "In cases in which there is no stalemate or a stalemate exists objectively but is not recognized by one or both parties, the third party may need to consider direct leverage to ripen the conflict: affecting the military balance by helping the weaker side, raising the price of fighting to one side or both in order to bring about stalemate, or (as in Bosnia before Dayton) by direct intervention in support of the mediation" (1999, 242).

This viewpoint demonstrates that mediators are often seen as levelers of the playing field—protecting the weaker belligerents from complete domination by a stronger power. If a mutually hurting stalemate is to be created, then this often means that third parties need to make conflict costly for those powerful states that do not expect much harm to come to them in battle. In addition, if in some instances egalitarian settlements have some intrinsic value related to fairness, then mediators need to lean harder on actors with more bargaining power to prevent them from getting a disproportionate share.

IMPLEMENTATION ASSISTANCE

Heavy mediation that is forward looking and offers monitoring or enforcement during agreement implementation provides another means of overcoming bargaining failures. A mediator that can monitor and enforce in the future may help bolster the costs of reneging on an agreement by either increasing the probability of detecting cheating or increasing the costly consequences of cheating.[41] So, even if the red lines of the belligerents are prone to move over time, as capabilities and resolve shift, settlements can remain agreeable when the mediator continues to incentivize peace. Also, third parties can attempt to facilitate implementation when a combatant that intends to comply is simply unable to follow through on its promises. When self-policing is difficult, third parties can try to provide necessary resources to identify and punish spoilers or to prop up a regime that is politically vulnerable to a backlash that would result from policing its own people.

For example, an important reason why British mediation, primarily under the auspices of Peter Carrington, succeeded in finally resolving the Rhodesian Civil

---

41. Walter (1997, 2002) has found empirically and Schmidt (2004) has found formally that in third-party intervention in general, when the root of a crisis is an enforcement problem, strong intermediaries are often needed to resolve the credible commitment issue.

War when earlier attempts failed was that Britain promised continued monitoring and enforcement assistance during the transition process (Walter 2002). More generally, mediation efforts often naturally evolve into monitoring, peacekeeping, or peacebuilding once the conflict is over. UN Secretary General Ban Ki-moon gives some examples of what such activity might look like:

> Mediation does not end once an agreement is signed. Formal and informal good offices or mediation are required throughout implementation. Different aspects of the agreement, such as restoration of security and basic services; disarmament, demobilization and reintegration; return of refugees and internally displaced persons; promotion of human rights; security sector reform; child protection; adoption of a constitution; holding of elections; rebuilding institutions; establishing transitional justice mechanisms; and restarting the economy, are addressed at different times and details need to be carefully negotiated and carefully sequenced. (2009, 14)

Even non-UN actors are often asked or expected to provide implementation assistance. For example, Syrian President Hafez al-Assad, well before accepting an invitation to what would become the Madrid Conference, insisted on having guarantees from Baker's team that the cosponsors of the talks would guarantee the results (Baker 1999).

Also related to implementation assistance, third parties can sometimes directly resolve situations when the timing of any agreed transactions might create vulnerabilities—as when the relinquishing of a good or issue before the step is reciprocated might create a window in which the opponent no longer feels compelled to fulfill its obligations. In such situations, mediators can serve as trustees and provide the medium of exchange, ensuring that both sides receive their agreed-on concessions at the same time. An example of implementation assistance related to issues of timing is the actions of the International Body (George Mitchell from the United States, Harri Holkeri from Finland, and John de Chastelain from Canada), which facilitated the process that led to the Good Friday Agreement in Northern Ireland. The International Body was initially charged with the primary task of figuring out how decommissioning (disarmament) could be accomplished because it was understood that no peace would last in Northern Ireland if the paramilitary groups could continue to threaten one another with their high levels of armament. This mediation group was able to move the peace process forward by coordinating the delicate timing of the political and arms concessions, such that neither side had the opportunity to benefit greatly from backing out of its pledges once the other side had carried out its promises (Chastelain 1999).

When actors face potential time inconsistency or other commitment problems, they might thus lean on a third party to help maintain an agreement. Even when third parties struggle to eliminate defection from an agreement, they can reduce the seriousness of such noncompliant behavior. That is, third parties might not be able to credibly enforce all violations of a peace agreement because of resource limitations or waning interest in the long run. Even so, they can more credibly commit to intervene in the most serious violations that pose more of an existential threat, that, among other things, could upset a strategic balance, generate regional instability, or cause a humanitarian crisis. Because third parties have more of an incentive to guard against serious violations of a negotiated arrangement that they brokered, they can decrease the *vulnerability* of the disputants to future defections even though they may struggle to decrease the *frequency* of future defections. Through the reduction in vulnerability, the presence of a mediator that promises implementation assistance can make it easier for combatants to reach a bargained settlement.

INFORMATION EXCHANGE

Let us now turn to light mediation. Third parties can try to reduce uncertainty and help the prior expectations of the actors—about conflict costs and outcomes—converge on the actual values so that appropriate offers become more identifiable. In considering this role of mediation, the existing literature has emphasized the direct provision of information by the third parties to the combatants.[42] Mediators in some cases pool information—from material that the combatants have privately divulged or from their own intelligence activities—and then disseminate it as a resource to the actors at the negotiation table. For example, during the disengagement talks between Israel and Egypt following the 1973 October War, the U.S. negotiators presented data about the precise locations of unexploited oil reserves and three-dimensional models of the terrain in the Sinai—information that was more accurate than had been available to Egypt and Israel (Stein and Lewis 1991, 17). As another example, Richard Holbrooke and Wesley Clark used state-of-the-art mapping technology to help Slobodan Milosevic agree to a corridor between Gorazde and Sarajevo during the negotiations at Dayton (Holbrooke 1998, 283–85).

More indirectly, the mediator may simply be keeping the lines of communication open so the actors can exchange their own information more easily. The

---

42. See, for example, Kydd (2003, 2006); Rauchhaus (2006, 2011); Princen (1992); Moore (1986); Carnevale and Pegnetter (1985); Savun (2008); Smith and Stam (2003). Fey and Ramsay (2010) more strongly assert that mediators can only serve an informational role when they have access to independent sources of information.

role of the third party here primarily involves preventing the misunderstanding of information transmitted between the negotiating parties and not necessarily providing *new* information. The emotions of conflict, cultural peculiarities, and inaccurate media coverage can distort the intended messages between disputants, and mediators can help clarify meanings.[43] Shuttle diplomacy (in which the mediator meets separately with each disputant) is especially useful in this regard because the face-to-face meeting of belligerents at the bargaining table can heighten their confrontational rhetoric and decrease the exchange of meaningful communication.[44] Actors in a bilateral setting may also be unwilling to share information that they think will be manipulated by the other side for political advantages. As a witness to the communication flows, a mediator can assuage such reluctance by decreasing the ability of the actors to leak false information. The Norwegian mediation team in Sri Lanka, for example, found this to be an important part of the mediation between the LTTE and the Sri Lankan government.[45] In this way, mediation reduces the transaction costs and risks of communication when various barriers are in place.[46]

As another indirect information conduit, mediation might serve as an updating device, similar to seeking a second-opinion in choosing medical procedures. If it is possible for separate actors to reach different conclusions from the same data, then the opinion of a mediator may simply allow actors to update their perceptions of a given situation without the mediator actually providing more information. An example of this is, again, the case of Sri Lanka, when the Norwegian delegation frequently relayed messages from one side to the other and was asked to provide its interpretation of the messages. The Norwegian delegation was also frequently asked to advise on the content of the messages sent, so as to decrease the chances that the messages would be unclear to the other side. The Norwegians did not actually know more about the situation nor were they perceived as wiser, but their views were actively considered because the opposition groups were uncertain about whether their interpretations or perceptions of what the other side would interpret were correct.[47]

Light mediation using proposal making can also foster an agreement when the disputants are uncertain about what is mutually acceptable. A mediator

---

43. See Touval (1982).

44. In his letter to the UN Security Council, Ban Ki-moon (2009, 9–10) makes a similar point.

45. I thank Erik Solheim for his perspectives on this conflict expressed during an interview at the Norwegian Ministry of Foreign Affairs, July 1, 2005.

46. For additional treatment of mediation as a means of reducing the transaction costs of information in the economics literature, see Mitusch and Strausz (2000); Schroeter and Vyrastekova (2003); Jarque, Ponsati, and Sakovics (2003).

47. Interview with Erik Solheim at the Norwegian Ministry of Foreign Affairs, July 1, 2005.

might resolve some of the confusion when there is a large disparity in the offers being made by proposing an alternative that both actors should find preferable to fighting. In addition, if the actors cannot decide on one outcome in the set of possible alternatives, a mediator can attempt to create a focal point. The mediator also may weed out proposals it knows to be outside the set of mutually acceptable arrangements so that they do not obfuscate the viable offers or inflame tensions. For example, Henry Kissinger decided not to present an Israeli plan to Syrian President Hafez al-Assad during disengagement negotiations because he knew that Assad would reject it and Kissinger feared that it would cause a fatal blow to progress in the negotiations (Kissinger 1982, 965).

POLITICAL COVER

Light mediation can in addition provide political cover when disputants face high domestic audience costs for unpopular, although potentially prudent, concessions. When locked into a conflict because of domestic pressure, leaders might turn to a third party to help sell their constituents or other political elites on a more concessionary tack.[48] The need to save face is a similar situation in which a leader encounters costs from backing down and needs to concede without losing support at home.[49] This is not to say that leaders use mediation to convince their domestic publics that a bad deal is worth taking. On the contrary, when the leader deems a settlement to be prudent and the domestic audience is uncertain about whether it actually is, the involvement of a third party can help convince the selectorate at home that certain concessions are worthwhile. Within the bargaining framework, the effective provision of political cover entails that leaders will face fewer costs for conceding and will then be able to find more alternatives mutually preferable to conflict.

One means of doing this is for mediators to share the burden of responsibility for the concessions. The role of the mediator as a proposal maker can be especially relevant in that the belligerents do not have to own up to the authorship of a potentially unpopular agreement if the third party is the first mover in suggesting the deal. For example, Kenneth Stein and Samuel Lewis recognize the importance of political cover in Middle East negotiations and note that "Israeli cabinet members also have often relied on U.S. mediators to put forward certain

---

48. Allee and Huth (2006), Gent and Shannon (2010), and Simmons (2002) have similarly demonstrated that actors seek legal dispute resolution using third parties as a means to gain domestic support for unpalatable concessions.

49. See Rubin (1981); Druckman (1973); Pruitt (1981b); Carter (1984). Note that saving face can also be used more broadly to also include the social-psychological costs (e.g., embarrassment) of conceding or the fear of looking weak to an opponent (Pruitt and Johnson 1970; Touval 1982; Ott 1972; Young 1972).

difficult positions so that the blame for accepting an unpopular compromise can be put on U.S. 'pressure,' not on their own government" (1991, 13). More simply, third parties often provide a negotiation environment that is away from the public eye and thus free from constant domestic scrutiny of who made each proposal and counterproposal. In such an environment, the hope is that disputants will not feel as compelled to adopt a hard-line stance and create the image of being averse to compromise. The 1978 Camp David initiative (considered at length later) demonstrates this well.

Although being able to shift, or blur, responsibility for concessions is one reason that leaders may desire mediation, this probably applies more to binding third-party conflict management—as in arbitration or adjudication—or at least to mediation by a powerful third party that could turn into heavier involvement if needed to induce compromise. Without a binding resolution or the involvement by a third party with considerable sway, a leader is less able to shift responsibility to the third party. Domestic audiences that do not agree with a mediated outcome will question why their leadership acquiesced to a third party that has no authority or ability to impose a settlement.

Even though the potential to blame a third party for concessions is limited during mediation, intermediaries can otherwise provide needed domestic political cover by informing the domestic audiences about the merits of the concessions. The mediator can signal to the domestic public that the agreed-on outcome was nominally fair. General citizens and other political elites might be uncertain about whether a deal is in their interests and look to the approval by an expert third party of terms that are prudent for both sides.[50] By receiving inside information about a peace process, the third parties are more informed than the domestic audiences and can signal to them (e.g., by supporting a proposed peace plan) that any resulting concessions are in the interests of the disputants. UN Secretary General Ban Ki-moon has reported on the importance of such political cover:

> Viable agreements also need to be acceptable to the majority of constituents. While mediators and parties usually seek to maintain confidentiality with regard to the internal dynamics of the mediation process, a communications strategy remains important as talks continue, in order to establish appropriate expectations and to prepare the public for the outcome. Once an agreement is signed, a more robust media campaign

---

50. According to Pruitt, this is why it is important for mediators to "sponsor *concession exchanges*" (1981b, 208). For work on how security institutions such as the UN Security Council can provide credible signals to domestic audiences about the prudence of foreign policy actions, see Chapman and Reiter (2004); Chapman (2007).

is needed to inform the population of the opportunity for constructive change and to engage them in active participation in reconstruction. (2009, 13)

Algeria played such a face-saving role in the Iran hostage crisis because domestic audiences in both the United States and Iran made it prohibitively costly for the two sides to meet on one another's turf or even to conduct direct negotiations.[51] Algeria, by relaying the messages and hosting the parties during the signing of the documents, allowed the negotiations to occur, which led to a mutually acceptable agreement. The negotiations took place in relative secret, with the exact role of Algeria left ambiguous, obscuring which parties were most responsible for the concessions made. Algerian support for the release of the hostages also proved to be a useful signal to backers of the Iranian revolution that were skeptical of any deals with its Western adversary.

Long-Term Consequences of Mediation

We have seen that mediators can perform a variety of tasks to assist combatants in managing and resolving their conflicts. These mechanisms explain how intermediaries can improve the bargaining environment so that immediate resolution can more easily be reached; they also have implications for conflict relapse. To grasp fully how these tactics shape the bargaining environment, it is important to consider both a short and a long time horizon. As I flesh out more fully in chapters 5 and 6, there is likely to be a tension between these two time horizons.

The benefits that mediation provides apply primarily to the near term only. This holds for each of the mediation functions we have considered. First, the use of leverage to expand the set of acceptable alternatives makes the attractiveness of peace greater, but only in an immediate sense. Second, providing information and facilitating the exchange of information can realistically do little to reduce uncertainty about what is likely to happen in the future—it is difficult enough to get an accurate sense of the lay of the land in the past and the present, which are actually observable. Third, providing political cover can tackle only the political situation at hand. And, last, even the promise of implementation assistance is not guaranteed to improve settlement durability because third-party involvement cannot endure indefinitely. As a result, we can expect that mediators have a strong record of promoting peace in the short term but probably not in reducing the long-term propensity for the recurrence of conflict.

---

51. See Cohen (1996); Christopher (1985); Sick (1985).

Third parties can only secure a long-term peace when they enable the adversaries to reach a self-enforcing arrangement. Such an arrangement entails less willingness of the belligerents to challenge the resulting order and a greater ability to resolve future challenges peacefully if and when they arise. But the inclusion of a mediator in a peace process can actually disrupt the ability for the actors to find the self-sustaining means of avoiding future conflict. When actors bring in a third party to resolve tensions they feel in the present, both a greater need for renegotiation and a greater potential for bargaining failure in the future can arise. Table 2.2 summarizes these effects.

First, mediation can create or worsen time inconsistency problems, especially through its use of leverage. Most directly, the use of leverage can create only temporary incentives for combatants to make peace, and the relative attractiveness of conflict will return once those artificial incentives are removed. Particularly when a mediator tries to level the playing field by promoting a more egalitarian settlement when the bargaining power is far from equitable, such settlements come under tremendous stress once the pressure of the third party no longer restrains the side with stronger bargaining power from demanding a better share of the good or issue under dispute. Third-party incentives may not last long, for reasons relating back to our discussion about how mediation is an impure public good that is typically underprovided by third parties who have many items on their diplomatic agendas. Even the promise of implementation assistance, through monitoring or peacekeeping, can lead to more future demands for renegotiation by the actors because the third party typically cannot stay involved indefinitely and the actors who are dependent on the external security guarantees eventually will have to find an arrangement that is mutually preferable to conflict on their own. The attenuation of mediator involvement over time when leverage is used can greatly increase the need for renegotiation and thus risk relapse into conflict.

Second, mediation can actually heighten the degree of uncertainty in the bargaining environment in the future and thus make any renegotiation that does occur more difficult to resolve peacefully. If heavy mediation occurs early in the lifespan of a conflict, then actors may not be able to learn enough about the capabilities and resolve of their opponents to bargain with better clarity the next

TABLE 2.2 Mediation and the recurrence of conflict

MEANS OF INFLUENCE	IMPACT ON NEED FOR RENEGOTIATION	IMPACT ON EASE OF RENEGOTIATION
Expand alternatives	Worse if involvement fades	Worse if abbreviates learning
Implementation assistance	Worse if involvement fades	No major direct effect
Information exchange	No major direct effect	Worse if creates dependence
Political cover	No major direct effect	Worse if muddles signals

time tensions arise. What a "natural" and mutually acceptable agreement looks like may not be clear after such intervention because the primary reasons for reaching the earlier peace were the artifacts of incentives provided by the third party. In addition, when the disputants rely too much on the third party for information about their adversaries, they may not fully develop the means to learn from and adjust to the behavior of their foes to avoid renewed conflict. Moreover, the signals that actors use to deter one another, particularly when the actors attempt to generate audience costs as a means of indicating resolve, can become obscured when third parties have provided political cover in the past and enabled the actors to untie their hands.

Third, and not shown in table 2.2, all types of intermediary involvement are susceptible to manipulation by disputants with insincere motives. When third parties facilitate a peace process, the risk arises that the participants are seeking only a short-term lull in hostilities or support from domestic or international audiences who desire peace. When such objectives exist, we expect there will be future challenges to the existing order and more difficulty in resolving those challenges because that is what one or more of the actors intended all along. The previous existence of insincere motives also greatly increases the mistrust among the actors and the fear of future exploitation, further dampening the prospects of preventing conflict relapse.

We now have a theoretical basis for the trade-off that disputants and third parties confront when choosing mediation. To reap short-term peaceful dividends, the actors face the dual future risks of greater demand for renegotiation and greater difficulty in moving any renegotiation toward a peaceful conclusion. The dilemma becomes more pronounced when we consider higher levels of mediator involvement. More intrusive mediation, particularly with a heavy reliance on leverage, has the strongest likelihood of enabling the combatants to find an agreement in the present. Mediators with such an active level of involvement, however, also struggle the most to enable the combatants to reach a self-enforcing agreement that will be stable in the absence of third-party influence. The more the third parties become involved, the more they create only temporary incentives for peace, interrupt learning, foster dependencies, and muddle signals.

It would be a mistake, however, to conclude that mediation, especially of the heavy-handed and active variety, is then something that should generally be avoided. As I reveal in the next chapter, many belligerents appear to anticipate this trade-off and find mediation worthwhile precisely when they value an immediate peace highly. To the participants and the concerned observer, the choice of mediation can be a true dilemma in the sense that something must be given up when choosing either to go forward with mediation or to forgo it. This theoretical framework and my subsequent analysis will help identify the extent of this dilemma and the conditions under which it is maximized.

In this chapter, I have provided the theoretical basis for the rest of the book. Mediation is the inclusion in a peace process of a third party with mutual consent of the parties involved and without binding authority or the use of violent coercion. The tactics that an intermediary may employ range from merely facilitating discussions to using substantial leverage to move the belligerents toward peace. To provide the foundations of a deductive theoretical framework, I have discussed the incentives for mediation, on both the supply and demand sides, and then considered mediation in the context of crisis bargaining. Bargaining failure often occurs because of information asymmetries, domestic political constraints, or commitment barriers. Mediation can address these barriers by expanding the alternatives, assisting in implementation of the agreement, providing information, or providing political cover. Although these functions comprise the potential benefits of mediation in the short term, they are not generally effective in securing durable resolutions to conflict because, in addition to not necessarily helping in the basic struggle to shape future preferences for peace, they can interfere with the natural resolution of the conflict and the learning processes of the combatants. The provision of artificial incentives that fade over time, the obfuscation of the future bargaining environment, and the potential for insincere motives all can make future renegotiation both more likely and more difficult. Moreover, the short-term and long-term trade-off at the heart of the mediation dilemma becomes starkest whenever third parties become more active and intrusive in the conflict dynamics and peace processes of the combatants.

WHY ACCEPT MEDIATION?

If it is true that the breakdown in diplomacy leads to war, it is also true that the breakdown of war leads to diplomacy.

Geoffrey Blainey, *The Causes of War*

To explore the impact of mediation on the conflict bargaining environment, we can, as I do in chapters 4 and 5, observe how the variation in conflict outcomes changes in the presence of third-party involvement. Alternatively, we can look at the conditions that give rise to mediation to understand the purpose for which the actors intend to use it. We can learn much about the intended purposes of a treatment by studying the symptoms that lead to its adoption.

By forming and testing our expectations about when actors find mediation in their interest, we can deal head on with the puzzle that arises when considering the long-term risks of mediation in conjunction with its frequent occurrence. If mediation is expected to do relatively poorly in the long run, why would combatants or third parties ever sign up for it? If there are both short-term benefits and long-term struggles associated with third-party involvement, then the mediation selection process should reflect that dilemma. It is doubtful that the actors involved are ignorant to the risks of third-party conflict management; therefore, when mediation occurs, the participants must have interests that supersede the potential for any resulting peace to be more fragile than what could be attained in the absence of outside involvement.

The argument I focus on in this chapter simply posits that any long-term instability is more worthwhile when the short-term benefits of peace are substantial. When the actors are desperate for a reprieve from fighting, even if only temporary, they will avail themselves of that option and accept the potential long-run risks of mediation. Moreover, a short-term break from conflict appears even more attractive when the future is heavily discounted, such that the benefits today are substantially preferable to the benefits tomorrow.

The supply-side incentives for mediation also become relevant. Third parties with strong interests in the outcome of a dispute or in the achievement of short-term peace can influence the viability of mediation. This can also help explain why mediation so frequently occurs even though the combatants are left with a less durable settlement as a consequence. The observable implications of these arguments can be quantitatively tested and applied to historical examples.

Aside from taking a first cut at assessing the dilemma that actors face in considering mediation, we gain an additional benefit from examining mediation selection, in that it allows studies of mediation outcomes (such as those in the following chapters) to address problems of causal inference that arise from the nonrandom assignment of mediation. Studying the effects of mediation without a firm understanding of when mediation occurs would be like studying the effects of a medical treatment without knowing the baseline characteristics of the population to which the treatment has been administered. The set of crises that lead to mediation is likely to be very different, in terms of the ex ante likelihood of mediation success, than the set of crises that does not lead to mediation or that leads to intervention of another type. For example, if mediators generally intervene in intractable situations, the conflicts that do not undergo mediation are likely to be more amenable to full resolution and mediation will appear to have less of a positive impact than it really does. This is a form of endogeneity bias or selection effect.[1]

Once the selection processes are understood, analysts can then carefully interpret the potential for biased inferences and can construct appropriate research designs to assess the relationships more accurately. Note that this is true of both quantitative and qualitative research. Both types of analyses must account for the nonrandom selection of mediation when forming causal inferences about its effects. The appendix at the end of the book provides more discussion of how selection effects are likely to apply to many of the common data sets used in the study of mediation.

Willingness to Accept the Costs and Risks of Mediation

Given the potential long-term risks of third-party involvement, we expect mediation to occur when the costs of conflict are high and the future is substantially

---

1. For a more thorough account of selection effects with regard to the study of mediation, see Gartner and Bercovitch (2006). Note that this is different from selection bias, which is a problem in studies that examine the set of mediated cases only to determine what causes mediation success.

discounted. In such situations, the short-term benefits are extremely attractive, with any long-term risks more of an afterthought. Mediation rarely occurs in the absence of violent conflict, that is, as a preventative resolution mechanism or between conflict spells. A common explanation is that the actors often need to feel the sting of bargaining failure before they turn to alternative dispute resolution mechanisms.[2] When actors face costly and seemingly unending conflict, they are more likely to try other options, even if the alternative mechanisms are themselves costly and without guarantees of success. Relative to the costs and risks of severe conflict, mediation can appear cheap and nearly risk-free.

This explanation thus contends that the choice of mediation is one of desperation and relates to the expectation in the ripeness literature that mediation is more likely to occur during times of hurting stalemate. When the bilateral path has produced heavy costs, the combatants may feel that staying the course will surely bring more pain, whereas seeking third-party assistance at least will provide the chance of resolving the remaining bargaining barriers at less cost. If mediation fails to produce a stable peace, the disputants might not find it much worse than the nasty state of affairs prior to mediation. It becomes a worthwhile gamble. And even if mediation leads to long-term instability, the participants could actually be better off when conflict resumes because the third-party influence may curtail the severity of conflict, if not the likelihood, and the third party may have provided positive incentives as a part of the negotiation process.

It should not be assumed, however, that combatants seeking mediation want a full resolution of their costly conflict as an end in itself. Conflict is not something into which actors just accidentally fall; it is a chosen path that they take to maximize their payoffs in coercive diplomacy. They will have understood the risks of high conflict costs when refusing to settle at an earlier point in the bargaining process, and they will not want to pursue an alternative, less costly course of action if it offers no hope of more efficient bargaining. The argument here is that costly conflict makes other conflict management strategies relatively less costly or risky, but it is crucial that an alternative strategy such as mediation at least have some potential to decrease the barriers to bargaining that led to the onset of conflict in the first place.

Consistent with this view, high costs of conflict can lead disputants to want a limited cease-fire, during which they can explore their options for a full peace or renewed conflict. In other words, they may simply desire a breather during which negotiations can take place with some chance of success but with no delusions

---

2. For analyses that find that a costly and lengthy conflict heightens the probability of mediation, see Greig (2005); Greig and Diehl (2006); Bercovitch and Jackson (2001); Svensson (2008). For additional studies relating desperation to the desirability of mediation, see Bercovitch (1996); Terris and Maoz (2005); Böhmelt (2010a).

about the prospects for full resolution. In this case, participants recognize the costs associated with mediation and are willing to risk potential backsliding because it at least gives them a chance to make progress at the bargaining table, which has ostensibly not happened via bilateral bargaining. The negotiating parties may have also built the potential for such cease-fires into their decision calculus even before choosing to enter into conflict.

>   Hypothesis 3.1 *Mediation is more likely in disputes with high levels of severity.*

The *shadow of the future* refers to how strongly actors discount future outcomes today. When the future is relatively meaningless, we say that an actor has a short shadow of the future, and this is precisely the type of situation that will make mediation more attractive if its benefits are primarily in the short run. With such preferences, actors could enjoy the immediate benefits of mediation even though they may eventually give way to greater instability further down the line.

One variable that can shape the shadow of the future is regime stability. In unstable regimes, leaders' major concern is their own political survival. Transitioning regimes are adopting new institutions that they are unfamiliar with, and a small misstep may result in the current leaders being whisked out of office along with the failed institutions. Moreover, the presence of domestic instability typically indicates a high degree of contentious politics such that any decision of major importance, such as to fight or concede, will be hotly contested by opposition groups that want to portray the regime as weak or not acting in the national interest. Making decisions in the long-term interest of lasting peace is likely to be a low priority for such leaders because they will be unable to enjoy the downstream benefits of a policy if domestic instability persists and they soon lose office. As one example of such eagerness to achieve the short-term stabilizing benefits of mediation during times of desperation, in early 2001 Joseph Kabila, president of the Democratic Repbulic of the Congo (DRC), immediately accepted the prospect of talks in Washington and sought an end to the ongoing war enveloping the Great Lakes region of Africa after replacing his assassinated father as president. Options that have a high probability of short-term gains, particularly when accompanied by a period of stability, will thus be highly regarded by leaders in unstable regimes even if there is a low probability of sustained benefits.[3]

---

3. Note that the logic here is not necessarily at odds with Goemans's (2000) notion of gambling for resurrection in which leaders that are almost certainly going to lose office and then face severe punishment will attempt to seek a military victory to regain political control. The Kabila example provides a case of a leader that has a tenuous hold on power and is looking for short-term stability but is not at the point of needing an unlikely victory to stay in power.

A similar logic applies to leaders early in their tenure. New leaders have less ability to think in terms of long-term benefits and, instead, need to focus on consolidating power. Many new leaders are new precisely because general instabilities exist that preclude the ability to plan far in advance. Although revolutions and coups are obvious cases of instability, even new leaders that accede to power because of the collapse of a coalition government in a parliamentary system can experience domestic instability that will make immediate results more salient than long-term ones. Other new leaders may come to power via normal periodic transitions, as in many presidential systems. New leaders in such cases may not be symptomatic of instability per se, but they are still prone to have short shadows of the future. For instance, they will want to capitalize on elevated political capital—which can be lost quickly as U.S. President Barack Obama and French President Nicolas Sarkozy have recently discovered—following an electoral victory before the opposition parties can strengthen. As an example of new leadership injecting a sense of desperation for results, the peace process in Northern Ireland moved past a critical impasse in 1997 in part because both the United Kingdom and Ireland experienced leadership transitions as Tony Blair and Bertie Ahern became the new premiers and immediately pushed for progress in the talks (Chastelain 1999). The point is that new leaders have a greater desire for immediate results, with less emphasis on outcomes further down the line or on bolstering their legacies.

The idea that regime stability and leadership tenure shape a leader's discounting of the future and thus his or her preference for mediation relates to the saving-face function of third-party involvement. The short shadow of the future generated by new and unstable leadership leads not only to a general preference for short-term benefits but, much more specifically, to a need for immediate political cover. Notice that mediators may be sought to provide such short-term political cover both sincerely and insincerely. When a leader is unable or unwilling to make the concessions necessary to end a conflict because of domestic opposition, then he or she is likely to sincerely seek third-party assistance. Existing research has found that new leaders are more prone to make concessions,[4] which means we expect new leaders to have a strong need for short-term political cover that makes the concessions palatable at home. To the extent that a mediator can provide political cover for concessions—through owning responsibility

---

4. In this vein, Gelpi and Grieco (2001) argue that leaders early in their tenure have a greater willingness to make concessions because they are vulnerable and unable to take on the burden of sustained military combat. Chiozza and Choi (2003) and Beardsley (2010) indicate that the impact of tenure on a leader's preference for mediation is conditioned by regime type.

or signaling the prudence of concessions—this preserves the type of short-term political capital that new leaders and leaders in otherwise unstable regimes covet.

New and unstable leaders, however, may also face the opposite problem—having a domestic audience that is overly eager to end a conflict when the leader believes he or she will benefit more from fighting than conceding. Because leaders with a tenuous hold on power are less able to bear the political costs of fighting an unpopular war, they may seek mediation insincerely for a different type of political cover. In this case, the leader will try to go through the motions of a mediated peace process to convince the opposition at home that compromise is earnestly being pursued when, in actuality, the leader fully intends to remain intransigent at the negotiation table and return to conflict while blaming the other side for being unreasonable. For example, as we explore later, the DPRK is often suspected of pursuing mediation solely to play this part to domestic and international audiences, and Israeli and Palestinian leaders frequently accuse one another of the same. Opponents and third parties should be hesitant to pursue mediation when they suspect an actor of having such incentives, but uncertainty of the motives can allow for such imperiled mediation to occur nonetheless. Moreover, skeptical participants face a difficult choice between dealing with a negotiating partner potentially acting in bad faith and giving that actor the ability to use any refusals as evidence that it is not the side responsible for the ongoing hostilities.

Both types of political cover, because they merely help the leaders stay in power, meet more of a short-term need. So, leaders with a high demand for political cover will care less about conflict management strategies that primarily accrue in the long run. Their immediate needs of political survival will trump the desire for long-term gains.

> Hypothesis 3.2 *Mediation is more likely in disputes involving unstable regimes or new leaders.*

One implication of the political-cover logic is that the need to save face should be stronger for the challengers in a dispute than for the defenders of the status quo. Challengers are the actors that most clearly have chosen to enter into a dispute, and they must justify that choice to their publics, which can make backing down costly. The act of initiating a dispute signals to domestic audiences that the leader is optimistic about the chances of revising the status quo; however, then subsequently backing down can indicate incompetence and otherwise go against the audiences' own perception of what an acceptable agreement looks like as informed by the leader's initial justification (Bueno de Mesquita, Siverson and Woller 1992). Defenders, on the other hand, do not generally choose which disputes are brought against them and have fewer political constraints in making concessions. Because the audience costs of concessions are typically higher for challengers, we expect the challengers' need for political cover to be greater. This logic is consistent with the argument from existing studies that democratic leaders are especially more selective in choosing when to initiate a conflict because they face stronger political sanctions at home if they challenge and lose.[5] Following this argument, we can test whether regime stability and leadership tenure of just the challenging states do well in explaining the involvement of third parties in disputes.

Supply-Side Factors

As mentioned in the previous chapter, third parties can have a variety of selective incentives for serving as mediators. In particular, some can benefit from attenuating the conflict spillover costs, reducing a humanitarian crisis, or shaping the outcome in their favor. Even when third parties anticipate the long-term trade-off involved in mediation, they can still find serving as a conflict manager worthwhile. This is especially true if they primarily benefit—strategically, politically, economically, or morally—from helping to resolve the conflict immediately but do not bear many of the costs when the conflict recurs. Saadia Touval actually advocates that third parties discount the future and intervene forcefully whenever possible: "I believe that mediators ought to give greater weight to the likely near-term consequences of their choices because predictions of the near term are generally more reliable than those of the more distant future. Mediators can be certain that an ongoing war will produce casualties. Less certain is the proposition that ceasefires tend to break down, leading to the renewal of war and causing higher casualties in the long term" (2002, 183).

When outside actors will benefit from reducing negative externalities, have humanitarian interests, or have preferences about the final allocation of the good or issue under dispute, they can lobby the combatants to let them mediate.[6] Even when the combatants are hesitant about mediation because of the costs or risks involved, third parties may be able to compel the disputants to undergo assisted negotiations. Such enticements may include some form of tangible aid or threat, but probably they more often involve less tangible promises of improved relations and preferential treatment that can be consequential, especially if the third party

---

5. See Bueno de Mesquita and Siverson (1995); Reiter and Stam (1998); Gelpi and Griesdorf (2001). In a similar vein, Reiter (1995) argues that leaders often avoid preemptive wars because of the political burdens of initiating conflict. Slantchev (2003, 2004) and Filson and Werner (2002) also argue that the initiators of conflict are the actors most prone to revise their expectations of success downward as war progresses.

6. For an assessment of when third parties will offer to provide mediation in interstate and intrastate conflicts, see Greig (2005); Greig and Regan (2008). For a network perspective of how close ties with third parties can influence the incidence of mediation, see Böhmelt (2009).

is an important player in the international system. For example, the offer of U.S. mediation in Honduras following the June 2009 coup presumably was accepted because the key players in Honduras recognized that maintaining favorable relations with the United States was important and that the United States had strong interests in the outcome related to both its desire to strengthen democracy in Latin America and to stand firm against Venezuelan meddling. Also, the pressure to mediate does not have to come from the would-be mediator per se if interested third parties are content to have another actor broker a deal. For example, from 1967 to 1969, U.S. inducements in the form of arms assurances provided an incentive for Israel to agree to participate in the negotiations under the auspices of Gunnar Jarring, special representative of the UN (Touval 1982, 149).

Conversely, an absence of interest by third parties in providing mediation can lead to a free-rider problem and an under-provision of mediation even when the combatants desire it. Either way, it should be the case that mediation is positively associated with third-party interest. Heightened outside-actor interest in conflict management should increase the propensity for mediation to occur while indifference should decrease the propensity.

> Hypothesis 3.3 *Mediation is more likely in disputes with a high degree of salience to potential third parties.*

Empirical Record

To assess these hypotheses, I use quantitative methods to explore aggregate relationships while accounting for potentially confounding variables. This statistical approach not only allows the analyst to test whether the implications drawn from the arguments are actually observed in the real world; it also allows us to see the substantive effects of the relationships. The purpose, then, is not just to test if there is *some* relationship between two variables in the observed data but much more than that. The methods are useful in understanding the magnitudes of the relationships. For this reason, my focus here is on the substantive interpretations of the findings.

I next present a brief overview of the data and variables. More information regarding the coding of these variables and the model specifications, as well as the full regression results, are presented in the appendix at the end of the book.

Two data sets are used: the International Crisis Behavior (ICB) data and the Issue Correlates of War (ICOW) data (version 1.1, created by Paul Hensel and Sara Mitchell). The ICB data are useful because they cover the entire globe from 1918 to 2006 and include cases in which militarized violence is a perceived possibility but does not necessarily occur—its threshold is neither too restrictive to only include conflicts that have escalated nor too relaxed to include conflicts with no potential for escalation. Of the 729 crisis dyads in the data, 170, just over 23 percent, experienced mediation.[7]

Because the ICB data contain only one observation per crisis dyad, and thus are unable to provide information about dynamic third-party activity within a crisis, I also use the ICOW data. These data contain information on territorial claims in the Western Hemisphere and Western Europe from 1816 to 2001; river claims in the Western Hemisphere, Western Europe, and Middle East from 1900 to 2001; and maritime claims in the Western Hemisphere and Western Europe from 1900 to 2001. The principal justification for using the ICOW data is that they allow the analyst an opportunity to assess each conflict management event over the course of a claim at different points in a conflict. Using an event-history approach with these data, it is possible to model not only whether third-party conflict management occurs but also when it occurs. Factors related to conflict severity, a short shadow of the future, and third-party pressure that are expected to have a positive impact on the incidence of outside involvement should also decrease the time until conflict management occurs. Note that some of the third-party conflict management attempts in the ICOW data involve arbitration and adjudication. Although the results are robust to a competing-risks setup that separates the occurrence of mediation from the occurrence of arbitration and adjudication, for simplicity of interpretation, the results presented here relate to models of the occurrence of general third-party conflict management.

To capture conflict costs, the analyses with the ICB data use four variables: an indicator of violence level, the length of the crisis (log transformed), the presence of an ethnic dimension in the conflict, and the latent military capability ratio (log transformed) that the strongest actor in a dyad has. A four-point indicator of violence most directly measures conflict costs. Crisis length and the ethnic conflict indicators primarily capture the difficulty of resolving the crisis peacefully, whereas the capability ratio measure captures the potential for the crisis to be mutually hurting. The ICOW analyses similarly use the number of fatal militarized interstate disputes (MIDs) that have occurred in a dyad over an issue in the current year, the number of fatal MIDs that have occurred in a dyad over an issue in the past five years, and the natural log of the capability ratio within the dyad.[8]

The models run with the ICB data use three variables to account for the potential interests of third parties in mediating. The first variable counts the

---

7. The value 23 percent is for all crisis dyads, which translates into approximately one-third of all crises.

8. ICOW dispute length is not included here as an indicator of costliness because so many of the disputes never became militarized.

number of neighbors of each actor in a dyad and sums them together to get a total count of the number of neighbors.[9] The logic is that having more neighbors implies having more actors that are potentially adversely affected by spillover or that have particular interests in the outcome of the dispute. When conflicts occur in relative isolation, there should be fewer third parties interested in becoming involved as a conflict manager. The second variable counts the number of democratic neighbors. Sara Mitchell (2002) has argued that there is a higher preference for third-party conflict management within democratic communities.[10] In addition, domestic political incentives to intervene in salient neighboring conflicts will weigh more heavily with democratic leaders, who will also tend to be more active in international organizations that frequently supply mediation. A third variable uses a five-point measure of the salience of a crisis to the international system, with low values indicating isolated regional relevance and higher values indicating widespread ramifications. The ICOW analyses also use the number of overall neighbors and the number of democratic neighbors as indicators of third-party incentives to become involved, although an analogous geostrategic salience variable does not exist for these data.

To measure instability, the number of years since a substantial change in a regime's institutions is taken as one indicator. The number of days (log transformed) since executive leadership turnover is taken as another measure of the extent to which the future is discounted. Some models use the averages of these measures to characterize the stability and leadership tenure of the actors within each dyad—because the choice of mediation must be mutual, both sides in a dyad have to see some need for it. To demonstrate robustness, other models use the measures that pertain only to the challenger, which is, recall, the actor most likely to need political cover for backing down or making concessions.[11]

To get an even better grasp on the role of instability, it is useful to isolate the set of democratic dyads to explore how the effect of instability is conditioned by regime type. That is, democratic leaders who are early in their tenure or in unstable polities should perceive an even shorter shadow of the future than authoritarian leaders. Authoritarian leaders often can anticipate being in power indefinitely, whereas democratic leaders face strict institutional constraints. Moreover, democratic leaders, by the nature of their greater accountability, should need political cover more for both conceding and remaining in conflict when there are substantial portions of the polity that object to such important

---

9. This approach intentionally double-counts actors that are neighbors to both combatants because such actors are especially affected by the dispute.

10. See also Crescenzi, Kadera, and Mitchell (2007).

11. The challenger-specific models are possible only with the ICOW data because challengers and targets are not identified in the ICB data.

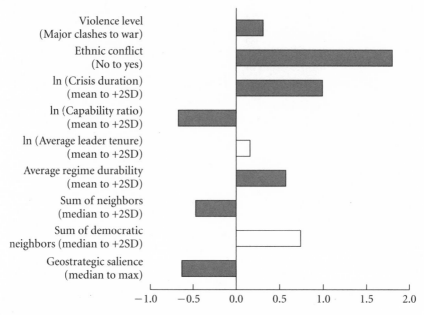

FIGURE 3.1   Relative risks of mediation in all crisis dyads. Values are relative changes in the predicted probability of mediation incidence. Shaded bars are statistically significant ($p < 0.05$, one-tailed test). SD, standard deviation.

Source: ICB data.

decisions. For these reasons, we expect the tenure and regime durability variables to have an even stronger effect on mediation incidence when democracies are involved. Democratic leaders with a short tenure or with a tenuous hold on power should be the most likely to seek mediation, whereas authoritarian leaders with a long tenure and in a stable regime should be the least likely.

The results generally confirm our expectations. Figure 3.1 presents the substantive effects of the results using the ICB data. These are relative risks of mediation occurrence, calculated as the difference in the predicted probability of mediation when moving the independent variable as indicated, divided by the baseline predicted probability.[12] Interval-level and ordinal variables are increased by two standard deviations (2SD) and dichotomous variables are increased from 0 to 1.[13] The shaded bars indicate statistical significance, and empty ones indicate statistically insignificant relationships.

---

12. Multiplied by 100, the value for relative risks gives the percentage change in the risk of occurrence. The baseline configuration has all the interval-level independent variables set at their means, all the ordinal variables at their medians, and the dichotomous variables at zero.

13. For the ordinal variables, the changes are rounded to the nearest integer. The geostrategic salience variable is increased to its maximum because that is the closest possible value to the two-standard-deviation (2 SD) increase.

All the variables indicating severity and costs of conflict are statistically significant and in the expected directions. Mediation is more likely in a violent war, when there is ethnic conflict, the crisis is long, and there is power parity. When actors are relatively desperate for a reprieve, they are more willing to accept the costs and risks associated with mediation. Many of these relationships are also substantively meaningful. Mediation is almost three times more likely in ethnic conflicts, twice as likely when the natural logarithm of the crisis duration increases by 2SD, and less than half as likely when the indicator of capability imbalance increases by 2SD.

Regime durability has an unexpected positive relationship with mediation, and the tenure variable is statistically insignificant. But so far we have not accounted for the potential conditioning effect of regime type. Leaders in democracies should respond differently to issues of instability and tenure than other leaders. The results in figures 3.2 and 3.4 later in the chapter take into account the potential conditioning effect of regime type.

The evidence does not demonstrate as much support for our supply-side expectations. The total number of neighbors and the geostrategic salience have a substantial negative correlation with mediation, and the number of democratic neighbors is not statistically significant. An increase by 2SD (rounded) in the number of neighbors of a crisis dyad—which is an increase by thirteen—decreases the probability of mediation by almost half, and an increase in geostrategic salience from its median to its maximum decreases the propensity for mediation by even more. These findings are interesting because they suggest that when neighboring and powerful states in the international system have strong interests in a crisis, the disputants actually *resist* mediation. On further consideration, this is understandable because many disputants prefer to limit meddling by external actors wishing to shape the regional and global orders in their favor. As we see later, more intrusive interventions tend to produce greater risks of long-term instability, and so disputants have reason to be especially hesitant about allowing very eager third parties to become involved. When outside interests are too strong, the disputants are wary about third-party conflict management. Indeed, many of the crises with high geostrategic salience and many neighbors involve great powers, which are best able to keep external actors from interfering. Presumably for this reason, mediation rarely occurs in conflicts between great powers.

Figure 3.2 presents the relative risks of mediation from a model that is restricted to the set of democratic dyads. Regime durability and tenure, as expected, are both negatively correlated with outside involvement when the dyads are restricted to joint democracies. Mediation is more likely among relatively unstable and new democratic regimes. These findings corroborate the argument that actors find mediation most attractive when they strongly discount the future. In competitive

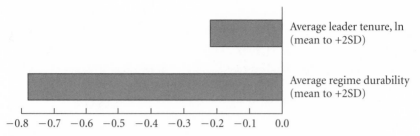

FIGURE 3.2   Relative risks of mediation in democratic crisis dyads. Values are relative changes in the predicted probability of mediation incidence. Shaded bars are statistically significant (*p* < 0.05, one-tailed test). SD, standard deviation.

Source: ICB data.

democracies, new leaders and those governing through infirm institutions have relatively short shadows of the future because of the need to consolidate power, the restrictions of term limits, and the needs for political cover from any unpopular foreign policy decisions. It is worth noting that the regime stability variable has much more of a substantive impact than the tenure variable: an increase by 2SD in regime durability decreases the probability of mediation by 78 percent, whereas a 2SD increase in the measure of leadership tenure decreases the probability by just 22 percent. This should not be surprising because regime stability is a more direct measure of how precarious a leader's political standing is, and many new democratic leaders could conceivably feel quite comfortable if they recently received a strong electoral mandate.

Using the ICOW data, figure 3.3 displays the relative risks of outside involvement when the independent variables increase by 1 unit for the fatal MID counts and by 2SD for the other variables.[14] The results presented are from two different models. One model measures tenure and durability using the averages across the actors in each dyad; this model is the basis for most of the results reported. The other specification, which produces robust results as seen in the appendix, measures tenure and durability using the values from the challenging state. Figure 3.3 indicates that the risk of experiencing third-party conflict management increases by 200 percent (i.e., it triples) when there is a fatal MID in the current year of the dispute and that it increases by 48 percent when there has been a

---

14. These values were calculated from Cox duration models and are simply the relevant hazard ratios minus 1. A hazard ratio is the ratio between the hazard rate with the treatment and the hazard rate without the treatment—where the hazard rate is the probability of experiencing the event conditional on having not experienced the event yet and thus can be thought of, in this case, as a type of risk of experiencing third-party conflict management.

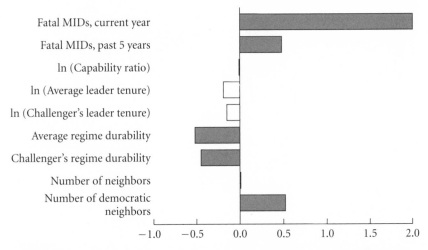

FIGURE 3.3 Relative risks of third-party conflict management in all dispute dyads. Values are relative changes in the risk of third-party conflict management when variables increase by either one unit for the counts of fatal MIDs or two standard deviations for the other variables. Shaded bars are statistically significant ($p < 0.05$, one-tailed test). MIDs, militarized interstate disputes.

Source: ICOW data.

fatal MID in the previous five years. These findings confirm the expectation that actors are more desperate for at least a short-term reprieve when they are suffering heavy conflict costs. In such instances, the immediate needs of each actor to reduce costs become stronger than long-term concerns about whether any lulls in hostilities will only be temporary, intentionally or not. Interestingly, the capability ratio variable is not statistically significant when the ICOW data are used.[15] One potential explanation for this is that this indicator is not as useful of a measure of a hurting stalemate in disputes that are predominantly low level and not militarized.

Even though the measure of the total number of neighbors is statistically insignificant, the results show that disputes in democratic communities are more prone to experience outside assistance; this effect is both statistically significant and substantively meaningful. An increase by nine democratic neighbors for a dyad (four or five for each actor) increases the probability of third-party conflict management by 52 percent. In democratic communities such as Europe and, more recently, the Americas, there is stronger pressure for third-party conflict

---

15. This variable does become statistically significant, with the expected sign (negative), when the sample is restricted to the set of democratic dyads.

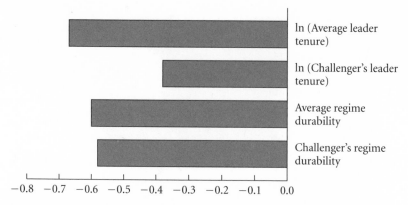

FIGURE 3.4   Relative risks of third-party conflict management in disputes involving democratic states. Values are relative changes in the risk of third-party conflict management when variables increase by two standard deviations. Shaded bars are statistically significant ($p < 0.05$, one-tailed test).

Source: ICOW data.

management. This at least provides some indication that neighboring interests can have a positive effect on the propensity for outside involvement, not just a negative one. In light of the discussion about hesitation by combatants to involve overly eager third parties, it is likely that disputants in democratic neighborhoods are less threatened by the potential meddling of other democracies and are more likely to acquiesce to their advances, especially if the democratic neighbors work through international organizations.

To better assess the role of political instability using the ICOW data, figure 3.4 again restricts the sample to just the democratic states and focuses on the tenure and durability variables.[16] The results confirm our expectations—both relationships are negative and statistically significant in each model specification. We observe that outside involvement is less likely as stability—measured by both tenure and institutional durability—increases among democratic disputants. Moreover, the effects are quite strong because an increase by 2SD in three of the measures leads to a decrease of well over 50 percent in the risk of outside involvement. That is, short shadows of the future and greater needs for political cover correlate with more third-party conflict management, whereas better political stability correlates with less. It is interesting that the relative magnitudes differ between the ICOW and ICB analyses. When we use the ICB data, regime

16. When the variables capture the dyadic averages, the sample consists of the democratic dyads; when the variables capture the challenger's characteristics, the sample consists of the democratic challengers.

durability appears to have a much starker impact than leadership tenure. One explanation may relate to existing findings, which show that vulnerable leaders need political cover less in more severe conflicts (ICB crises tend to be more severe than ICOW disputes).[17]

To sum up the findings from the quantitative analysis, we find that, first, mediation is more likely to occur when the actors face costly and difficult conflict situations, as when the fighting is intense, has occurred for a long time, involves ethnic dimensions, and is between actors of similar strength. Second, democratic states with domestic instability and new leaders are more likely to seek mediation. These findings indicate that actors tend toward mediation when they are desperate for peace or otherwise discount the future greatly in favor of short-term political gains. We thus begin to get a sense of how states face a trade-off when considering mediation and are much more willing to take on the long-term risks when the immediate cessation of hostilities is highly attractive. Third, it appears that supply-side factors do matter, but not necessarily in ways initially expected. We see some evidence that democratic communities can encourage the practice but that disputants may actually resist mediation by heavily interested third parties.

Illustrative Cases

Here I introduce three illustrative examples in which the logic just discussed and tested has played out in practice. In subsequent chapters, I will continue to glean information from these cases. Although each of these cases did experience mediation, we see in chapter 5 that they had different outcomes with regards to the long-term stability of their mediated peace; we then focus on key factors that maximize or minimize the trade-off in mediation outcomes. For now, I present these cases as examples of the various mechanisms that drive the choice for costly and risky mediation.

Kissinger and Carter in the Middle East

Although Henry Kissinger and Jimmy Carter had different approaches to peace in the Middle East, I treat their efforts together here because the final Egyptian-Israeli peace treaty cannot be understood without following the peace process

---

17. See Beardsley (2010). This explanation is not complete, however, because it does not explain why regime stability does not also matter less in the ICB analysis.

from 1973 to 1979. This case demonstrates how the high costs of conflict, need for political cover, and third-party pressure can shape the incentives for mediation to occur. Because of these incentives, Israel and Egypt were willing to accept the risks from third-party involvement.

Conflict costs are the first important factor driving the incentives for mediation. As the hostilities in the 1973 October War wound down, the immediate aims of Egypt centered on protecting the Third Army from complete collapse, recovering the Sinai Peninsula, and resolving issues related to the occupied territories and the Palestinian question.[18] The need to save the Third Army, and generally to avoid further military losses, made its initial desperation for negotiations quite high. Even though Sadat claimed to have achieved his goals in the October War, he was keenly aware of the burdens of the war, and this motivated him in his peace initiative.

> Why did I think we could achieve so much through peace? By a simple calculation: how much war had cost Egypt and the Arab world since 1948. Until the October War, 99 percent of the economic burden was borne by Egypt. Even after the October War, when the entire Arab world made a lot of money out of oil and added to their wealth, Egypt by contrast was drained of its resources. So whenever the Israelis created problems during the peace negotiations, my thoughts would go back to the burden we had to bear, and I would opt for peace.
>
> I also thought of the direct results of the October War. What did that war achieve for us? We regained a very small portion of the Sinai and we managed to reopen the Suez Canal. Against this we have to set the cost to Egypt of 14 billion pounds, plus all the losses in men and equipment. (Sadat 1984, 106–7)[19]

The Egyptian economy was heading toward ruin because, in part, it bore the greatest security burden in the protracted conflict between the Arab states and the Israelis. It was also becoming clear that continual conflict with Israel was not ever likely to yield much of a payoff, given that the strategic advantage for Egypt at the start of the 1973 war was potentially as good as could be expected and yet the result was, objectively, closer to defeat than to victory.

Israel too had high immediate costs of conflict, even as it encircled the Third Army. The Israeli military suffered heavy casualties at the start of the war, and the people became desperate for peace as the war unfolded in the midst of a stalled

---

18. See Touval (1982, 236).
19. Carter (1982, 283) also recognizes Sadat's war weariness as a crucial factor in bringing him to the negotiating table. See also Baker (1978, 130, 243).

economy.[20] Kissinger (1982, 748–49) recognized the growing support for a settlement on disengagement, noting that Israel would have needed to maintain the deployment of several divisions to continue holding the territory gained on the west bank of the Suez and that Israel needed to find a way to recover its prisoners of war sooner rather than later.

The mounting price of war, not only from the immediate fighting in October 1973 but also from the toll of a quarter century of nearly constant hostilities, thus helps explain why Israel and Egypt embarked on a disengagement process with Kissinger at the helm. Both sides were relatively desperate to try something new and would not have thought that the costs and risks of mediation were all that significant in relation to the burdens of the status quo. Both sides, and especially Egypt, were also eager to tap more into U.S. technology and aid as a means to bolster their economies, which would further increase the attractiveness of pursuing a peace process under Kissinger's auspices.[21] The rising desperation on both sides was not lost on Kissinger, who claims, "From the outset, I was determined to use the war to start a peace process" (1982, 468).

The costs of conflict were certainly salient to the disengagement talks in the immediate wake of the October War, but they also were influential in later initiatives that included the Camp David summit.[22] In that regard, as bilateral talks stalemated after the initial promise of Sadat's bold trip to Jerusalem in 1977, the risk of renewed conflict resurfaced as impatience grew. Moreover, Egypt had been spending substantial amounts on its security forces during the lull in hostilities, with over half of its GNP going to military expenditures in 1975 (Telhami 1990, 69; Baker 1978, 130). With such high security expenses, the costs of nonagreement were substantial enough to keep the parties eager for settlement and more willing to bear the risks and costs of mediation.

Another factor motivating mediation throughout the step-by-step and the Camp David peace processes was the importance of political cover for the leaders in the midst of fragile domestic and international political situations. Aaron David Miller notes that the leaderships on both sides of the Arab-Israeli conflict have been "held accountable 24/7 by domestic politics, public opinion, and their own conception of how the terms of any agreement would shape their current political situation and place in history" (2008, 37). Negotiating with Israel, widely viewed by Arabs at the time as an illegitimate state, was politically costly domesti-

---

20. See Stein (1999, 97).

21. See Baker (1978, 137–38).

22. In fact, the lengthy quotation from Sadat's memoirs expresses his justification for his peace initiative that began with his trip to Jerusalem in 1977 and that led to the Camp David process in 1978.

cally and regionally for Arab leaders. Sadat recognized that if he could not go all the way with Israel to reach a comprehensive settlement that resolved the issues related to the Palestinians and the occupied territories, he would certainly need substantial political cover to make an Egyptian-Israeli treaty viable.[23] Moreover, both Israel and Egypt claimed victory after the October War, so it was politically delicate for either side to consider concessions that would be necessary for a peace agreement.

More specific to the Israeli leaders' need for political cover, this period saw the end of the relatively firm control of power by the Labor Party and can be characterized as politically unstable (i.e., not conducive to a long shadow of the future). Public support for government policies on salient issues such as national security had to be carefully nurtured and protected. The Israeli domestic public was closely attuned to the U.S. leaders' stance toward Israel because the fate of Israel had been so intertwined with its superpower ally. This actually created competing incentives for pursuing U.S. mediation. On the one hand, Israeli leaders could win political support when making decisions that improved U.S.-Israeli relations. On the other hand, by giving the United States a prominent role in the negotiations, the leaders faced a risk of stirring domestic concerns whenever they ran afoul of U.S. interests. In fact, Yitzhak Rabin (1979, 300) faults the aggressive posture of the Carter administration toward him as the key reason why the Labor Party lost control of parliament in 1977.[24] The ability for a third party to hold sway with a domestic public can offer the opportunity for saving face, but it also can increase the risk of losing face when preferences differ from those of the third party.

The importance of political cover can be seen through comparing these mediation initiatives to other conflict management attempts. An interesting facet of the Arab-Israeli conflict during this time period is that we do observe some of the alternatives to mediation that were considered, and one reason why they failed to make progress was the abundance of rampant political posturing in the absence of political cover. That is, Sadat and Begin tried a bilateral initiative that began with lower-level negotiations through secret Moroccan and Rumanian channels and that became public with Sadat's speech to the Knesset in 1977. But the bilateral talks soon bogged down, in part because neither side could make the moves necessary for progress when under constant domestic and international scrutiny.[25] In addition, the parties tried the Geneva Conference, initially created as a

---

23. On Sadat's need to save face, see Carter (1982, 345); Quandt (1986, 203).

24. It is, of course, difficult to assertain the truth of such a claim made by someone assigning blame for a failed bid for election.

25. On the importance of domestic political constraints in the bilateral initiative, see Stein (1999, 231).

charade of sorts. One problem with the Geneva Conference, as witnessed in the opening statements on December 21, 1973, was that the parties had strong incentives to grandstand and show off to their domestic and international audiences instead of negotiating sincerely with one another. Kissinger (1982, 794) writes, "Each of the contending parties could sustain its experiment with peace only by proving its constant vigilance to the hard-liners back home." Another problem, and ultimately what doomed a return to the conference later, was that the representation of the Palestinian Arabs became a political dilemma: the Israelis would lose substantial political capital if there was a formal Palestinian delegation because this would imply recognition of the Palestine Liberation Organization (PLO) as a legitimate entity; on the other side, the Arab states would bear immense criticism if they consented to the exclusion of a Palestinian delegation and tried to speak on their behalf.[26]

Through mediation, especially the type characterized by Kissinger's shuttle diplomacy and Carter's secluded summit, the greater public was left in the dark about the content of the negotiations and thus could not decipher who offered which concessions and whether the Palestinian Arabs were getting a fair shake or not. In contrast to the bilateral initiative and the Geneva Conference, negotiations under the auspices of Kissinger and Carter could more easily proceed and deal with very difficult substantive issues instead of being sidetracked by political posturing. Mediation in these cases was thus motivated in part by actors confronting dicey political situations and needing to save face.

Turning to supply-side interests, the United States was initially eager to become involved as a third-party conflict manager to improve its influence in the Middle East relative to that of the Soviet Union and to get the oil embargo lifted.[27] There was also fear that renewed hostilities between Israel and Egypt would bring the United States and USSR into serious confrontation, giving the United States a substantial stake in reducing regional tensions.[28] We can see directly how the superpower rivalry—easing during this period of detente but still a strong concern—motivated U.S. incentives to mediate in Kissinger's adroit denial of substantial Soviet involvement in the peace process. Keeping the Soviets at arm's length, thereby enhancing U.S. sway in the region and minimizing the friction points between the superpowers, was an important goal for Kissinger. To do this, he had to create the perception that the Soviets were involved in the peace efforts

---

26. See Stein (1999, 170, 205); Quandt (1986, 132).

27. For a thorough discussion of the importance of superpower competition in shaping the incentives for U.S. involvement, see Telhami (1990). In his memoirs, Carter (1982, 278) cites oil dependence as crucial in U.S. incentives to mediate. See also Quandt (2001, 125–26); Horne (2009, 237); Ben-Ami (2005, 149).

28. See Brzezinski (1985, 83); Quandt (2001, 104, 125).

while separately making progress on his own. A key function of the Geneva Conference in December 1973 was thus to involve the USSR and the UN as collaborators and to give the peace process legitimacy when the intention all along was to make progress on the disengagement agreements between Israel and Egypt after the conference and without Soviet involvement.[29]

The motivations for Camp David are arguably even more closely tied to third-party incentives than the motivations for the disengagement talks because the latter occurred in the shadow of massive battle losses, while the former occurred during a period of relative calm in relations between Israel and Egypt. Almost immediately on taking office, Carter began a Middle East peace initiative, and during his tenure he was the most willing of any U.S. president to take political risks for peace in the Arab-Israeli conflict.[30] His zeal for peace strongly shaped the incentives for Israel and Egypt, both of which highly valued alignment with the United States at this point, to come together under his auspices. The U.S. president clearly saw his role as important in making the Camp David process happen, as Carter (1982, 316) writes in his memoirs, "There was only one thing to do, as dismal and unpleasant as the prospect seemed—I would try to bring Sadat and Begin together for an extensive negotiating session with me." Cyrus Vance (1983, 164), secretary of state at the time, also highlights that the administration believed, even before it took office, that progress on peace in the Middle East depended on the United States taking a proactive stance: "President Carter and I agreed that his administration would take an immediate, leading role in breathing new life into the Middle East peace process, building on the foundations laid by our predecessors."

Note, however, that the Camp David negotiations did not occur until September 1978, almost two years into Carter's term. So, Carter's eagerness to mediate the conflict did not immediately produce a third-party assisted peace process and may have even delayed the type of negotiations seen at Camp David. Just as we have seen in the quantitative analysis, disputants often resist the advances of third parties that are too interested in becoming involved; Carter was actually rebuffed early in his presidency. Israeli and Egyptian frustrations with Carter's push for a renewed Geneva Conference, as well as their aborted bilateral attempt, are suggestive of the incentives and disincentives that disputants consider when choosing conflict management approaches. Mainly, they indicate that parties often have a preference to keep the negotiations as limited as possible if they can.

---

29. See Kissinger (1982, 749–50, 755, 843); Isaacson (1992, 538–39); Quandt (2001, 135). Brzezinski (1985, 83, 87) notes a similar motivation for the push by the Carter administration for a return to Geneva.

30. See Stein (1999, 43–44); Telhami (1990, 13).

Both Israel and Egypt wanted to avoid the spectacle of another Geneva Conference because of all the compromises that would be needed just to convene the conference, chief among them agreeing on how to incorporate Palestinian representation and how to limit Soviet and UN involvement.[31] Israel and Egypt initially preferred a bilateral attempt to reach a comprehensive settlement and only later, after the bilateral initiative fizzled, saw merit in another U.S.-led peace process. Disputants will often prefer to start with a bilateral approach because of the costs and risks associated with including an intermediary.[32] This also suggests that forum shopping for conflict management is sometimes a trial and error process. Disputants may start with a bilateral initiative and then later incorporate a third party when their initial attempt fails and they become more impatient for resolution and the assistance that third parties can bring.

Carter in North Korea

A later example is Jimmy Carter's mediation as a private citizen in the North Korean nuclear crisis. This case, too, demonstrates the importance of conflict costs and supply-side incentives in choosing mediation but in important new ways. Here the high costs were anticipated and not actually related to heavy battlefield casualties. So, we see some evidence that expected costs alone can increase the incentives for the actors to desire mediation. Moreover, the supply-side pressure was not from a major power using its geostrategic influence but, rather, from a private citizen using less tangible political influence. Soft power can be relevant in addition to traditional power when we consider the incentives for mediation.

The DPRK signed the Nuclear Non-Proliferation Treaty (NPT) in December 1985, but delayed signing the mandatory International Atomic Energy Agency (IAEA) safeguards for six years.[33] Only after the United States removed its nuclear forces from the Korean peninsula in 1991 did North Korea finally agree to the safeguards of seven declared sites in January 1992. Also, in December 1991, the DPRK and the Republic of Korea (ROK, or South Korea) agreed to a "Joint Declaration on the Denuclearization of the Korean Peninsula," in which both sides promised to not pursue nuclear weapons and to allow mutual inspections. Between May and January 1993, the IAEA conducted six ad hoc inspections of the declared DPRK sites. The inspectors found discrepancies between

---

31. See Weizman (1981, 241); Rabin (1979, 320–22); Quandt (1986, 132); Ben-Ami (2005, 158).

32. Ezer Weizman, the Israeli defense minister, was especially leery of maintaining a high degree of dependence on the United States and preferred initially to develop face-to-face negotiations with the Egyptians (Weizman 1981, 126–27).

33. For an overview of the DPRK nuclear crisis, see Mack (1994); Cronin (1994).

the declared inventory and the observed levels, creating the suspicion that the DPRK had diverted fissile material prior to inspections. But the IAEA inspectors were denied the necessary access to verify the accuracy of this suspicion. In addition, after a tip from U.S. intelligence, the IAEA requested special inspection of two suspected nuclear waste storage facilities that were not included in the list of declared sites. On March 12, 1993, the DPRK refused to allow the special inspections and declared its intent to withdraw from the NPT. On April 1, the IAEA Board of Governors reported the DPRK noncompliance to the UN Security Council, which passed Resolution 825 on May 11 calling for North Korea to comply with its safeguards agreement.

After a year of high tensions and failed diplomatic initiatives, the situation escalated in mid-May 1994 after the DPRK began extracting the 8,000 spent fuel rods in the Yongbyong 5-megawatt reactor. On June 13, the DPRK officially submitted its intent to withdraw from the NPT, and on June 15, the United States began consultations with other Security Council members, as well as with Japan and South Korea, about a two-phase sanctions plan. The United States had also begun mobilizing its forces in the region and strongly considered a tactical strike on the Yongbyong complex because it feared that the DPRK might launch a preemptive military strike in response to the threat of sanctions and in advance of a full U.S. deployment (Wit, Poneman, and Galucci 2004).

Amid this growing crisis that was threatening to spiral out of control, Jimmy Carter acted as a mediator on June 15–18, 1994. On June 6, Kim Il Sung, who knew that the former president kept an open mind toward compromise with the DPRK, confirmed a standing invitation for Carter to mediate. The Clinton administration debated whether to allow Carter to go because he held a more lenient stance on whether the DPRK should be allowed to reprocess nuclear material—it was permitted under the NPT, but prohibited by the North-South joint declaration—and was much more dovish on sanctions.[34] Ultimately, Clinton allowed Carter to go, hoping that his status as a former president might afford Kim the opportunity to back down from his nuclear program without losing face at home.

The expected costs of conflict shaped the propensity for mediation in this case. Even though hostilities never actually broke out, their heightened potential to do so, perhaps the highest since 1953, and the prodigious destruction they would entail made the attempt at mediation worth a shot. In June 1994, the Clinton administration was in the final stages of both seeking sanctions from the UN

---

34. On the deliberations by the Clinton administration regarding Carter's visit, see Wit, Poneman, and Galucci (2004, 203, 243).

Security Council and mobilizing forces in the region. If the crisis had continued along the course it was taking, the risk of full-scale war would have increased substantially and the costs of such a war would have been enormous. Thus, although the direct immediate costs of conflict were not high in June 1994 (violent hostilities had not yet erupted), the expected costs of continuing in crisis—the probability of war multiplied by its costs—were high.

As discussed in chapter 2, disputants may have both sincere and insincere motives for mediation. Thus far I have discussed the high expected costs in this crisis in terms of sincere motivations—the attempt to find an alternative path of reaching a settlement in the midst of the potential for severe escalation. But the costs also probably created incentives, especially on the DPRK side, to pursue mediation insincerely with the end of stalling. The DPRK, with its nascent weapons program and foundering economy, presumably saw an opportunity to use the peace process as a means both to delay the threat to its weapons program and to extract aid from the international community. We will return to this likely motivation later as a key explanation for why tensions eventually renewed after this bold peace initiative and also consider how the Clinton administration tried proactively to reduce the DPRK exploitation of the process.

The United States was not oblivious to the potential for the DPRK to use the mediation initiative as a charade, but its perceived expected costs of the crisis made the mediation gamble worth taking. Moreover, supply-side pressure on the U.S. side helps explain the occurrence of mediation in this case. Carter was primarily motivated by the possibility of renewed war on the Korean peninsula if additional sanctions were levied, as well as the humanitarian consequences of such sanctions, and felt that he could use his experience and profile to, at a minimum, open up a line of communication and potentially help the actors find a way out of the escalating tension.[35] To achieve these ends, Carter would have gone to the DPRK in June 1994 even without permission from the Clinton administration (Creekmore 2006, 44, 68). This threat to visit with Kim Il Sung without Clinton's blessing placed pressure on the administration to consent to the initiative. Had Carter gone to the DPRK—as a third-party consultant, not a mediator—without Clinton's support, Clinton might have looked weak and he would not be able to take credit for any progress that resulted. Realizing that it would be better for Carter to go with permission than without, Clinton eventually, but reluctantly, consented to having Carter play a mediation role. Again, this untraditional supply-side pressure is noteworthy because the likely devious objectives on the DPRK side would have created substantial counterincentives

---

35. See Carter (2007, 23); Troester (1996, 76).

to avoid mediation. Carter helped convince Clinton that the mediation initiative was still worth the gamble, unlikely as it was to produce a satisfying settlement.

Roosevelt at Portsmouth

Theodore Roosevelt's mediation between Russia and Japan in 1905 at the Portsmouth Naval Shipyard also demonstrates the dynamics discussed in this chapter. Foremost, this case confirms that mediation becomes quite likely when both sides are hurting and become eager for a way out. One of the interesting elements of this case is that the actors reached a point of mutual suffering even though it did not look like a traditional hurting stalemate. That is, Japan eagerly sought mediation immediately after one of the most resounding victories in military history because of just how costly the conflict had become. This case also provides insight into the role of supply-side influence in leading to mediation.

The conflict between Russia and Japan that eventually led to the outbreak of war in 1904 was set in motion in 1895, after Japan defeated China in the first Sino-Japanese War.[36] The Treaty of Shimonoseki, signed on April 17, 1895, terminated this war. In an earlier agreement between Japan and China, Japan was to receive the Liaodong (Liaotung) peninsula and Port Arthur, important acquisitions for the Japanese establishment of a powerful presence on the Asian mainland. This, however, threatened the interests of the European powers who also had plans to increase their influence in Asia. As a result, Russia, Germany, and France pressured Japan to give up its claims to the Liaodong peninsula in exchange for more of an indemnity from China. This gave the European powers greater access to China and helped bring about the lease of Port Arthur to the Russians in 1897. The Japanese perception of Russia as a threat continued in the coming years as Russia solidified its position in Manchuria after the Boxer Rebellion in 1900. Meanwhile, Japan began establishing itself as the dominant power in Korea, which brought Japanese and Russian interests in East Asia into close competition. Japan wanted to be recognized as the dominant power in Korea while limiting the Russian presence in Manchuria.

On February 8, 1904, Japan launched a surprise attack on Port Arthur, thus beginning the Russo-Japanese War. With most of its military forces based in Europe, Russia experienced early difficulties in the conflict. Japan defeated the Russians at the battle at the Yalu River and then crossed the Yalu to defeat the Russians again at Liao-Yang in late August 1904. After months of struggle, Japan

---

36. For an overview of the motivations for war and of the war events, see Auslin (2005); Randall (1985); Schimmelpenninck van der Oye (2005); Teramoto (2008).

captured Port Arthur on January 1, 1905 and then defeated the Russians again at Mukden in March. This set the stage for the Russian defeat at the Battle of Tsushima Straits on May 27–28, 1905. Russia had sent its Baltic fleet around the world to cut Japan off from its land forces, but Russia lost sixteen warships in the battle, Japan virtually annihilating the entire fleet.[37] This capped a series of confrontations in which the Japanese were able to defeat the Russians, but with high casualties and without completely devastating the Russian ground forces.[38]

Realizing that pursuing the war was taking a huge financial toll, on May 31, 1905, Japan asked Theodore Roosevelt to mediate. His invitation to host peace talks was formally accepted by the Japanese leadership on June 10 and by the Russians on June 12.[39] It is worth noting that Roosevelt had made gestures toward mediation in January 1904, even before the war began, but Japan initially preferred to seek a bilateral agreement to end the conflict.[40] Japan began testing the waters for mediation in March 1905, after Mukden, and entreated Roosevelt to mediate immediately after its victory at Tsushima. Russia became amenable to negotiations after its public became quite critical of the conflict and the ongoing Russian Revolution became more of a threat to Tsar Nicholas's rule.[41] The formal negotiations began on August 9 at the Portsmouth Naval Shipyard in Kittery, Maine. Komura Jutaro, the Japanese foreign minister, served as the chief negotiator for Japan; Sergius Witte, president of the Council of Ministers, served as the first plenipotentiary for Russia.

The possibility of continued conflict costs generated the primary impetus for the peace initiative and for greater involvement by Roosevelt as the initiative stalled. Although Roosevelt initially distanced himself from the negotiations—he in fact had pledged not to mediate when he sent the initial invitations to the peace conference—and retired to his summer home in Oyster Bay, New York, the threat of the failure of the negotiations and ongoing conflict motivated the Japanese delegation to request that he take a more active mediation role.[42] Moreover, both Witte and Komura pushed back the end date of the conference multiple times

---

37. Perhaps this was not so surprising; Russia had not established itself as a naval power, as seen in Rudyard Kipling's remarks just prior to the war: "I've been hearing details of the Russian fleet that are rather quaint. They seem to have all the makee-look but very little of the makee-do aboard vessels" (1903).

38. On the costs to the Japanese, see Steinberg (2005); White (1964, 206, 288–90).

39. For accounts of the invitation and responses, see White (1964, 208–13); Dennett (1959, 189). For the formal language of the invitation, see *Papers Relating to the Foreign Relations of the United States* (1906, 807, 817). Trani (1969) and Princen (1992) also provide accounts of earlier considerations of a mediation initiative.

40. See Lukoianov (2008, 41).

41. On the relationship between the instability in Russia and the peace process, see Saul (2005, 494).

42. See White (1964, 237–38).

to avoid leaving empty-handed.[43] In other words, Roosevelt did not have to do very much to encourage the sides to stay at the bargaining table; the adversaries demonstrated significant resolve on their own to prolong the negotiations in the face of impending failure.

It is quite significant that Japan was so eager to enter into mediation after its successes at Mukden and Tsushima. The conflict had become so costly that Japan did not want to continue its successful campaign against Russia. Even in victory, Japan suffered many casualties fighting against the well-entrenched Russian positions. In the future, the costs of the war for Japan would only have increased because it was not well situated for a protracted land war with Russia outside a limited portion of Manchuria and it could never feasibly conquer Russia.[44] In the first 240 days of the war, Japan had suffered nearly 58,000 casualties, compared to 28,000 for Russia (White 1964, 186). The Japanese economy was also struggling, worsened by the ongoing warfare that was financed completely through foreign loans (Princen 1992, 116). Had Japan borne fewer costs, it is doubtful that Japan would have been as eager for a quick end to the conflict or to stay at the bargaining table despite not being able to get all that it had expected.

At the same time, third-party pressure, especially on Russia, also shaped the preferences for mediation, particularly in regard to choosing the mediator. The Russo-Japanese War generated much international interest because it involved two great powers fighting for dominance in a part of the world where many other great powers were interested in securing trading and territorial rights. The terms of settlement of this conflict would not only affect the state of affairs in East Asia, but it would also lead to a change in the relative power held by both Japan and Russia. After the Spanish-American War, Roosevelt's interest in the global standing of the United States heightened, and he particularly focused on the power struggle in East Asia (Trani 1969, 7). He understood what was at stake and had a clear preference for a certain outcome. Demonstrating that a mediator's aims are often far from altruistic, Roosevelt remarked to a French ambassador, "From my point of view, the best [outcome] would be that the Russians and Japanese should remain face to face balancing each other, both weakened" (quoted in Princen 1992, 109).[45]

Roosevelt's eagerness to mediate eventually awarded him the opportunity to do so. Japan initially spurned his offer, demonstrating the reluctance of many combatants to allow foreign actors with strong interests to meddle in their secu-

---

43. See Trani (1969); Princen (1992).
44. On the precarious position of Japan, see White (1964, 185–205).
45. See also Dennett (1959, 202).

rity affairs. Nevertheless, Japan and Russia eventually warmed to the idea of Roosevelt mediating. France, Germany, and Britain all might have been suitable mediators, but Roosevelt had actively cultivated a good rapport with the Japanese.[46] Moreover, Russia sought U.S. financial backing, and Witte hoped to use the peace initiative as a gesture of goodwill to court support.[47] Leaning on Russia further, Roosevelt appealed to Kaiser Wilhelm of Germany to urge Tsar Nicholas II to consider Roosevelt's mediation offer. As a result, in a June 3 letter, Wilhelm expressed to Nicholas II his belief that Russia should admit defeat after Tsushima and consent to U.S. mediation (White 1964, 209). The combination of pressures, from both within and without, on the parties to negotiate led to the acceptance of Roosevelt's invitation one week later.

To understand the impact of mediation, we must first understand what the actors hope to achieve through it and the conditions under which it is most prevalent. Studying the incidence of mediation also helps preempt a question that arises when the short- and long-term trade-off of mediation is explored in chapters 5 and 6: Under what conditions would actors consent to mediation if it decreased the stability of peace? In this chapter, I have examined the conditions under which mediation is most prevalent. The first two hypotheses are that mediation occurs when the costs of conflict are high and the shadow of the future is short. In such situations, the short-term benefits are extremely attractive, with any long-term risks being more of an afterthought. A third hypothesis is that mediation is more likely to occur when there are strong pressures from third parties. The results from the ICB and ICOW data confirm that third-party peacemaking is more likely during severe conflict in unstable or new democratic regimes and in democratic communities. It also appears, however, that mediation is less likely to occur when the third parties are too eager to intrude and shape the outcomes as peacemakers. The cases of Kissinger and Carter in the Middle East, Roosevelt at Portsmouth, and Carter in the DPRK illustrate these important factors that shape preferences for mediation. We will return to these cases in subsequent chapters to observe the impact of mediation in both the short and long terms.

---

46. See Princen (1992); Trani (1969).
47. On the Russian incentives, see Lukoianov (2008, 50).

RAISON D'ÊTRE

Short-Term Benefits of Mediation

> We have no desire to be the world's policeman. But America does want to be the world's peacemaker.
>
> —Jimmy Carter, State of the Union Address, January 25, 1979

In the previous chapter, we find that mediation is more likely when actors confront severe and long conflicts that provide mounting costs for the disputants and when leaders discount the future in favor of short-term political consolidation. For mediation to be as prevalent as it is, in light of expected nontrivial costs and long-term risks, it must then provide the actors with, at a minimum, short-term relief from hostilities, assuming that seeking mediation is a rational response to the desperation for peace. The short-term peaceful dividends considered here include the ability to achieve a formal agreement, the willingness to make concessions, and the reduction of tension in the brief period after a crisis has ended.

Mediation and Formal Agreements

The theoretical framework I present in chapter 2 reveals that through leveraging the costs of conflict, promising future involvement, facilitating information revelation, and providing political cover for concessions third parties can help the disputants find an alternative that is mutually preferable to fighting. Even though mediation is not expected to have much of a long-term positive influence, third parties can make the immediate bargaining process more efficient. These effects should be manifested in an increased probability that the combatants will reach a voluntary formal agreement. Formal agreements are costly to make, especially in terms of procedural effort, and can entail costs for reneging (including any enforcement provisions that are triggered and reputational costs), so actors will generally sign only when they are strongly satisfied, at least in the immediate future, with the terms.[1]

Some debate exists about whether peace treaties are merely demonstrations of intent by the negotiators, so that compliance frequently follows because the only states willing to sign are those that would have complied anyway.[2] Others argue that peace agreements strengthen the durability of peace because of the valuable informational and coordination functions they provide.[3] Regardless of whether formal agreements in and of themselves contribute to a stable peace, they nonetheless still represent the desire of the parties to abide by a negotiated settlement.

If formal agreements are epiphenomenal, anything that increases their likelihood must positively shape the bargaining environment to bring the actors to favor settlement over fighting. According to this perspective, formal agreements are merely a product of and reflection of a bargaining environment that is disposed toward peace when the parties sign an agreement. The argument is that, through mediation, the bargaining environment becomes amenable to peace and the actors consequently become more likely to declare their intentions to commit to a negotiated settlement.

If, instead, formal agreements are not deemed epiphenomenal, they are costly to break, which means that actors must be sufficiently satisfied with the bargain to fully buy in. Mediation in such a state of the world can be considered an important step in the peace process, with the agreement itself as one of the final steps. In either conception of what formal agreements actually do, we still expect that when mediation is effective at helping the actors reach a mutually satisfying bargain, formal agreements, especially robust ones with multiple provisions, become more attainable.

Although actors can resolve their crises satisfactorily in other ways than a formal agreement, from a purely probabilistic standpoint, the likelihood of crisis actors being willing to sign an agreement should increase when the bargaining process is less encumbered. Other crisis outcomes such as perpetual stalemate or complete capitulation become less likely when the actors more easily recognize a

---

1. For extensive coverage of the costliness of formal agreements, see Fortna (2004c).

2. On the potential for formal agreements to be epiphenomenal, see Downs, Rocke, and Barsoom (1996).

3. In support of this argument, Fortna (2004c) and Mattes and Savun (2009) find that stronger agreements tend to be followed by longer peace spells. Lo, Hashimoto, and Reiter (2008), however, extend Fortna's analysis and find that agreement strength does not have a statistically significant relationship with the stability of peace after conflict, casting some doubt on the utility of formalizing peaceful settlements.

set of mutually acceptable alternatives. Such outcomes are clear cases of bargaining failure, leaving room for more successful outcomes that include formalized peace agreements. For these reasons, if the theoretical framework is valid, we should observe that crisis actors are better able to identify and commit to a negotiated settlement when mediators are present to expand the set of mutually agreeable options, decrease their vulnerability to cheating, decrease misinformation, or provide a fig leaf for concessions.

There are probably also supply-side pressures that contribute to a higher rate of formal agreements in mediated conflicts. To the extent that third parties believe that formal agreements are good for peace, whether because of possible constraints they create against defection or because they reduce uncertainty about what the terms are, they will encourage the parties to adopt a formal agreement at the conclusion of the negotiations. More selfishly, third parties may gain political benefits for their contributions to tangible outcomes such as signed resolutions. It is easier to take credit for being a promoter of peace if there is a resulting document with the third party listed as the peace broker. If the presence of heavy-handed third parties that desire formal agreements merely as ends in themselves provides an additional reason for mediation to result more often in formal agreements, we may question whether achieving a formal agreement is actually a decent metric for mediation success, even in the short run. In response, we must recall that mediation is inherently consensual. Third parties are limited in how much pressure they can place on the combatants to adopt a bad deal. As the pressure for an undesirable outcome mounts, it is likely that the combatants will refuse further negotiations under the auspices of the offending intermediary. Moreover, the combatants should have some sense about how much the third party values formal agreements. So, many of the cases in which third-party pressure contributes to the achievement of a formal agreement are likely to involve combatants that are hoping for and/or expecting such an outcome.

> Hypothesis 4.1 *Crises with mediation have a higher probability of achieving a formal agreement than crises without mediation.*

The ICB data are useful for assessing quantitatively the relationship between mediation and formal agreements.[4] Note that the formalized nature of

---

4. These formal agreements are distinct from formal terms that are imposed on a defeated state. The dependent variable for this hypothesis should be a measure of short-term bargaining success; in contrast, imposed agreements better indicate bargaining failures in which the combatants avoid resolution until one side claims victory. For reasons I elaborate on in the appendix, the ICOW data are less useful for an analysis of whether mediation increases the propensity for formal agreements because of the great heterogeneity in conflict management attempts and the fact that we do not observe cases in which there was no conflict management.

the agreements is important from both a theoretical standpoint (formal agreements better indicate a successful bargaining outcome because of the greater effort needed to negotiate the specific terms, define what compliance looks like, and decide on any enforcement provisions) and a practical standpoint (formal agreements are easy to identify, so measurement error is minimal). Some of the analyses that follow disaggregate formal agreements because it is important to know whether mediation leads only to weak cease-fires instead of more robust agreements. In this regard, four types of short-term outcomes are identified: (1) no formal agreement, (2) nonrobust agreements (basic cease-fires), (3) robust agreements (with a provision for peacekeeping, confidence-building measures, arms control, or further conflict resolution), and (4) strongly robust agreements (with multiple provisions).

The models include as controls contextual variables, such as conflict severity and timing, similar to those that Virginia Page Fortna (2004c) finds to be related to the strength of formal agreements and the duration of peace after formal agreements. These are discussed in the appendix to this book. Probit and ordered probit estimation techniques were used with these data, and the findings are robust to an approach that accounts for potential selection effects that could plague inferences because mediation is not randomly assigned.

The regression results confirm that mediation has a positive effect on the realization of formal agreements and on the robustness of the formal agreements. Figure 4.1 depicts the predicted probabilities of agreements from probit and ordered probit models with the control variables set at their medians for categorical variables and at their means for interval-level variables. The propensity for formal agreements more than doubles in crises that experience mediation. The increase in the propensity for strongly robust agreements is even starker, with a more than threefold increase. Notable recent crises with mediation that resulted in strongly robust peace agreements include the Pretoria agreement that ended the war in the DRC in 2002 and the Dayton Accords that ended the war in Bosnia in 1995. Notable recent cases that did not have mediation and did not end in a formal agreement are the 2006 crisis over the Iranian nuclear-weapons program, the 2003 invasion of Iraq, and the 1999 Kargil war between India and Pakistan.

Mediation and Concessions

Allowing the actors to reach formal agreements is only one short-term benefit of mediation. Much of the existing literature, which emphasizes the leverage and informational functions of mediators, overlooks the potential role of the third party as political cover for unpopular concessions. If mediation frequently

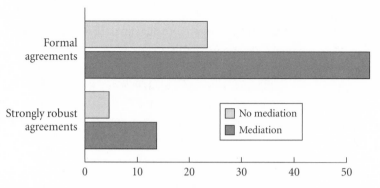

FIGURE 4.1 Propensities for formal agreements with and without mediation. Values are predicted probabilities. Changes in propensity are statistically significant ($p < 0.05$, one-tailed test).

Source: ICB data.

provides a fig leaf for unpopular compromises, then we should logically expect that the probability of concessions will be greater when a third party assists in conflict management. Chester Crocker notes the danger in overlooking the role of political cover in a mediator's toolkit and states that mediators would do well to "focus greater attention on inducements for the cohesion and reassurance of negotiating partners. This includes detailed knowledge of the domestic pressures and constraints they face, and it implies a willingness to help with political support and 'cover'" (1999, 242).

The expectation here is that mediation can promote the disputants' willingness to make concessions, but it is worth recognizing that a partially countervailing tension can arise. Concessions are often necessary for a peaceful arrangement to be reached, but making too many concessions might cause the opposing side to perceive that it can completely defeat a combatant and reach its ideal point without negotiation. A mediator must balance between encouraging necessary concessions and curtailing the optimism of the actors with stronger bargaining power. Such a concern is likely to limit the extent to which mediation produces concessions. This is especially pertinent when heavy-handed third parties try to level the playing field and foster a hurting stalemate because, in doing so, they may intentionally or unintentionally discourage concessions by the weaker actors. For example, as we have seen in chapter 3, Teddy Roosevelt believed that U.S. interests were served well by a stalemate between Russia and Japan in East Asia, which helps explain his insistence that Russia not be pushed too heavily on concessions. Kissinger's mediation in 1973 also shows that Kissinger was keenly aware of the difficulties that would arise if either Israel or Egypt achieved too much of an upper hand.

Hypothesis 4.2 *Crises with mediation have a higher probability of achieving concessions than crises without mediation.*

To assess the relationship between mediation and the prevalence of concessions, the dependent variable in the models using the ICB data measures whether either side in a crisis made a compromise or was defeated—two outcomes that entail substantial concessions. The ICOW data, which more explicitly capture whether an agreement contains concessions, can also be used to test this hypothesis if the unit of analysis is limited to the set of agreements reached.[5] There are a few ways to define the occurrence of concessions in the ICOW data. Because leaders in challenging states potentially face the most domestic opposition to concessions, we can see whether mediation does especially well in encouraging concessions from the challenger. To see whether mediators might encourage only limited concessions, so as to not embolden the other side, it is also useful to distinguish between low-level concessions and major (high-level) concessions in the dyad as a whole.

The (probit) regression models again indicate that mediation plays a role in providing short-term benefits, namely concessions in this case. Based on the ICB data, mediation increases the propensity for a crisis to end with concessions. The results using the ICOW data are also supportive but not without nuance; mediation has a positive and statistically significant effect on whether challenger concessions and minor concessions occur in an agreement but not whether there are major concessions. It appears that the political cover afforded by a mediator only goes so far, presumably because some third parties want to limit the concessions that are made.

Figure 4.2 presents some of the substantive interpretations. The graph of propensities illustrates that mediation increases the likelihood of general concessions in the ICB data by 26 percent compared to crises without mediation. More starkly, in the ICOW data the propensity for challenger concessions more than doubles and the propensity for small concessions increases by 64 percent when mediation occurs compared to agreements without either mediation or binding third-party involvement. Some well-known recent crises that included both mediation and concessions are the 2006 Israeli-Hizbollah war, the war in Kosovo, and the war in Bosnia.

---

5. Limiting the observations to the conflict management attempts that produced agreements allows an apples-to-apples comparison of units when there is extreme heterogeneity in conflict management attempts and an absence of observations during periods without conflict management. Note that the models here do distinguish mediation attempts from other third-party conflict management attempts.

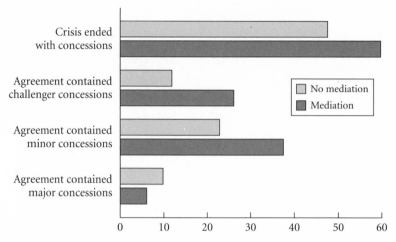

FIGURE 4.2   Propensities for concessions with and without mediation. Values are predicted probabilities. Changes in propensity are statistically significant ($p < 0.05$, one-tailed test), with the exception of that pertaining to major concessions.

Sources: "Crisis ended" data from ICB; "agreement" data from ICOW.

It is worth noting that additional types of third-party involvement, such as arbitration and adjudication, also have the potential to provide political cover for concessions.[6] Results confirming this expectation are shown in the appendix. One of the possible mechanisms of political cover, blame shifting, is unlikely to be a dominant factor in mediation. Because mediation is nonbinding and permissive, it is simply difficult for leaders to shift the onus of responsibility for unfavorable terms on to the mediator unless the third party has significant leverage over the disputants. However, legal dispute resolution (arbitration and adjudication), given its binding nature and legal legitimacy, has a greater potential to allow blame shifting to occur. Although leaders undergoing mediation can still use the presence of a third party as a signal to the domestic public that the concessions are prudent, the point is that mediators are more limited in their potential for providing political cover than arbitrators and adjudicators. This expectation is borne out by the data—binding third-party conflict management attempts that produce agreements in the ICOW data have even stronger positive effects on the potential for concessions.

---

6. Indeed, early efforts to explore the importance of political cover centered on legal dispute resolution (Simmons 2002; Allee and Huth 2006).

The absence of a significant relationship between mediation and major concessions, with a negative sign no less, when using the ICOW data is telling. While the political cover provided by third parties is able to encourage minor concessions, mediators may actually prevent one side from having to make major concessions, consistent with a view of mediation as a means of leveling the playing field for weaker belligerents. If this is the case, it would support the notion, explored in depth in the next chapter, that mediators can interfere with the natural trajectory of settlement and promote outcomes that are not self-enforcing. That is, if mediators tend to discourage major concessions from being made, this could increase the sense of dissatisfaction that combatants—specifically those to which the concessions would have been made—feel after third-party pressure diminishes.

Short-Term Peace

An expected third manifestation of the short-term benefits of mediation is that tensions will be calmer and crises less likely to recur for a few years after a mediated dispute concludes. If mediators truly help disputants reach arrangements that are mutually preferable to hostilities, then fighting should be more easily avoided in the immediate aftermath of a conflict that experienced mediation. Even if mediation struggles to decrease the long-term stability of peace, it takes time for the influence of the third party to diminish or for the actors to shift in bargaining power such that the new settlement becomes unsatisfactory. It is doubtful that mediation would be able to increase the potential for actors to make formal agreements and concessions, as we have found, if it did not improve the prospects for peace at least in the short run.

Even when mediation does not help find a mutually satisfying bargain, the presence of a third party can give the disputants an incentive to lay low at least for a short while. Whatever the outcome of a crisis or conflict, the disputants will be hesitant to immediately resume hostilities if doing so will incur the wrath of a strong third party or motivate other actors in the international system to side with the opponent. If states balance against those that appear most threatening,[7] then actors have an incentive to not unnecessarily create a perception of being a threat through blatant acts of aggression such as immediately going on the offensive after a mediated peace process. Similarly, a combatant that pursues mediation insincerely, either to stall for time or to create the perception among

---

7. The seminal work on such threat balancing comes from Walt (1987).

domestic and international audiences that it is doing its best to achieve peace, still has an incentive to restrain aggression immediately after a mediation initiative concludes. The lingering involvement of a third party can decrease the battlefield gains that stalling helped generate, and immediate aggression can alert the relevant observers to the insincerity of the effort. One example that points to the incentive to lay low after a mediation initiative, even when the result is not mutually acceptable, is the militia attacks in East Timor immediately following the referendum for independence from Indonesia—agreed to after Portuguese mediation—that triggered a strong international military response against the militias and sympathetic elements of the Indonesian military.

> Hypothesis 4.3 *Crises with mediation have a higher probability of experiencing short-term tension reduction than crises without mediation.*

To present the evidence that mediated disputes end up with stronger short-term stability than unmediated conflicts, we can see whether the mediated crisis dyads are more likely to experience tension reduction after five years, as coded by the ICB data.[8] Tension reduction implies, at a minimum, the absence of subsequent crises within the five-year window and also typically involves the attenuation of nonmilitary contentious behavior, such as economic and political sanctions. The ICOW data are also useful for testing this hypothesis. Although these data do not contain an equivalent variable of tension reduction, they do provide information on whether a formal agreement that was reached is followed by an end to the disputed claim within two years.

Figure 4.3 presents the propensities for tension reduction in ICB crises and ICOW disputes, again from probit models. As the graph demonstrates, tension reduction in the five years after a crisis is more than twice as likely with mediation. Moreover, mediated agreements in the ICOW data are 57 percent more likely to experience an end to a disputed claim within two years than unmediated agreements. Both findings are statistically significant. The crises between Russia and Georgia over the Abkhazia and South Ossetia autonomous areas (in 2002 and 2004), the conflict between India and Pakistan during the Kargil war (1999), and the Indian parliament attack (2001) serve as examples of crises that did not experience mediation or tension reduction. In contrast, the 2002 crisis following the attack on the Indian Kaluchak army base was mediated, and it was followed by a period of relative tension reduction.

---

8. This is an extension of Beardsley et al. (2006).

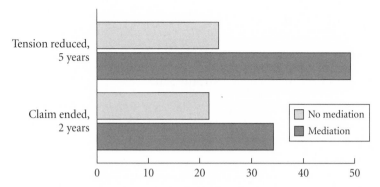

FIGURE 4.3 Propensities for short-term tension reduction with and without mediation. Values are predicted probabilities. Changes in propensity are statistically significant ($p < 0.05$, one-tailed test).

Sources: "Tension reduced" data from ICB; "claim ended" data from ICOW.

In sum, the results are strongly supportive of the claim that mediation does promote short-term peace well. The ICB crises with mediation are more likely to experience (robust) formal agreements, concessions, and short-term reduced tensions. The ICOW mediation attempts are more likely to produce agreements that include concessions and that lead to the end of a claim within two years. Moreover, all these findings are robust to model specifications that account for the nonrandom assignment of mediation, as detailed in the appendix. Combined with the findings in the previous chapter, this shows that mediation is an attractive conflict management strategy because it enhances the prospects for immediate peace.

Illustrative Cases

The quantitative tests confirm the hypotheses regarding the multiple short-term benefits of mediation. To explore additional facets of how mediation shapes the bargaining environment of combatants, we now turn to historical cases of mediation in practice. In each case, the mediator was able to move the peace process forward, toward formal agreements and concessions. Here the focus is on *how* the third parties were able to reduce the immediate barriers to efficient bargaining. I thus give substantial attention to the ways in which the mediator provided leverage, implementation assistance, information, and political cover (see chapter 2). The means by which the third parties engaged the disputants should have affected the long-term outcomes as well, and the question of whether these efforts led to just a short-term peace or to a more lasting pattern of peaceful behavior is taken up in the next chapter.

Kissinger and Carter in the Middle East

Throughout the efforts by Henry Kissinger and Jimmy Carter in the Middle East, they used substantial leverage on the participants in the negotiations to make progress toward bargained settlements. At the height of the October War, Kissinger tailored his approach to increase the incentives for a peaceful settlement and to reduce the extent to which either side thought that continuing hostilities would lead to greater bargaining advantage. Kissinger insisted that Israel not make a preemptive strike when the Arab forces began mobilizing, waited before authorizing an airlift to aid Israel, and pressured Israel to spare the Egyptian Third Army so as to not precipitate a clear Israeli victory. Furthermore, he delayed movement on a UN cease-fire—even giving Israel the green light to violate the cease-fire reached on October 22—until Israel had sufficient advantage to prevent the perception of an Arab victory.[9] The intended plan was to create the feeling of a stalemate so that progress could be made and the best alternative to settlement, protracted battle, became less attractive.

Immediately after the parties implemented the cease-fire, the United States employed even more direct pressure, especially in trying to get Israel to allow supplies to reach the Egyptian Third Army and to drop its insistence that a prisoner exchange happen before the supply lines were established. Kissinger warned that, unless Israel become more flexible on these issues, the Soviet Union was likely to intervene, and he threatened that the United States might supply the Third Army itself, might not veto a UN resolution for withdrawal, and might not respond favorably to Israeli aid requests.[10] The promise of aid and the implicit threat of withholding such aid, not only to Israel but also to the Arab states, became common positive and negative inducements throughout Kissinger's diplomatic involvement in the Middle East. The use of aid as a carrot for progress toward peace can be seen in how U.S. aid to both Israel and Egypt more than quintupled from 1973 to 1979 (Mearsheimer and Walt 2007, 26, 31).[11]

After the Sinai I agreement—the first disengagement settlement—was reached, the United States continued to apply substantial pressure in hopes of

---

9. On Kissinger's strategic manipulation of the security environment during the war, see Dallek (2007, 525–26); Touval (1982, 228); Del Pero (2006, 138); Pressman (2008, 100–105); Horne (2009, 272, 281); Mearsheimer and Walt (2007, 43–44); Stein (1999, 91).

10. See Touval (1982, 234).

11. See also Ben-Ami (2005, 153); Pressman (2008, 82). For accounts of how such aid proved influential, see Quandt (2001, 133, 139, 146); Isaacson (1992, 558–59).

maintaining momentum. For example, following an aborted attempt to reach an additional disengagement agreement between Israel and Egypt in March 1975, Kissinger and new President Gerald Ford pursued a policy of reassessment that pressured Israel to be more concessionary. As part of the reassessment, the administration threatened to reconvene the Geneva Conference, which Israel did not find desirable because it would probably result in a unified front calling for Israeli withdrawal to 1967 lines, and to delay economic and military aid to Israel.[12] The importance of U.S. pressure is seen in the fact that agreement on Sinai II became possible in August, just five months after the earlier failure. The importance of the reassessment policy itself, however, is debatable because Ford and Kissinger eventually had to back away from their threats due to strong domestic criticism.[13] John Mearsheimer and Stephen Walt (2007, 37–38) argue that such domestic constraints reduced the credibility of any U.S. sticks waved at Israel; moreover, they contend that it was the renewed promise of carrots in the form of aid that actually contributed to the second disengagement agreement. Whether through positive or negative inducements or both, the point here is that U.S. leverage served an important role in attaining the Sinai II settlement.

Carter used leverage even more directly and has been criticized for being too heavy handed in his approach, especially toward Israel, early in his presidency.[14] The Carter administration even had planned at one point to collude with Sadat to maximize the pressure on Israel to make concessions (Brzezinski 1985, 242; Quandt 2001, 196). This tough approach with Israel led to some domestic political backlash and infuriated the Israelis, especially when Carter publicly called for the creation of a Palestinian "homeland."[15] Zbigniew Brzezinski (1985, 88), the national security advisor at the time, notes that the resulting tension with pro-Israeli factions at home was a foreseen consequence of the pressure that the Carter administration felt it needed to place on Israel. According to Ezer Weizman (1981, 372), the Israeli defense minister during this time, the approach worked because the heavy use of "unprecedented pressure" against Begin was a key factor in allowing Begin to finally agree to dismantle the Sinai settlements,

---

12. On the threat to reconvene the Geneva Conference, see Rabin (1979, 251). On the aid threat, see Rabin (1979, 255–65); Stein (1999, 176).

13. For arguments about how the reassessment policy proved influential, see Touval (1982, 271); Shlaim (2000, 336). For arguments about how reassessment failed to achieve its intended result, see Miller (2008, 122, 151–52); Isaacson (1992, 634).

14. Of Carter's first meeting with an Israeli prime minister as president, Kenneth Stein writes, "Kissinger was tough and angry with Israeli leaders, but he never told Israelis to swallow discomforting ideological positions. By contrast, Carter took the conclusions of a consensus document, which had been drafted without any Israeli input, and imposed them on Rabin, believing them to be fair, equitable, and adequately acceptable" (1999, 192). See also Stein (1999, 249); Weizman (1981, 286, 365).

15. On the significance of this language, see Stein (1999, 193); Quandt (1986, 60).

which was the last barrier at Camp David. Weizman writes, "Only Jimmy Carter had the power to bang their heads together and force them to reach agreement" (1981, 367).

Pressure on Israel was especially needed during this time because Israel was more vulnerable to commitment problems. One issue was that Sadat's major concession at Camp David was the recognition of Israel and subsequent exchange of ambassadors. But ambassadors can always be withdrawn and recognition can be revoked—the significance of the initial gesture will endure, but it is conceivable that future administrations in Egypt could claim that they have never accepted the right of Israel to exist. That it became nearly impossible for Israel to renege—once it had abandoned the Sinai and dismantled its settlements—but not for Egypt is quite informative and helps explain why Israel was much more reluctant to concede. The occupation of the Sinai was the main source of leverage for Israel, even though the Sinai carried relatively little intrinsic value for Israel, and once it was gone it could not be regained without another full-scale war. Meanwhile, Egypt still could potentially and more easily take back much of what it had promised. Kissinger was keen to recognize a similar tension in the early days of the disengagement talks. He writes in his memoirs,

> All the tangible concessions—above all, territory—had to be made by Israel; once made, they were irrevocable. The Arab quid pro quo was something intangible, such as diplomatic recognition or a legal state of peace, which could always be modified or even withdrawn. Hope that Israel might at last be accepted by its neighbors was dimmed by knowledge that for other countries recognition is where diplomacy begins, not ends; by doubt that any change of Arab policy would be either genuine or permanent. (Kissinger 1982, 619)[16]

Even on Sadat, whose interests were more closely aligned with Carter's, the U.S. president exerted substantial pressure. In the last hours of the Camp David negotiations, Carter had to lean heavily on Sadat for him to make more concessions and to accept the weak linkage between the two frameworks (Carter 1982, 395; Vance 1983, 226). Carter made it clear to all involved that failure to reach an agreement was not an option at Camp David, which of course was the primary justification not to cap the length of the negotiations.[17]

Carter also used aid leverage to increase the pressure on Begin and Sadat to compromise. The United States ultimately promised $3 billion worth of aid to Israel and $1.5 billion to Egypt at the conclusion of their peace treaty (Quandt

---

16. See also Rubin (1981, 15).
17. On Carter's insistence to the negotiating parties, see Weizman (1981, 345).

2001, 235). Moreover, Carter explicitly linked the provision of aid to the successful conclusion of talks. Secretary of Defense Harold Brown, for example, stated publicly in Egypt in February 1979 that no supply of arms would be possible without a signed agreement.[18] Even without the explicit connection between progress in the peace process and arms provision, the degree to which Israel depended on U.S. military and economic aid was such that the preservation of favorable relations with the United States was always a key source of influence. In this regard, Weizman catalogs the degree of military dependence: "Since the guns had fallen silent at the end of the Yom Kippur War, we had received U.S. military assistance of stunning proportions, far exceeding what our forces had possessed in the Six-Day War. By my reckoning, some 20 percent of our defense system is maintained by the American taxpayer, to the yearly tune of a billion dollars in military aid to Israel" (1981, 245). On top of this, the United States provided economic aid, which as Brzezinski notes "amounted to around $10 billion since 1973, almost $3,000 for each Israeli citizen, an unprecedented level of aid to a single and not a particularly poor country" (1985, 236).

Manipulating the sense of dependence, Carter frequently threatened poorer relations with the United States if the parties remained intransigent. At the crucial moment on the eleventh day of negotiations at Camp David, when the Egyptian delegation packed its bags and threatened to leave, Carter wanted to make sure that Sadat knew this would severely damage U.S.-Egypt relations and push the United States to side more with Israel. Carter describes this deciding moment:

> I explained to [Sadat] the extremely serious consequences of his unilaterally breaking off the negotiations: that his action would harm the relationship between Egypt and the United States, he would be violating his personal promise to me, and the onus of failure would be on him. I described the possible future progress of Egypt's friendships and alliances—from us to the moderate and then radical Arabs, thence to the Soviet Union. I told him it would damage one of my most precious possessions—his friendship and our mutual trust. (1982, 392)

Similarly, the potential for worse relations with Israel proved to be a key source of leverage. This was on full display in a March 1978 meeting between Carter and Begin in which Carter threatened to decry Begin's intransigence to the U.S. Congress (Brzezinski 1985, 246). Later, when Carter was trying to reach an agreement on the Egyptian-Israeli treaty, he again threatened to tell the U.S. Congress that

---

18. On this specific linkage between aid and the peace progress, see Touval (1982, 317); Weizman (1981, 381).

Israel was responsible for any failure (Touval 1982, 315). Weizman was especially fearful that a failure at Camp David would lead to a severe rift between Israel and the United States. "Israel had managed to survive for thirty years without a single day of peace," Weizman writes, "but I doubted whether we would be able to survive without the political, military, and economic support of the United States" (1981, 367).[19] Along with the threat of poorer relations with Israel, Carter maintained an implicit threat of closer relations with Egypt and the other Arab states as a means to leverage Israel toward compromise. For example, Brzezinski (1985, 247–48) describes how Carter increased the proposed number of planes to be sold to Egypt and Saudi Arabia in response to frustration with Begin's refusal to budge over settlements.

The flip side of the threat of poorer relations was the implicit promise of better relations with Washington as a motivator for cooperating during the peace process.[20] In his memoirs, Carter (1982, 366) describes how both Begin's and Sadat's desire for an agreement with the United States before an agreement was reached between Egypt and Israel "magnified" his influence. This desire stemmed from both the status that being recognized as an important ally of a superpower could bring and the leverage that such prior deals between intermediary and disputant could create over the other parties at the table. The importance of U.S. ties as a source of leverage could specifically be seen during day four of the Camp David negotiations, when, as Carter recalls, Begin "pointed out that there had to be two agreements at Camp David; the most important was between the United States and Israel, and the other, of secondary importance but obviously also crucial, was between Israel and Egypt. The most important one would have to come first. He wanted the world to know that there were no serious differences between Israel and the United States" (1984, 18–19). Egypt also benefited greatly from strengthening ties with the United States because of how dependent Israel was on the Americans for its security. If Sadat could align himself with U.S. interests, this would weaken the Israeli bargaining position and make concessions much more attainable.[21]

Kissinger and Carter did not completely rely on pressure to move the negotiations forward. Once negotiations started progressing on the Sinai I agreement, the United States relied more on political cover and assurances to address the various vulnerabilities created during the peace process. One source of vulnerability was the political pressure on Sadat from Arabs at home and abroad who

---

19. See also Weizman (1981, 341). Note that Weizman is arguably overstating the case here because Israel had fared well enough prior to the massive increase in U.S. assistance during the 1970s.

20. On the significance of this implicit carrot, see Telhami (1990, 13).

21. See Telhami (1990, 70).

were loath to negotiate with the Jewish state that most saw as illegitimate. During the disengagement talks, the Israeli leadership also feared the wrath of the Israeli public for what some would interpret as a unilateral withdrawal from the Sinai.[22] By taking responsibility for making proposals and transmitting messages directly, Kissinger allowed progress to be made without the leaders' having to pay prohibitively costly audience costs.[23] It was important to relay the messages secretly. For example, a brief crisis arose during the negotiations of the Sinai I agreement when Kissinger intended to deliver an Israeli proposal directly to Sadat—so that there was less of an appearance that it was actually an Israeli proposal—but the proposal was leaked through other channels. Knowing the importance of keeping Israeli authorship hidden, Kissinger writes that "it was essential to keep this Israeli concept secret for several reasons: Egypt would find it easier to accept if it appeared to result from American influence, rather than to be an Israeli demand. It would become a public benchmark, making it harder for either side to yield in the subsequent bargaining" (1982, 803).

The motivations for the Geneva Conference in December 1973 demonstrate well how Kissinger's mediation helped the parties save face. Although Geneva was primarily a front to legitimize the disengagement talks that Kissinger orchestrated over subsequent months, it still served one of the key functions of mediation discussed in this chapter—namely political cover. Sadat needed to present the appearance of working with his fellow Arab allies, and Golda Meir's government also stood to benefit from the publicity provided by the Geneva Conference.[24] Israeli elections were scheduled for December 1973, and it looked good for Meir to have members of her government negotiating at Geneva, with no risk of embarrassing concessions because of the prior agreement to limit the substance of the talks.

Carter also was responsive to the needs for fig leafs to cover difficult concessions. One of the chief motivations for holding talks at Camp David was to exclude the media, thereby keeping hidden who was responsible for proposing any particular concession and preventing the negotiators from locking themselves into a hard-line stance by grandstanding to their domestic and international audiences. Carter justified the decision as "imperative that there be a minimum of posturing by Egyptians or Israelis, and an absence of public statements, which would become frozen positions that could not subsequently be changed" (1982,

---

22. See Kissinger (1982, 824). The Israeli public, however, was much more enthusiastic about peace with its Arab neighbors after the October War because the war had demonstrated that the Israel Defense Forces (IDF) were not as invincible as previously assumed (Ben-Ami 2005, 148).

23. On the importance of this role, see Quandt (2001, 143).

24. On the saving-face function of the Geneva Conference, see Stein (1999, 118–21).

318).[25] In the months before Camp David, the Egyptian and Israeli media were becoming increasingly critical of the leadership in the opposing country, which contributed to the collapse of the bilateral peace initiative.[26] Insulation from the press was thus an important prerequisite for new progress. More generally, Carter's mediation focused on undoing some of the positions taken prior to Camp David and even during the summit. Weizman, for example, recognized the need for Carter to help Sadat retreat from the strong demands he initially proposed at Camp David. He writes that Sadat "may have climbed too far up on his high horse, in which case he would need an American ladder to help him down. . . . The American team, headed by Carter, Vance and Brzezinski, now went about steadying the ladder for Sadat's descent. The second week at Camp David was marked by American efforts to flush Israelis and Egyptians out of the defensive positions each side had clung to" (Weizman 1981, 362).

Aside from domestic discontent, another source of vulnerability that mediation was able to address arose from fear that the other side might exploit any strategic advantages created while the forces in the Sinai were repositioned. The U.S. negotiators provided a number of assurances and guarantees that took such forms as monitoring and promises of aid. For example, many of the major issues of contention in the negotiation of the Sinai II agreement related to security vulnerabilities, such as the potential abandonment of early-warning facilities in the Sinai.[27] The United States helped diminish such concerns by offering guarantees, promising to monitor compliance, and ensuring that both sides had adequate early-warning capabilities. As another example, when negotiations broke down between the signing of the Camp David Accords and the signing of the peace treaty, the United States made important guarantees that included assisting Israel in relocating its Sinai airfields to the Negev and promising to maintain Israeli oil supplies for fifteen years if Egypt failed to grant Israel access to the oil wells that it would be abandoning in the Sinai.[28]

At each point in the peace process—at the disengagement agreements, the Camp David Accords, and the Israeli-Egyptian peace treaty—the United States provided both sides with additional letters that clarified disputed language and

---

25. See also Carter (1984, 18); Stein (1999, 252). Even with the relative isolation at Camp David, the Israeli delegation had reason to fear that the Egyptians would leak a copy of Sadat's initial proposals to the international press as a way to force more Israeli concessions and to project blame onto Israel in the event of failure of the negotiations (Weizman 1981, 353–55).

26. See Weizman (1981, 349).

27. See Rabin (1979, 245, 268–70).

28. On this particular example, see Weizman (1981, 371, 374); Carter (1982, 424); Vance (1983, 250–51); Dayan (1981, 276–77); Quandt (2001, 233). On the importance of U.S. guarantees more generally, see Quandt (2001, 167); Rabin (1979, 270); Shlaim (2000, 337); Rubin (1981, 27); Stein (1999, 113).

promised U.S. commitments into the future. The protagonists themselves provided similar auxiliary letters that clarified issues or committed them to certain courses of action meant to augment the agreements. For example, as part of the Sinai I process, but separate from the signed agreement, the United States signed a ten-point memorandum of understanding and sent separate letters to Israel and Egypt with further details.[29] As part of the disengagement process between Israel and Syria, the United States separately submitted documents that offered its interpretation of the limitation of forces, pledged to monitor the agreement, laid out its stance should a violation of the agreement occur, clarified the right of Israel to defend itself against terrorist attacks, promised aid, insisted that the disengagement line was not a final boundary, and promised to work toward both full implementation of UN Security Council Resolution 228 and representation of the Palestinians in future negotiations.[30] The Sinai II agreement also contained a supplemental annex and guarantee letters in which the United States clarified the intended length of the agreement (three years), committed itself to serving as a trustee, guaranteed the sides against violations, promised monitoring, offered technical assistance regarding the early warning systems in the Sinai, pledged to compensate the parties, and promised not to negotiate with the Palestine Liberation Organization (PLO) as long as it did not recognize Israel.[31] Finally, supplemental letters were exchanged at the conclusion of the Camp David Accords and the Egyptian-Israeli peace treaty. In letters to Begin and Sadat and in memorandums of understanding, Carter and his administration offered clarifications, promised economic and military aid, pledged action in response to any violations to the treaty, committed the United States to monitoring force reductions, promised that it would establish a multinational force to keep peace in the event that a UN force could not be sustained, and guaranteed oil supplies.[32]

These auxiliary agreements served a number of purposes. First, by having the content of the letters separate from the signed documents, the negotiating sides were able to avoid political punishment for concessions that they had actually made but that were largely unknown to their domestic and international audiences.[33] In addition, both sides were able to further their objectives of strengthening ties with the United States—with the U.S. guarantees of the agreements, the Americans became more fully committed to upholding the interests of the

---

29. For more on the side agreements that were part of the Sinai I process, see Touval (1982, 247–48); Stein (1999, 151–52).

30. On these side agreements, see Touval (1982, 259); Stein (1999, 161).

31. On the supplemental agreements that were part of Sinai II, see Touval (1982, 265–67); Shlaim (2000, 338); Stein (1999, 179).

32. On these letters, see Touval (1982, 318); Quandt (1986, 313–14; 2001, 235).

33. See Dayan (1981, 280).

signatories.[34] Furthermore, by clarifying the language in the agreements, the letters reduced the fear that either side would try to interpret them in a more favorable light than was intended and take action that would violate the spirit of the agreements. Finally, by promising U.S. commitments, the auxiliary letters decreased the signatories' concerns that their cooperation would be exploited by the other side and decreased their own incentives to renege on the agreements for fear of U.S. punishment. This especially helped ameliorate the many timing and sequencing issues that the protagonists confronted while seeking settlement. One of the timing issues that troubled Sadat throughout the peace process was the timing of the exchange of ambassadors relative to the timing of the Israeli withdrawal (Sadat 1984, 98). Sadat feared that if relations were normalized before withdrawal, Israel would have received something that it greatly desired—recognition—and then would not have as much incentive to carry out its promised withdrawal. Carter convinced Sadat to exchange ambassadors within nine months of the signing of the Egyptian-Israeli Peace Treaty and in auxiliary documents promised to monitor violations, which assured Sadat that he would be able to initially evaluate Israel's good faith commitment to withdrawal before providing the last piece of full recognition.

Another mediation tactic that Kissinger and Carter used which did not rely on the use of leverage was the role of proposal maker. While both tried to be careful to not taint any proposals as an "American plan," which would have been unsavory in its parochialism,[35] they did take responsibility in assembling the positions of each side and proposing various combinations. In doing so, Kissinger and Carter were able to clarify what was actually being negotiated and could create focal points in the midst of countless combinations of potential alternatives. Carter especially made use of a single-document approach to mediation, in which the sides negotiated one proposal, assembled by Carter after taking into account the preferences of both sides, and revised it as needed instead of considering multiple proposals at the same time.

The result of this combination of mediation tactics was thus three disengagement agreements, the Camp David Accords, and the Egyptian-Israeli peace treaty. Kenneth Stein stresses the importance of U.S. mediation in producing the Camp David Accords and the Egyptian-Israeli peace treaty: "It was the presence

---

34. Of the Sinai I auxiliary documents, Kenneth Stein writes, "Israel might have signed a disengagement agreement with Egypt, but its core premises were strengthening American monitoring of the negotiating process and deepening American relations with Israel. The quest for an Arab-Israeli peace became a series of Egyptian and Israeli accommodations channeled through Washington" (1999, 152).

35. Begin was especially fearful of the U.S. offering its own proposals (Vance 1983, 217).

of Carter's passionate determination to find an Egyptian-Israeli solution that, finally, made the difference. Coming on the heels of Kissinger's achievements, Carter's tenacity resulted in negotiated results, not perfect by anyone's standard, but signed agreements nonetheless" (1999, 45). Weizman also highlights Carter's indispensable role in reaching the Camp David Accords when he writes, "Finally, at the moment when it seemed that all the effort had proved fruitless, Jimmy Carter did what no other leader had been able to do" (1981, 340). After recalling that we actually observed a bilateral peace initiative without U.S. mediation fail, Brzezinski similarly concludes that U.S. involvement was the key ingredient to successful progress in the Middle East:

> The fact is this: without the United States neither the Egyptians nor the Israelis were able to move the peace process forward on their own. In spite of Sadat's bold and generous initiative, the Egyptian-Israeli bilateral talks quickly bogged down, and it became apparent, even to the Israelis and the Egyptians, that American mediation would be necessary to bring Sadat's initiative to a constructive conclusion. . . . In the course of 1978, Jimmy Carter, by running major personal risks and by providing effective personal leadership, did succeed in getting Israel and Egypt to take a giant step toward real peace and normal relations. (1985, 122)

As a final note, and corroborating the empirical results, we observe that Kissinger and Carter were instrumental in allowing concessions to be made, but we also see their hand in *restraining* major concessions that might have destabilized the peace process by emboldening the side receiving the concessions. This is especially seen in Kissinger's aversion to having either side in the October War feel defeated. Instead, Kissinger hoped to demonstrate "the futility of the military option" to "give impetus to the search for peace" (1982, 468).[36] It is also telling that Kissinger cut the Kilometer 101 talks short when he discovered that Aharon Yariv and Mohamed Abdel Ghani el-Gamasy, the Israeli and Egyptian principal negotiators, respectively, had moved beyond their purview of discussing the technicalities of disengagement and had begun to make progress on a political settlement. Kissinger actually feared too much progress because it would reduce the perception of mutual stalemate and prematurely deflate the momentum for the Geneva Conference and the subsequent mediation initiative. He writes, "we were not, to be frank, too eager for a breakthrough at Kilometer 101 before the Geneva Conference. . . . If disengagement disappeared from the agenda, we would be forced into endless skirmishing over broader issues on which I knew we would

---

36. See also Stein (1999, 32, 84).

not be able to deliver quickly, if at all" (Kissinger 1982, 752).[37] Again, Kissinger's mediation was an important ingredient allowing concessions to be reached, but it also reined in more substantial concessions that could have unraveled the entire process.

Carter in North Korea

Former U.S. President Jimmy Carter's mediation in the 1994 DPRK nuclear crisis also demonstrates the short-term benefits of mediation. Carter's efforts were crucial in bringing about the Agreed Framework and the temporary lull in tensions that followed. Here we see how Carter was able to shape the bargaining environment so it was conducive to agreement.

Carter met Kim Il Sung on June 16, 1994, in Pyongyang. After a brief time, Kim agreed to allow the IAEA inspectors to remain in place in return for U.S. pledges to provide light-water reactors that would replace the extant graphite ones and to not launch a nuclear strike against the DPRK. Carter, mediating as a private citizen, knew that he did not have the authority to formalize any agreements, so he used the international media to his advantage. Without approval from and against the wishes of the Clinton administration, Carter went on CNN and declared that tensions had been significantly reduced as a result of Kim's pledge. The Clinton administration was worried that this might pin the United States into a position that did not get it much new and also feared that the DPRK was just trying to stall.[38] As a result, the administration issued a statement promising to seek a new round of talks if the DPRK not only agreed to keep the IAEA inspectors in place and to pursue the replacement of its graphite reactors but also completely froze its nuclear energy program. This raised the bar on what had been agreed between Carter and Kim, and Carter had to smooth things over on June 17. During the meeting, a CNN camera caught on tape comments by Carter that could have been taken as a promise that the Clinton administration would not continue to pursue sanctions.[39] Kim reaffirmed his previous pledge and also agreed to a meeting with South Korean President Kim Young Sam, indicating a potential momentous change in relations between those two countries. Carter returned to an elated South Korean president in Seoul and then to a generally frustrated Clinton administration in Washington, which felt that Carter's pre-

---

37. See also Stein (1999, 112).

38. On these fears, see Wit, Poneman, and Galucci (2004); Creekmore (2006, 176); Troester (1996, 78–79).

39. Carter (2007, 32) recalls that these comments were taken out of context; see also Creekmore (2006, 189).

emptive deal, in addition to his open criticism of the sanctions, had weakened its bargaining position (Wit, Poneman, and Galucci 2004, 235–46).

Unexpectedly for all involved, the DPRK accepted the conditions for a third round of high-level talks—including a complete freeze of its nuclear program—without objections on June 22.[40] The third round of talks began on July 8 in Geneva and continued through multiple sessions until the United States and DPRK signed the Agreed Framework on October 21. Under the framework, the DPRK pledged to freeze its nuclear program, remain as an NPT state, and implement the full IAEA safeguard protocol. In exchange, the United States, in conjunction with the newly established Korean Energy Development Organization (KEDO), funded mostly by the ROK and Japan, pledged to provide two light-water reactors and sufficient heavy fuel oil to cover DPRK energy concerns. Clinton also provided a personal letter of assurance. This effectively terminated the first DPRK nuclear crisis and thereby averted a serious dilemma for the Clinton administration if it had found that it needed to carry out its threats, avoided a renewal of major war on the Korean peninsula, and began an eight-year period of relative peace during which the DPRK was unable to produce or extract plutonium.[41]

Carter's mediation demonstrates well a few of the dynamics discussed in the theoretical framework and explored in the previous quantitative tests. Foremost, it reveals the important function that manipulating domestic and international audiences has in enabling formal agreements such as the Agreed Framework to become possible. As a private citizen at odds with the Clinton administration, Carter had very little leverage available to him. His primary source of leverage was his notoriety as a former president of the United States, and he used that to maximum advantage via the international press. Carter quickly appeared on camera to announce the progress in the talks because he feared that the DPRK regime would change its mind or later deny it had made any promises. Even in the short span between Carter's meeting with Kim Il Sung and the interview with CNN, the DPRK had already tried to back away from its commitments (Creekmore 2006, 177). By appearing on CNN, Carter placed the negotiations on the record to avoid any future fabrication of what had been said when there might be a strategic advantage from doing so. The presence of an international audience made it difficult for the DPRK to continue evading firm commitments. Had Kim

---

40. This sign of acquiescence from the DPRK was a clear departure from previous promises (Wit, Poneman, and Galucci 2004, 239).

41. On the counterfactual of what would probably have transpired in the absence of Carter's peacemaking attempt, Wit, Poneman, and Galucci conclude that "without President Carter, war would have been more likely, but not inevitable" (2004, 243–45).

Il Sung backed out of his public promises to Carter, sanctions would have been much easier to pass in the Security Council.[42]

Appearing on CNN also placed pressure on the United States—fearful, if not certain, of Kim's insincere motives in pursuing talks—to moderate its demands, lest it be perceived as the intransigent party and give actors such as China a reason to back Pyongyang in the crisis.[43] Carter even boasted after his appearance on CNN that his interview had "killed the sanctions resolution" (quoted in Creekmore 2006, 179). In the midst of such pressure, the United States thus asked for a nuclear freeze as a step above what Carter had delivered, but still a step below its earlier demands for full safeguards and disclosure of the previous discrepancies.

Carter thereby made intransigence more costly to both sides by publicly stating that an agreement was near. Note that Carter's manipulation of the audience costs is related to, but not the same thing as, providing political cover. Whereas saving face relates to reducing the costs of unpopular concessions, the type of manipulation here increases the costs of continued belligerence. That is, at Camp David Carter tried to play a face-saving role by keeping the negotiations secret, but in the DPRK, Carter did the reverse and broadcast the positions so as to prevent backsliding. At Camp David, Carter feared that hostility toward concessions in Israel and in the Arab world would constrain bargaining; in the DPRK, Carter saw an opportunity to use public opinion to his favor. This type of leverage acted most strongly on the decision calculus of the Clinton administration. By publicly declaring in the international media that an agreement was imminent and that the United States should not pursue sanctions, Carter increased the costs of bargaining failure. Clinton would have faced steep opposition had he followed through on his threats of sanctions, much less air strikes, when an agreement was supposedly in reach and such measures had been deemed not necessary by a former commander-in-chief.

Perhaps less meaningful than the constraints placed on Clinton but not insignificant, Carter's involvement also shaped the audience costs of nonagreement for the DPRK. Kim Il Sung would probably have faced increasing international pressure, most significantly from China, if he had not allowed the IAEA inspectors to remain after having promised Carter to do so and had not agreed to terms such as those in the Agreed Framework when the Americans were willing. That is, if Kim had balked at the promise of fuel aid and future reactor construction, it would have been clear that the DPRK was the intransigent party and more

---

42. The DPRK faced fewer costs from reneging in 2002—during the second nuclear crisis—than in 1994 because the United States was occupied militarily elsewhere in the world in 2002 and it had an arguable claim that the previous agreement was null because the KEDO light-water reactors had failed to materialize.

43. On Carter's intent to shape U.S. options, see Carter (2007, 34).

concerned about attaining weapons than providing energy for its people. Subsequent actions by Kim Il Sung's son, Kim Jong Il, who has not demonstrated much restraint in the face of international pressure, even from China, rightly leads us to question how important the international audiences were in moving the DPRK toward the Agreed Framework. Nonetheless, the freeze of the plutonium program and the adoption of the safeguards represents a substantial change from the previous state of affairs. The freeze prevented the DPRK from simply extorting concessions from the United States and the ROK without giving up anything, as it has at other junctures since the Agreed Framework collapsed. The freeze and safeguards were significant concessions that prevented the DPRK from adding to its fissile material, and they certainly stand out as a high point in what the DPRK has been willing to accept in its lengthy history of nuclear negotiations. Moreover, this new willingness to settle cannot easily be explained as a response to U.S. pressure because Carter's efforts also decreased the credibility of U.S. threats of sanctions and air strikes.

In addition to ratcheting up international pressure, Carter also enabled the DPRK to change its course of action while saving face at home. Clinton admitted that giving the DPRK an "escape hatch" was the major benefit of allowing the Carter mediation to proceed (Wit, Poneman, and Galucci 2004, 240–43). As former president of the only superpower, Carter's visit conferred a certain amount of prestige and respect on the DPRK regime.[44] If one of the motivations behind the DPRK nuclear program is to secure support among the military and party elites for achieving a technological feat about which only few states can boast, then a visit by a former U.S. president could bring similar respect to the regime and compensate for the nuclear freeze.[45] Kim Il Sung could thus back away from a confrontational tack without appearing to have been left empty-handed.

Finally, Carter's mission increased the clarity of the demands by both sides, which further helped them reach the Agreed Framework. Because the DPRK is so closed and has no diplomatic contact with the United States, accurate information about the aims of the DPRK is scarce. In fact, Carter was surprised by how poor the intelligence was regarding the DPRK during his briefings before his trip (Carter 2007, 25). By establishing contact and simply opening a mechanism through which both sides could communicate their demands, it became increasingly possible to reach a peaceful settlement.

The Agreed Framework that Carter helped bring about lasted less than eight years. Although the nuclear freeze in place during that time did temporarily halt

---

44. See Creekmore (2006, 21).

45. For a related account of the political motivations behind the nuclear ambitions of Pyongyang, see Solingen (2007).

the DPRK proliferation activities, this was not a permanent fix. Ultimately, the DPRK has gone on to seek uranium enrichment capabilities, test two nuclear devices, and acquire a small arsenal of nuclear weapons. The point here is that Carter's mediation, despite being by a private citizen, was able to bring a successful short-term abatement to tensions on the Korean peninsula. Even though the lull in tensions was not permanent, it is almost certain that the DPRK arsenal would be more developed today had the Agreed Framework not been negotiated.

Roosevelt at Portsmouth

Returning to Theodore Roosevelt's mediation in the Russo-Japanese War, we again observe how a third party can reduce barriers to efficient bargaining, at least in the short run. Like Carter in the DPRK, Roosevelt lacked substantial leverage over the combatants and also had to be creative in pushing against entrenched positions. Perhaps ironically, Roosevelt received much acclaim for his efforts, including the 1906 Nobel Peace Prize, but his level of involvement in the negotiations pales in comparison to what we have seen in, say, Kissinger's and Carter's efforts in the Middle East. As we see in the next chapter, Roosevelt's combination of restraint and a well-timed push for peace might have been exactly what was needed in this case—although not in all cases—and can help explain why the peace established between Japan and Russia was relatively durable.

Japan began the 1905 negotiations with a list of demands. The most contentious were the demands for indemnity and rights to Sakhalin Island. Other issues were less contentious, such as those related to the Japanese control of the Korean peninsula and rights to the Liaodong peninsula, and were resolved in relatively quick fashion. The negotiations at Portsmouth stalled after a week primarily over indemnity and Sakhalin. Up to this point, the discussions had been very much bilateral, with Roosevelt not participating in the deliberation. In the days approaching the conference, the U.S. president had counseled both sides to reduce their demands—he lobbied Russia not to try to prolong the war because of its poor military position, and he advocated that Japan not press for indemnity, foreseeing that this would be a stumbling block toward peace.[46] But during the negotiations, Roosevelt remained at a distance, primarily at his summer residence in Oyster Bay, New York, intending to intervene only as a last resort. Roosevelt's early involvement as an intermediary thus primarily entailed the pure facilitation of the talks, with some function as a proposal maker before the conference technically had commenced.

---

46. For an overview of Roosevelt's approach to both sides, see Princen (1992).

The Japanese delegation eventually reached a point where it felt a last resort was needed, and on August 18, it asked Roosevelt to act. Roosevelt immediately entreated Tokyo and St. Petersburg to compromise. A direct appeal to Nicholas II via both telegram and Ambassador George V. I. Meyer was unconventional in going over the head of the Russian delegation but was important because Nicholas, in response, agreed to the possibility of giving up half of Sakhalin island and also allowed negotiations to continue (Esthus 1988, 143). Roosevelt's initial involvement as a more intrusive mediator, however, also created some confusion because his proposals were out of sync with what Witte and Komura had discussed in secret.[47] Despite this stumble, Roosevelt's involvement eventually had the needed effect of enabling the sides to reach an agreement.

Using his understanding of the Japanese plight as leverage, Roosevelt reminded the Japanese delegation that the failure of the negotiations would entail significant battlefield costs. He also lobbied for Germany, France, and Britain to endorse his proposed compromise and received it from the first two.[48] This increased the incentives for both Japan and Russia to accept the agreement because their domestic supporters and international allies presumably would be more willing to accept a compromise when other powers found it prudent. In addition, Germany and France applied diplomatic pressure to both sides to accept the deal.

After a few near-collapses of negotiations, both sides finally agreed to divide control of Sakhalin in half, and Japan gave up its indemnity demand. Komura actually had instructions from Tokyo to concede all of Sakhalin if needed, but Komura a hard-liner who was loath to concede too much, held out for half of the island (Princen 1992; Randall 1985). The Treaty of Portsmouth was successfully signed on September 5, 1905, but the publics of both Russia and Japan were outraged at the poor terms—in Russia for giving up territory for which there was no precedent, and in Japan for giving up the indemnity demands.[49] The outrage was most present in Japan because the public had not expected Japan to get such modest terms when it clearly had the military advantage. There were riots in Tokyo for three days after announcement of the agreement. Despite such opposition, Roosevelt's mediation had brought the combatants to agreement.

This case thus involves a balance of mediator restraint and carefully timed indirect leverage to reach a landmark accord. Roosevelt served as an agreement formulator and applied leverage primarily via international pressure only after his

---

47. See Esthus (1988, 131–35).
48. On these sources of leverage, see White (1964, 303); Esthus (1988, 137–40); Lukoianov (2008, 56).
49. On the public reactions, see Esthus (1988, 167–92); Lukoianov (2008, 60–61).

efforts as a pure facilitator had reached the limits of what they could accomplish. It is worth noting that the ultimate agreement was one that was fully consistent with Roosevelt's preference that no single dominant power would emerge from the conflict. This lines up neatly with the earlier findings that mediators often do well to encourage small concessions but not large concessions; too many gains by Japan, for example, would have upset the balance of power in East Asia. Roosevelt was banking, it turns out optimistically, on stalemate in the region to allow U.S. interests to grow.

The Tokyo riots do point to an interesting shortcoming in Roosevelt's efforts. One of the mediation tactics that Roosevelt was not able to use with much success was helping the actors save face while making concessions.[50] The fact that neither side enjoyed widespread domestic support for the terms of peace indicates that the general publics did not trust Roosevelt's insistence that both sides had received an adequate deal. Moreover, the jolt of anti-Americanism in Japan after 1905 suggests that Roosevelt *shared* the blame and did not *shift* it.[51] A couple factors might explain Roosevelt's inability to help the actors save face. First, tsarist Russia and Meiji Japan were not democracies with publics that had adequate voices, access to information, or the ability to see competing positions. There was thus no real mechanism for Roosevelt to sell the agreement convincingly when the leaderships of both sides were claiming military success yet had to form a compromise. For example, the Japanese public was largely in the dark about the sore state of the Japanese military and economy despite the battlefield successes, and Roosevelt was bound to secrecy on the matter, so it would have been difficult for him to convince the Japanese public regarding the prudence of the agreement for Japanese interests (White 1964, 317). Second, Roosevelt's mostly hands-off approach and general lack of substantial leverage limited his ability to claim that he was responsible for pushing the actors toward difficult compromise. In general, this case demonstrates that simply by serving as a mediator, third parties do not automatically generate political cover. They must be well-positioned vis-à-vis the domestic audiences of the combatants to increase acceptance of otherwise unpopular concessions.

Another factor of the mediation environment, related to audience pressures, that shaped the negotiation dynamics was Witte's manipulation of the press. Although the negotiations were supposed to be confidential, the Russian delegation leaked the Japanese positions to encourage the international public to see Japan as negotiating from an unreasonable position (White 1964, 245). In

---

50. For a discussion of Roosevelt's failure to get either side to back away from positions rooted in the preservation of national honor, see Lukoianov (2008, 58–59).

51. See Wolff (2008); White (1964, 324); Esthus (1988, 186).

addition, Witte publicly proposed making the discussions open—even though the sides had already agreed to keep them closed—and public opinion became even more favorable to the Russians after Japan turned down Witte's suggestion (Lukoianov 2008, 55). It is interesting that Witte was primarily playing to U.S. public opinion, confirming that international audiences are important, just as domestic audiences are. Witte apparently believed that public opinion within a mediating state could be a source of leverage at the negotiating table. This relates to the notion that the potential for closer relations with a third party can both motivate bringing in a third party as a mediator and act as a source of leverage during the negotiations.

Mediation provides observable benefits in conflict management and conflict resolution, at least in the short run. By providing incentives that make ongoing conflict less desirable, decreasing the barriers to information flows, helping the combatants save face, and promising implementation assistance, intermediaries increase the attractiveness of formal agreements and concessions. They also enable the actors to avoid an immediate recurrence of hostilities and try peace for at least a while. At the same time, however, third-party mediators may limit the size of concessions, so as to not exacerbate the extent to which the conceding party looks weak. These benefits of mediation are important in understanding why mediation occurs so frequently in the international system. In the next two chapters, I demonstrate that mediation is not without potential risks.

THE STRUGGLE FOR SELF-ENFORCING PEACE

In the arts of peace Man is a bungler.

—George Bernard Shaw

In chapter 4, I point to the benefits that mediation offers to conflict bargaining processes. Along with the findings in chapter 3, this helps explain why third parties are so frequently asked to assist in negotiation initiatives. Combatants, wanting to maximize progress toward peace settlements or otherwise escape costly conflict, are typically rewarded when they turn to third-party assistance. Mediation is not epiphenomenal; it produces meaningful peaceful dividends.

The evidence explored thus far demonstrates that intermediaries are useful conflict managers, but it does not suggest that they constitute a conflict-resolution panacea. Each of the outcomes explored in chapter 4 pertains to short-term benefits, but third parties are particularly limited in what they can do in the long run. Much more, their involvement, especially the more heavy-handed it is, can make permanent strides toward a lasting peace more difficult. In this chapter, I provide the theoretical basis for such struggles and consider the conditions under which mediation is more (or less) prone to increasing the fragility of peace in the long run.

General Barriers

Putting aside any potential long-term destabilizing effects of third-party involvement for the moment, it is worth considering the general problems that mediators face in achieving peaceful bargaining outcomes. Third parties may intend to expand the set of acceptable alternatives, assist in implementation, reduce information barriers, or provide political cover, but all third parties encounter some hindrances to realizing these benefits. Although identifying these barriers might seem to be common sense, the barriers are highlighted here to stress the difficult tasks that third parties take on when mediating.

Expanding the Set of Alternatives

Despite the emphasis on leverage in discussions of third-party conflict management, mediators face a number of hurdles in actually exerting leverage. It is often difficult for third parties to obtain the necessary resources and influence to sufficiently increase the opportunity costs of conflict and make peaceful bargaining more productive. Individuals, NGOs, and small states are obvious examples of third parties that are typically unable to achieve enough leverage to make much of a difference in shaping incentives relative to the stakes of conflict.

Strong great power states can also struggle to attain leverage against combatants. Third parties can credibly promise meaningful carrots such as aid only when the benefits to the third party of reaching an agreement are substantial. And the difficulty in establishing leverage also pertains to the use of sticks, or negative inducements. Because military force is generally outside the purview of mediation, sticks typically involve denying, or threatening to deny, preexisting benefits of the relationship between the third party and the disputant. In particular, third parties often threaten, explicitly or implicitly, to withdraw aid from or reduce diplomatic ties with a combatant. When such aid or ties do not exist in the first place (i.e., a combatant enjoys few benefits from a relationship with the third party), mediators are less able to use sticks to secure an agreement. Even when a third party has strong ties with a combatant, it may struggle to establish credible leverage for at least two reasons. First, the third party may fear overstepping its bounds, thereby precipitating its rejection as mediator. Second, because sanctioning a disputant with strong existing ties is likely to be costly to the third party this may decrease the believability of any threats that the third party makes.

Implementation Assistance

A primary hindrance to the ability of a mediator to provide implementation assistance for an agreement stems from the difficulty of credibly committing to long-term resource contributions. After third parties have assisted in conflict attenuation, it is easy for them to lose interest in monitoring and enforcement, especially because they can typically renew their involvement if the situation sufficiently deteriorates again. A key difference exists between the interest of a third-party in *becoming* involved or *renewing* involvement in an ongoing conflict and a third-party's interest in *remaining* involved after hostilities have abated. In an ongoing conflict, bargaining failure is a certainty. In a recently terminated conflict, bargaining failure is less certain because it is possible for peace to endure. For this reason, the incentives for the third party to be involved during a conflict are greater than the incentives for the third party to remain involved once a ceasefire has been reached.

If there are other conflicts that need third-party assistance, mediators tend to devote their attention to the more pressing conflicts at the expense of their commitments to securing peace in areas that might remain stable without continual involvement. In addition, third parties may simply run out of resources to uphold all of their international commitments because direct security threats take priority over helping others keep a fragile peace. This relates to our discussion in chapter 2 about how third-party involvements in peacemaking, peacekeeping, and peacebuilding entail the provision of impure public goods and have the potential to be underprovided. In addition, domestic political constraints against using sovereign revenue, or much more the blood of one's own troops, to pay for the security of others can restrain third-party commitments to long-term involvement, as seen recently in the limited contributions to the NATO mission in Afghanistan by various European countries. Partly for these reasons, Monica Toft (2009) finds that third-party security guarantees are not very effective in securing durable settlements. Third parties may also want to avoid the problem of providing a safety net for risky behavior for too long.[1]

The expectation that intermediaries are often unable to stay involved after an agreement helps us understand not only the difficulty of providing implementation assistance but also how the almost inevitable attenuation of third-party involvement can be detrimental to the stability of long-term peace.

Information Provision

Turning to the struggles of lighter forms of mediation, there are some limitations to the view that mediators provide substantial information that helps the bargaining expectations of the actors converge. Put simply, it can be difficult for mediators to access information to which the combatants themselves are not privy. Also, a combatant may hesitate to reveal private information to a mediator because the mediator has an incentive to make the revealed information public

---

1. On the perverse incentives of third-party involvement, see especially Kuperman (2008); Rauchhaus (2009).

to reduce misinformation.[2] For the same reason that an actor in a dispute is hesitant to be honest with its opponent, it will be reluctant to reveal its hand to a third-party conflict manager that has incentives to increase peace. In addition, few intermediaries have access to intelligence superior to that which the combatants themselves can gather and are also willing share such sensitive intelligence with another state. The combatants have strong incentives to gather as much information as possible about their opponents well before fighting erupts. It is thus rare—although still occasionally possible, as discussed in chapter 2—that a third party with less at stake can reveal more about an opponent than an actor already knows.

Moreover, mediators are prone to manipulating the flow of information to maximize the probability of a settlement.[3] If the belligerents suspect such manipulation, they will discount the information and get no closer to convergence. So, even if the third parties do know something that the disputants do not, it will be difficult to effectively convey that information. Third parties with clear preferences for a peaceful resolution struggle particularly to provide believable information because their incentives are to tell the combatants whatever is needed to achieve peace.[4] When mediators desire peace above all else, the actors will dismiss the third-party pleas to make a deal as cheap talk meant only to reach an agreement. As a result, third parties must at a minimum be perceived as having an incentive to tell the truth when they know that concessions are not in the best interests of combatants.

Thus far, we have focused on the barriers to direct information provision. Third parties can also facilitate the provision of information indirectly, for example, by reducing the transaction costs of information exchange (see chap. 2). The numerous barriers to direct information provision suggest that third parties frequently have to rely on such indirect functions when serving an informational role. The information that can be provided through indirect mechanisms, however, also has obvious limitations. Although third parties can reduce the costs and risks of revealing information, in many cases they cannot decrease the incentives of the actors to manipulate information flows, or bluff, for greater bargaining power. The ability of a mediator to strengthen the flow of communication still leaves the content of that communication to the discretion of the combatants.

---

2. Fey and Ramsay (2010) show that mediators can only provide information when they have independent access to information.

3. See, for example, Smith and Stam (2003); Princen (1992); Young (1967).

4. See Kydd (2003, 2006); Rauchhaus (2006, 2011); Smith and Stam (2003).

Political Cover

Finally, third-party political cover also has limitations. As mentioned previously, only strongly influential mediators with the ability to impose a settlement can credibly shift the blame for concessions. Moreover, third parties can struggle to signal the prudence of agreements to domestic audiences. The problem of cheap talk is not a problem just for mediators wishing to provide credible information to the combatants; the same problem exists in providing political cover when domestic audiences are unsure of whether or not concessions are prudent and look to a third party for verification. If the third party has a constant interest in judging all concessions as prudent regardless of the truth, there is little credibility in the third party's signal to the domestic audiences.[5] The general public and the other political elites will have a hard time changing their minds about whether a particular settlement is a good deal simply because a peacemaker has blessed it. Without the ability to signal credibly, and without a mandate to produce a binding resolution on the matter, mediators that are strongly interested in peace provide less adequate political cover.

For example, Teddy Roosevelt's mediation at Portsmouth failed to provide much political cover when both negotiating teams returned to despondent publics (see chap. 3). This was especially true for Komura and the Japanese delegation. There was little reason for the Japanese or the Russian citizens to find Roosevelt's praise for the agreement a convincing endorsement because there was no history of the United States, in general, or Roosevelt, specifically, looking out for the interests of these two countries. And, of course, we know after the fact that Roosevelt was looking out much more for U.S. interests in East Asia and in the Pacific than he was for the well-being of Japan and Russia. The United States at the time also did not have the international heft to be perceived as having imposed the agreement on the two sides, putting it at an additional disadvantage in helping the negotiators save face.

Beyond Temporary Benefits?

Although these barriers are useful in understanding what mediators must overcome, clearly they overcome such obstacles frequently. If third parties were generally unable to provide any benefits, mediation would seldom occur and even more seldom succeed in producing short-term peaceful outcomes. The

---

5. Chapman (2007) similarly argues that authorizations from international security institutions can convey information to domestic audiences only when the organizations are perceived as biased and thus not completely driven by the pursuit of peace.

discussion thus far helps explain only why mediation does not have a perfect success rate. Now we turn to why many of the benefits of mediation, although sufficient to justify its prevalence, are not likely to help much in the long term. In fact, as I show in the next section, mediation can actually make peace less stable over time.

The principal way for third-party conflict management of any kind to enhance the long-term adherence to a negotiated arrangement, when the relative bargaining power and red lines of the actors shift over time, would be to increase the probability that a settlement falls within the most stable region of the set of mutually satisfying alternatives to conflict (i.e., well above the minimum acceptable offer of each actor). The mediator needs to increase the ability for the actors to "get the terms right," making future renegotiation less necessary.[6] In actuality, many third parties struggle to have much of an impact in this regard. Given the barriers to mediation, it is asking a lot of mediators to discover with reliable accuracy the most stable arrangements, especially when the disputants themselves have been unable to do so, and then convince the disputants to settle on those arrangements. It is difficult enough for a third party to understand the current bargaining environment better than the disputants do; it is even more difficult for a third party to understand the future bargaining environment better.

When third parties are unable to lead the combatants to the most durable agreements, either the third parties must stay involved indefinitely or the preferences of the actors about a satisfactory agreement must remain relatively static for the benefits of mediation to have staying power. If, as is likely, the bargaining positions of the combatants change over time and the third parties are unable to, as needed, maintain leverage, elucidate the changing bargaining environment continuously, and provide ongoing political cover, third-party involvement will have only temporary benefits. Because of this, with or without mediation, the actors often will eventually need to renegotiate in the future and again face the risk of a bargaining breakdown.[7]

Moving in the Wrong Direction

Third-party intervention can also have long-term negative consequences. A conflict episode terminates when the combatants expect the returns from making a deal or sticking with the status quo to exceed those from continuing to fight; through the mechanisms discussed, mediators can shape the conditions that

---

6. See Werner and Yuen (2005).
7. On the causes of renegotiation, see Werner (1999b).

make accepting a deal or the status quo more attractive in an immediate sense. If and when the involvement and influence of the mediator fades, however, conditions are prone to make both renegotiation and renegotiation failure more likely. Three potential factors can contribute to the long-term fragility of a mediated peace: the artificiality of external leverage, the obfuscation of the future bargaining environment, and insincere motives.

Artificial Incentives

Most directly, positive and negative inducements can generate or worsen time inconsistency problems—related to the concept of an obsolescent bargain—in which an arrangement is preferable to conflict at the time of negotiation but not at a time afterward. When third parties successfully promote a settlement that would not have been mutually satisfying in the absence of third-party leverage, contentment with the agreement is likely to falter eventually when the third party is no longer in the picture. Under the auspices of third-party leverage, temporary arrangements become possible because of the inflated incentives for agreement, but temporary they remain as long as the arrangements are not mutually preferable to conflict in the absence of such pressure. As Suzanne Werner and Amy Yuen state, "Once third-party attention wanes, the settlement becomes obsolete as a divergence between the settlement agreed to and the belligerents' expectations about what they could gain by renewing the war emerges" (2005, 269).[8] Yitzhak Rabin, writing in his memoirs about the signing of the Egyptian-Israeli peace treaty, is quite cognizant of this potential for third parties to leave behind a fleeting peace:

> I hope that now that the formal treaty is signed, the countries that spoke so promisingly of peace and coaxed and cajoled the sides at every opportunity—the United States, Canada, and the European nations—will pay more than just lip service to peace. Just as there was little chance of Europe's developing as a democratic part of the world after World War II had it not been for the Marshall Plan, without providing concrete economic support to Egypt—and to Israel—those who preach peace will not be able to prove their vision is truly valid. (1979, 330)

The use of leverage leads to short-lived settlements especially when third-party interests do not well align with the set of arrangements that will be most

---

8. Beardsley et al. (2006) present some additional empirical support for this expectation. They find that manipulative mediation is a superior tactic in reaching short-term agreements but not better in achieving post-crisis tension reduction. Gurses, Rost, and McLeod (2008) also find that superpower mediation tends to decrease the stability of peace.

self-enforcing—the arrangements that both actors will prefer to fighting long after the third party is gone. Third parties often have their own incentives for intervention, which can interfere with the combatants' reaching a self-enforcing peace. On this, Greg Mills and Terence McNamee write,

> A great failing of much interstate and intrastate conflict resolution of the past fifty years is that local actors have not "owned" the peacebuilding processes in their own countries. The international community, particularly the United Nations, has often developed and sustained solutions that express the political will of its most powerful members and its own bureaucratic interests rather than those of the parties to a conflict. (2009, 58–59)

Although some research has argued that biased third parties can be most effective in using leverage to elicit the abatement of conflict,[9] such third parties typically cannot be relied on to forge agreements that are the most enduring. By definition, biased mediators are primarily interested in shaping the distribution of a settlement. They may have no real interest in preventing the renewal of violence, and their incentive to continue managing the conflict will decrease after they have achieved their primary objective.

As we have seen in the previous chapter, attempts at conflict management using mediation are not more likely to lead to major asymmetric concessions by the disputants, and mediation might even limit the size of some concessions. Mediators may aid the side with weaker bargaining power and use their leverage to promote more egalitarian settlements that avoid massive concessions by one side. If this is the case, then such heavy-handed structuring of the terms of peace is not likely to be self-enforcing, especially when there is substantial asymmetry in bargaining power. When third-party leverage is removed, the side with more bargaining power will become dissatisfied with its allotment and will push for the concessions they otherwise would have received, threatening the viability of any settlement reached under the auspices of a mediator.

Even the attempt by an intermediary to have a positive long-run impact through promises of implementation assistance can be potentially counterproductive in addressing time inconsistency problems. The types of agreements that are difficult to reach without mediation but that result with third-party security guarantees are precisely those facing enforcement troubles—arrangements that might be acceptable at the time of the agreement but that are prone to backsliding. Once the inflated opportunity costs of future conflict from third-party guarantees

---

9. See, for example, Touval (1975); Favretto (2009).

again decrease to zero over time—as a result of the aforementioned fickle media-tor commitments—such agreements become less tenable. So, mediators are prone to promoting agreements that ultimately need to be renegotiated in the long run because of the inability of third parties to sustain their commitments indefinitely to those conflicts that, at the time of negotiation, needed it most.

Barriers to Learning

Involved third parties can also interfere with the natural learning processes in the conflict, which affects the prospects for successful renegotiation in the future. Scholars have theorized that belligerents often use war to learn about the capa-bilities and resolve of their opponents, thereby reducing problems of uncertainty in bargaining.[10] Wars often begin when the actors are unclear about what the set of mutually acceptable arrangements actually looks like, and they end when each side realizes which concessions to make. The conflict itself allows the combatants to observe the size and skill of the opposing combat forces, as well as the reaction to the violence of the leadership and domestic public. When an opponent fights with unexpected ability or resolve, concessions should be more readily forthcom-ing until eventually a mutually acceptable accord is reached.

When third parties intervene, especially when they do so early in a conflict and create strong incentives for peace, the belligerents might not learn enough about their opponents. If intrusive third parties interrupt the battlefield learning process, then the actors will be less able to find a mutually satisfying agreement on their own when the need for renegotiation arises. Uncertainty about the prob-ability of either side prevailing in war or about the full costs of such a contest will be greater than if the actors had previously fought to a point at which their expectations of how a conflict would play out converged. Note that I am not disputing here that one of the functions of mediation is to improve the informa-tion flow between belligerents. Instead, my point is that although mediation can sometimes reduce uncertainty when compared to bilateral negotiations, fight-ing has the potential to reduce uncertainty about the capabilities and resolve of opponents even more. So, peace processes that forestall fighting in many cases prevent a more full revelation of information.

In addition, mediation can substitute for direct interaction, so arrangements that are reached without mediation may prove more durable because the actors have been forced to develop bilateral mechanisms of learning and communica-tion that enhance future renegotiations. When the status quo is challenged again,

---

10. See especially Blainey (1973); Slantchev (2003, 2004); Smith and Stam (2003); Powell (2004a); Filson and Werner (2002).

negotiators that truly understand their opponents and how to communicate with them will find it relatively easier to reach a new bargain. Negotiators that do not will be more prone to renegotiation failure; in particular, they will be less able to read signals from, send signals to, accurately assess the trustworthiness of, or understand the political pressures facing an opponent. Diplomatic teams that previously were dependent on a mediator will be especially prone to such a fate. Note that this argument applies more to the dynamics among practitioners at the negotiating table and less to mediators affecting the way that people of various nationalities try to understand one another on a more general level. For example, one of the interesting consequences of Sadat and Begin's bilateral initiative that started in 1977 is that it provided a foundation for these two very different personalities to better understand one another's negotiating tendencies, even though it did not help them like one another better. This is a story, then, about interpersonal and interpolitical dynamics, and it is doubtful that Kissinger's and Carter's mediation attempts or Sadat's bold trip to Jerusalem changed much about what the Arab and Israeli people, with histories that have been intertwined for millennia, generally understand about one another.

Finally, the face-saving role of mediation can also decrease the quality of the information in the bargaining environment and make renegotiation more challenging. As discussed in chapter 2, generating audience costs for concessions can be a way for actors to signal their resolve and deter their opponents by tying their hands to a hard-line stance.[11] When such deterrence fails, these actors need political cover if they are to make prudent concessions and avoid conflict. A problem arises because the availability of political cover enables an actor to untie its hands and consequently obscure future deterrent signals. So, this provides an additional mechanism by which the presence of an involved third party can muddle the clarity of renegotiation environments.

Note that these ways of interfering with information and learning between combatants can make future disputes on other issues more difficult to resolve, as well as future disputes on the original issue. The general expectation explored empirically here is that mediation can make the long-term prospects for peace between two sides more fragile, regardless of whether the actors have only one issue that they keep renegotiating or multiple issues to dispute. Also, the argument about information obfuscation here means that, even if a mediator does well resolving one issue completely, future negotiations about other issues might be more difficult because of the third-party interference with more natural learning processes.

---

11. Fearon (1994) formalizes this argument.

Insincere Motives

The first two factors that can cause peace to be less stable over time can be pinned on third-party efforts, especially when the mediator is heavy handed. In addition, the combatants themselves often bear responsibility for the long-term risks associated with assisted conflict management. If the actors actually intend to resume fighting after the peace process, then mediation can play right into their hands and lead to greater instability. When actors merely want to stall or pretend that they sincerely desire peace, they will be eager to reach an initial cease-fire but quite hesitant to proceed toward full implementation of a peace deal. This behavior is consistent with a pattern of mediation outcomes in which cease-fire agreements are more likely to be reached after mediation but conflict is more likely to recur as time passes.

It is thus a mistake to assume that all instances of mediation involve combatants sincerely trying to resolve their bargaining difficulties. Situations often arise in which actors desire mediation simply as a stalling tactic when there are incentives to delay resolution and fighting. When faced with losses on the battlefield that are greater than expected, actors may desire a mediated cease-fire to regroup and resume the fight in the future from a stronger position.[12] Similarly, leaders who do not want to make the concessions that domestic and international audiences are pushing for can use their participation in a mediated peace process to blend in with others who are actually willing to settle. Although participating in mediation may not signal much to such audiences, not participating can signal an unwillingness to make the concessions.

One way to consider conceptually how mediation can be used for insincere motives is to imagine one of the actors being able to improve its bargaining position during mediation. This may occur if the actor were to secure its defenses during the negotiation period, thereby decreasing its costs of conflict, or rearm, thereby increasing the probability of victory. Another way for a disputant to improve its bargaining position is to decrease its audience costs for continuing conflict by convincing domestic and international audiences, through participation in mediation, that the culpability for bargaining failure lies elsewhere. In this way, the disputant gains a freer hand to push for a better bargain. If the bargaining position of an actor improves in any of these ways, the actor will have an incentive to make a challenge and push for more concessions at the end of the mediation period.

---

12. Such incentives might also give rise to a greater willingness to pursue a bilateral cease-fire, so the key comparison is that mediation becomes more attractive than continuing the conflict.

The pursuit of mediation for an objective other than peace is clearly something that is disruptive to long-term stability and mediation efficacy. Although it is important to consider the potential for mediation to be used insincerely, this effect is not likely to dominate the other causes of post-mediation fragility. The incentives for disputants to avoid mediation when they suspect that their opponents have insincere motives should limit the extent to which mere deviousness explains the instability of peace following mediated conflicts.

Testing the Observable Implications

As we have seen, mediation might inhibit long-term resolution of conflict via three mechanisms. First, and potentially most important, intermediaries can push for agreements that would simply not be viable in the absence of third-party pressure. This creates or exacerbates time inconsistency problems so that agreements that are satisfactory in the present will need to be renegotiated in the future. Second, third-party intervention can heighten the level of uncertainty in future bargaining environments—the belligerents might find renegotiation more difficult because of their abbreviated opportunity to learn on the battlefield, their failure to cultivate the necessary tools for successful unassisted negotiation, or muddled signaling from political cover. Third, mediation can enable combatants to use the downtime to improve their bargaining positions while they go through only the motions of pursuing peace.

The expectation that mediation makes long-term stability less likely does not obviate the short-term benefits of mediation. The need for renegotiation takes some time to materialize; few agreements would ever be reached if actors suspected that defection would be immediate. It takes time for the bargaining positions of the actors to change enough that they become dissatisfied with the new status quo. Capabilities and will are sticky and presumably do not fluctuate much from day to day. Militaries must be revamped, defenses must be secured, and politicians must either have a change of heart or be replaced for situations to become much different than when the conflict originally concluded. It also takes time for third-party involvement to wane and leave the actors with an agreement that is potentially not self-enforcing.

If the logic of the mediation dilemma holds, then we expect third-party conflict management to produce both short-term gains and long-term difficulty in sustaining peace. Mediation should do well in preventing the recurrence of conflict in the immediate aftermath of a crisis but less well in preventing a recurrence many years into the future. The corollary expectation is that, as time passes, the unmediated crises will produce more stable relationships than the mediated ones do. Unmediated conflicts that do not reignite soon after the end of a crisis tend to involve situations in which the combatants have managed to resolve their own bargaining problems. These types of relationships tend to have an advantage over those in which intermediaries leave the disputants with arrangements that, in the absence of continual third-party involvement, have a greater need for and difficulty of renegotiation.

> Hypothesis 5.1 *Mediators are more likely to prevent immediate crisis recurrence but less likely to prevent crisis recurrence further in the future.*

To test the hypothesis, we are interested in explaining the length of the peace spells from the end of a crisis until the beginning of a new one. Event history, or duration, methods allow models of such outcomes to be estimated. The ICB data are best suited for this analysis because the crises in the data are by definition abnormal periods of high tension, and it is useful to assess what contributes to a return to such tension after earlier settlement.[13] The event history models use a Cox semi-parametric specification because it does not require strong assumptions about the shape of the hazard function.

From Hypothesis 5.1, we expect that the impact of mediation on peace spells will start positively and strongly but diminish over time. In essence, the hypothesis suggests that the effect of mediation on the risk of recurrence is not constant over time (i.e., the hazard ratio is not proportional). By interacting the time since the previous crisis and the occurrence of mediation, we can allow for nonproportional hazards and directly model such an expectation.[14] Additional issues related to model specification, including tests for robustness to selection effects, are provided in the appendix to this book.

A nonproportional Cox model indeed reveals that the effect of mediation on crisis recurrence is conditioned by the time since the previous crisis. Immediately after a crisis has ended, mediated settlements have a smaller hazard rate than unmediated ones—dyads that did not have outside assistance are more prone to crisis recurrence than those that experienced mediation. But after four or five years, the unmediated peace spells tend to be more durable; over time, the mediated agreements emerge with a higher risk for recurrence. This relationship is

---

13. The ICOW data are less suitable to such a duration analysis. ICOW disputes often are not violently hostile, so recurrence does not necessarily have much meaning for the stability of peace. Moreover, ICOW disputes sometimes span decades and are deemed to end only when the analyst observes that there are no remaining issues relating to the claim. It is thus difficult to conduct analyses of the *recurrence* of tensions with the ICOW data; nevertheless, it is possible to assess the proclivity for violence after ten years as a means of gauging the long-term effects of mediation.

14. See Box-Steffensmeier, Reiter, and Zorn (2003).

exactly what we expect if mediators tend to make future renegotiation both more likely and more difficult.

Figure 5.1, which gives the instantaneous probabilities (annualized) of crisis recurrence over time, illustrates this effect. As we see in the figure, dyads less than four years removed from a crisis are less likely to relapse when they had mediation. After approximately five years, dyads that had mediation become more prone to relapse than dyads enjoying an unmediated peace.[15] Note that, even though the probabilities are low, the impact of mediation on recurrence at, say, ten years is quite high—more than doubling the probability compared to the baseline probabilities of recurrence without mediation. Moreover, the predicted values at each given year are instantaneous probabilities, so over time a heightened probability of crisis recurrence will accumulate and more strongly threaten the stability of peace. Crisis dyads without mediation are thus prone to higher recurrence soon after crisis termination, but if peace survives a few years in such dyads, that peace becomes much more stable than a peace resulting from mediation.

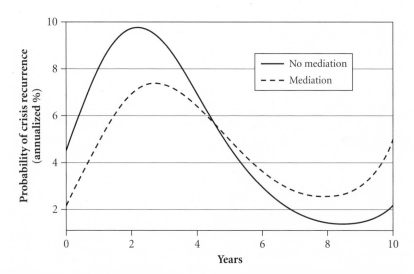

FIGURE 5.1 Impact of mediation and time on crisis recurrence. The difference between the lines is statistically significant ($p < 0.05$, one-tailed test) before 3 years and after 7 years.

---

15. The difference between the trends is statistically significant ($p < 0.05$, one-tailed test) before three years and after seven years after the end of a crisis.

Conditioning the Dilemma

At this juncture, it is prudent to explore the conditions under which the short- and long-term trade-off is minimized or maximized, and the steps that third parties can take to hedge against any long-term negative consequences. Intermediaries do not always enhance a short-term settlement at the expense of more permanent stability and certainly not all mediated peace spells end in the renewal of conflict. The question then becomes whether there are systematic explanations for why some instances of mediation are more prone to increase the fragility of peace than others.

Foremost, as we will see, the effects of mediation on both short-term success and long-term struggle are proportional to the amount of leverage used. The choice of whether to use heavy-handed tactics or not is thus a parallel dilemma to the broader dilemma of whether to use mediation or not. In this section, I also consider factors related to the characteristics of the disputants, third parties, and bargaining environment that further condition the extent to which the dilemma is manifested.

Leverage

As we have seen, three factors contribute to why mediation often creates a peace that cannot be sustained. Two of these factors are closely tied to the use of leverage and the third has a looser relationship. First, third parties that heavy-handedly manipulate the incentives for agreement are actually allowing time-inconsistent arrangements to be reached that the combatants would not find mutually preferable to conflict in the absence of the intervention. In such a situation, attenuation of the engagement role of the third party, gradually or suddenly, will directly translate into a greater need for renegotiation and a higher potential for renewed conflict. Second, reliance on leverage by a mediator to incentivize peace will most soundly disrupt the ability of the actors to learn from the conflict environment and develop the knowledge to carry out successful renegotiations. The third factor, related to insincere motives, can also loosely relate to leverage because a third party that pressures the sides into a cease-fire creates the requisite space and time for disputants with devious objectives to increase their bargaining power for use later when the third party is out of the picture.[16]

---

16. Similarly, previous research has found that disputants that suspect their opponents of insincere motives prefer weaker third parties to serve as mediators (Beardsley 2009).

The argument is thus that the increased use of third-party leverage will lead to ever-stronger short-term outcomes—more formal agreements, concessions, and lulls in hostilities—and ever-weaker long-term stability. The types of leverage relevant here include both immediate inducements and implementation guarantees. The former, in which the bargaining environment is manipulated only in the present, represents the most obvious form of artificial incentives. The latter type of leverage, in which mediators promise implementation assistance and security guarantees, rarely persists indefinitely and can also contribute to instability as years pass.

In considering the other end of the leverage spectrum, we suspect that third parties that rely purely on facilitation or political cover do not carry as great a risk of contributing to long-term instability. When mediators simply bring the parties together and help them communicate, any resulting peaceful arrangement will be close to those achieved bilaterally. Without external leverage, the belligerents must reach an agreement that is mutually preferable to conflict. Thus the primary risks of soft mediation to long-term stability are limited to a potential inability of the combatants to learn how to communicate bilaterally and the weakening of future signaling via audience costs, but these pale in comparison to the direct effects that artificial incentives can have on the bargaining environment.[17] Although low levels of intrusiveness are less likely to produce a higher proclivity for future relapse, such involvement is also less likely to yield the same short-run benefits as more manipulative tactics. That is, third parties should find it easier to directly shape incentives for short-term peace through direct appeals to costs and benefits than through informational or face-saving mechanisms.

If nonmanipulative mediation styles tend not to function better in the short run than manipulative mediation, but have less risk of contributing to long-term instability, we have another dilemma. Actors that allow substantial third-party leverage to be part of their negotiations have the best shot at short-term peace created by the external incentives. But this choice can make a relapse into conflict more likely in the long run because the participants become less able to reach self-enforcing arrangements. Alternatively, a less risky strategy of pursuing only facilitative mediation might not sacrifice much long-term hope for stability, but there is also less opportunity for short-term bargaining efficiency to be realized.

> Hypothesis 5.2 *The trade-off between short-term peace and long-term stability in mediation outcomes is starker when mediators use leverage.*

---

17. Similarly, Rubin (1981, 14–16) proposes that the advisory role of a third party can be much more enduring than a directive role that depends on constant third-party influence and that mediators that serve more of a process-oriented role have greater long-run success than mediators that serve more of a content-oriented role.

Because the absence of leverage leaves the mediator disadvantaged in being able to produce short-term peace, we should not expect that mediators would be strictly better off holstering their use of power. For example, Richard Holbrooke asserted strong U.S. involvement in Bosnia because he saw how ineffective the European peacemakers had been without using much leverage (Holbrooke 1998, 318, 331).[18] U.S. Ambassador Warren Zimmerman similarly laments the crucial impact that strong U.S. leverage could have had earlier in the conflict: "The refusal of the Bush Administration to commit American power early was our greatest mistake of the entire Yugoslav crisis. It made an unjust outcome inevitable and wasted the opportunity to save over a hundred thousand lives" (1996, 216). Separately, even Jan Egeland, a member of the Norwegian team that successfully facilitated the Oslo Accords, recognizes the merit of leverage in pushing for Middle East peace: "Maximum pressure must be exerted on all actors in the Israeli-Palestinian and wider Israeli-Arab conflicts for progress to be made on these burning issues" (2008, 183). Nonetheless, in the cases in which minimal leverage is sufficient to reach an agreement, the potential for sustainable peace can be high.

To test this hypothesis we need to distinguish among mediation styles. The ICB data have a three-part typology for mediation actions: facilitation, formulation, and manipulation.[19] The facilitative style is the least intrusive and involves a third party bringing the sides together either literally, when they are at the same bargaining table, or figuratively, during shuttle diplomacy. The mediator is serving only as a conduit for information flows and exchanges of proposals. When a mediator operates using the formulative style, the third party is taking a more active role by framing the issues and making substantive proposals. A manipulative style is the most intrusive and involves threats and promises (sticks and carrots) made by the third party to the belligerents. Because manipulation closely lines up with what is meant by leverage, the key independent variables here are thus indicators of whether manipulative mediation or some less intrusive form of mediation occurred. The results are discussed later in the chapter.

Characteristics of the Disputants: Patience and Sincerity

In terms of disputant characteristics, actors that can afford to be patient and wait for an agreement greatly exceeding what each party minimally prefers to conflict have a stronger potential of enjoying the benefits of mediation without the long-term risks. When actors rush to sign any agreement that is acceptable in the present, they are prone to adopt terms that will fall apart in the future, especially

---

18. See also Touval (2002, 135–69).

19. See Beardsley et al. (2006). For a more extensive overview of these three mediation styles, see Bercovitch (1997). The ICOW data, used here to test other hypotheses, do not include information on the tactics used.

if the arrangement depends on third-party leverage. When the belligerents do not have much pressure to settle quickly, they can more patiently wait until they find an arrangement that is not only immediately acceptable but also likely to persist given future changes among the actors and the third party. They can also spend time constructing a framework for future dialogue, such that, should the need for renegotiation arise in the future, mechanisms will be in place to prevent escalation to violence.

As we have seen in chapter 3, the desperation of the belligerents depends on the severity of conflict, so the most violent and difficult contestations are most susceptible to a rushed agreement. Mediation in the less severe conflicts is thus relatively safe from the long-term risks. The problem, of course, with a reliance on patient protagonists to ensure effective mediation is that actors have less need for mediation and the short-term peace that tends to come with it when they can afford to wait. Mediation is more likely, given the inherent downstream risks, when the actors are impatient. This relates to Richard Betts's statement that "Mediation is useful, but it helps peacemaking most where peacemaking needs help least" (1994, 24). Nevertheless, when mediation does occur among patient actors, there will be fewer rushed decisions and more of an opportunity to reach an agreement that endures.

Another reason exists for the expectation that mediation during violent and difficult conflict will be less able to secure long-term stability. When combatants are in the midst of severe losses, they are most prone to use mediation insincerely as a stalling tactic. If an actor perceives that there may be an opportunity in the future to negotiate or fight from a stronger position—for example, if there is a favorable change in seasons approaching, a potential leadership turnover in the adversary, or the likely joining of an ally—then the actor will want to bide its time without having to bear substantial costs in the meantime. Or, if the actor simply believes that it can rebuild faster than its adversary, it will want to call for a cease-fire after there have been heavy losses, so that it has time to regroup and fight from a stronger position. If mediation is more likely to be used insincerely when there are high levels of violence, we should observe greater instances of short-term peace arrangements that immediately follow mediation attempts during severe conflict, and such arrangements should have a higher likelihood of breaking down in the long run because this is exactly what the actors with insincere motives intended all along.[20]

---

20. Note that the impact of this explanation is necessarily limited because actors and third parties want to hedge their commitment to any peace process in which they suspect an opponent has insincere motives. Because true motives are private information and actors can also have sincere motives for mediation when there are high levels of violence, as discussed previously, it remains plausible that some relationship exists between high levels of violence and the use of mediation for insincere motives.

Hypothesis 5.3 *The trade-off between short-term peace and long-term stability in mediation outcomes is starker when the level of violence and the duration of conflict are high.*

To test this hypothesis using the ICB data, the base model of the impact of mediation on the duration of peace is run on a sample in which violence is at the level of either minor clashes or no violence and the duration of the crisis is less than the mean. These are relatively less severe crises in which the actors tend to be more patient.[21]

Characteristics of the Third Parties: Peacekeeping and Coordination

The extreme heterogeneity of the third parties available for mediation—from hegemonic states to private citizens—allows for an interesting study of which types create starker trade-offs between short- and long-term success. One dimension of variance among third parties is in their potential to exert strong leverage. A direct comparison of third parties with substantial potential for leverage to those with less potential, however, might not reveal much of a difference in terms of the ability for the mediator to secure long-term peace. Both powerful third parties and weaker third parties have strengths and weaknesses in their ability to bolster commitments to a peace arrangement.

The most powerful third parties are most prone to artificially inflate the incentives for peace and leave the actors with an arrangement that is not self-enforcing. Even if the third parties do not use strong carrots and sticks, their mere presence can alter the immediate costs and benefits of the various settlement alternatives in ways that are inconsistent with future costs and benefits. The combatants will make their decisions according to their expectations of what might happen if they choose otherwise. More concretely, peace will have a temporarily inflated value when a combatant expects that the third party will use substantial leverage if peace is not reached, even when the third party does not actually make overt threats. Similarly, a combatant might be enticed to seek immediate peace to get into the good graces of a consequential third party—or to stay out of its bad graces—for political or economic benefits. The involvement of a powerful third party therefore can shift the attractiveness of short-term peace and leave future stability in doubt as time passes, whether the third party intends this or not.[22]

---

21. The scarcity of ICOW disputes with any violence prevents a full analysis of the ICOW data, as discussed later.

22. For evidence of this logic applied to civil wars, see Gurses, Rost, and McLeod (2008).

Third parties without much potential for exerting leverage, especially relatively weak states, NGOs, and individuals, will be better able to avoid artificially and temporarily inflating the benefits of peace. This does not mean, however, that there will be a more stable peace after mediation by weaker third parties. When weaker third parties can apply leverage—for example, by manipulating domestic and international audience costs as Jimmy Carter did when mediating the 1994 DPRK nuclear crisis—the effect is typically fleeting because the opportunity for weaker actors to apply leverage tends to be ephemeral and resource constraints limit their ability to sustain their involvement over time. Moreover, other work has demonstrated that mediation by third parties without leverage is more likely to occur when actors have incentives to use mediation insincerely.[23] If weak mediators attract combatants that are hedging against exploitation, we have reason to suspect that an attenuation of stability should also be seen when mediation is conducted by weak third parties.

A direct comparison of mediation by weak third parties and strong ones might not lead to different expectations regarding long-term peace stability, but this does not mean that all types of third-party variation do not matter.[24] Variation in the ability of third parties to remain involved after a conflict is likely to matter much more than variation in latent capabilities. Part of my argument thus far has been that mediator influence is typically temporary, which means that the belligerents are often left with an arrangement that becomes unsatisfying as the ability of the third party to maintain the incentives for peace wanes. Some third parties, however, are able to remain involved in sustaining peace longer than others. Those that are able to constantly apply leverage and/or facilitate renegotiation run less of a risk of contributing to long-run instability. The long-term risks of mediation stem not from the potential failure of mediation per se but rather the potential failure of the post-mediation environment. When that long-term environment involves perpetual outside engagement, there is less reason for a time inconsistency problem to become worse because what was agreeable at the crisis termination will tend to remain agreeable under the constant watch of the third party and any need for renegotiation can continue to benefit from third-party assistance.

A survey of peacekeeping operations, many of which have been in place for decades, indicates that such third-party involvement could be well positioned to sustain long-term engagement after a mediation initiative concludes. Many lament the lack of involvement by the UN and other peacekeepers in various

---

23. See Beardsley (2009).

24. An analysis that does examine the latent leverage of third parties reveals no meaningful differences between mediator types.

conflicts, and the empirical evidence reveals that peacekeeping is often effective in stabilizing and maintaining peace in those areas in which they are sent.[25] Following up mediation with a peacekeeping force is thus one potential avenue to increase the potential for both short-term and long-term peace.[26]

> Hypothesis 5.4 *The trade-off between short-term peace and long-term stability in mediation outcomes is less stark when peacekeepers deploy to the post-conflict setting.*

Upon further consideration of what peacekeeping entails, we might temper our expectations about whether it can overcome the difficulties that mediation has in producing a robust self-enforcing peace. Although peacekeeping operations have tended to do well in preventing the outbreak of major war, it is not clear that they are well suited to provide the missing ingredient after mediation to achieve a more complete peace that also precludes lower-level contestation. In this regard, the relative security that peacekeeping provides can actually reduce further the incentives for the actors involved to push for a final settlement during a mediated peace process (Greig and Diehl 2005). Moreover, peacekeeping operations can interfere with a more natural and complete resolution, via victory, that is robust and sustainable.[27] Recent research has also found that peacekeeping does not do well in fostering the development of self-sustaining indigenous institutions.[28] This is not to say that the positive effects of peacekeeping found in the existing literature are illusory. Most simply, although peacekeeping may have some general benefits for the endurance of peace after both mediated and unmediated settlements, it may struggle to overcome the particular long-term effects from the shallow agreements that mediation tends to produce. So mediated arrangements with peacekeeping can still be more fragile in the long run than unmediated arrangements with peacekeeping.

Peacekeeping might also suffer from the coordination and collective action problems generally faced by global and regional security organizations that carry out peacekeeping. The space of common agreement among member states with disparate interests is typically quite small, which makes it difficult to maintain a consensus for a course of action—especially when peacekeeping mandates must be renewed at short intervals—or to otherwise carry out the mandate as intended.

---

25. See, for example, Fortna (2004a, 2004b, 2008); Doyle and Sambanis (2000, 2006).

26. For an account of the actual role of peacekeepers as mediators, see Wall, Druckman, and Diehl (2002).

27. Fortna (2009) notes that, although peacekeeping still works to reduce recurrence of conflict, one of the side effects might be the encouragement of more indecisive outcomes in conflict.

28. For example, see Sambanis (2007).

As an example of such coordination difficulty, Greg Mills and Terence McNamee (2009, 75) suggest that the involvement of over thirty contributing states and the lack of a common language have hindered UNIFIL from effectively keeping the peace in Lebanon. Speaking generally about the multiparty nature of many peacekeeping operations, Richard Gowan states, "Unsurprisingly, complexity is not conducive to efficiency. Peace operations work best when there is a single line of command to hold them together and set priorities. In reality, responsibilities tend to be spread thinly and sometimes irrationally" (2009, 3). So, the problem of the attenuation of mediator influence can also apply when peacekeepers deploy because of the difficulty of ensuring a consistent level of engagement amid such complexities.

This line of thought, in which coordination and collective action problems within and among third parties can contribute to the potential for mediation to lead to long-term instability, leads to an additional expectation that IGOs might be especially prone to weakening the stability of peace over time when they serve as intermediaries. How third-party actors are able to solve collective action and coordination problems directly informs their ability to remain involved in maintaining peace. When some decision nodes have veto power, as in the UN Security Council, it becomes more likely that consensus for involvement will fall apart over time.[29] Similarly, having multiple decision nodes also creates a collective action problem in which each actor or entity involved prefers to free ride on the efforts of other actors to sustain peace. Such incentives lead to an underprovision of the impure public good of continually fostering a peaceful relationship among former combatants.[30]

> Hypothesis 5.5 *The trade-off between short-term peace and long-term stability in mediation outcomes is starker when intergovernmental organizations serve as mediators.*

A similar logic applies to the involvement of multiple third parties, whether IGOs or not.[31] When follow-up involvement lands squarely within the responsibility of a single actor that has an ongoing incentive to promote peace, coordination and collective action problems are minimized. For example, observers of the war in Bosnia noticed the contrast between the earlier struggles by multiple European

---

29. Saadia Touval notes in this regard that IGOs are "incapable of pursuing coherent, flexible and dynamic negotiations guided by a coherent strategy" (2002, 177).

30. See Touval (1994, 45).

31. The inclusion of multiple third parties is different from the inclusion of a third party that is a coalition of distinct actors who have coordinated their efforts and represent more or less a single interest. A full assessment of such coalitions is left to future research; my focus here is on the situations in which the third parties have not tightly coordinated their involvement, which should directly translate into struggles in sustaining peace in the long run.

entities and the later relative effectiveness of U.S. intervention, concluding that mediation by a single actor that can take charge of the entire peace process is ideal.[32] Difficulty in getting multiple mediators on the same page should translate into greater long-term risks of third parties generating settlement incentives that simply will not last. In the most benign sense, the introduction of multiple decision nodes makes it more likely that the third parties will fail to respond to future threats to peace because of uncertainty over who is responsible for taking action. In this regard, Chester A. Crocker, Fen Osler Hampson, and Pamela Aall note that multiparty mediation attempts can create serious synchronization problems during the implementation phase of an agreement:

> Not only is there a waste of effort and resources that occurs when there is no clear leadership or delegation of authority in an intervention, but such management problems can also affect the fate of a peace agreement. Problems of handoff between one peacemaker and the next are all too frequently encountered when different mediators try to engage parties in negotiations over a prolonged period of time. These handoff problems are typically encountered in the transitional period between the successful negotiation of a peace settlement and its subsequent implementation. During this period, misunderstandings and conflicting interpretations about implementation are common. (2001, 507)

Multiple mediators, especially when they do not have similar interests, can also allow the disputants to play the third parties off of one another and thereby limit the leverage that can be maintained in the pursuit of full conflict resolution. When one third party tries to push the combatants toward carrying out the difficult compromises needed for a durable peace, the combatants can favor the involvement of another third party that is less demanding.[33] For instance, Wendy Betts faults the overabundance of mediators for the inability to move the Nagorno-Karabakh dispute from a simple cease-fire to a more permanent settlement: "The ineffectiveness of third party mediation in this conflict can be attributed to the availability of, and competition among, mediators, which reduced the amount of leverage that the mediators wielded for moving the parties toward a settlement" (1999, 174). Much more, third parties with divergent aims can directly undermine one another's efforts, as seen for example in how the U.S. and French involvements in the 2006 war in Lebanon at times directly competed.

---

32. See, for example, Touval (2002, 178).

33. Ban Ki-moon similarly reports, "For mediation to succeed, it must be guided by a lead actor. Multiple actors competing for a mediation role create an opportunity for forum shopping as intermediaries are played off against one another. Such a fragmented international response reinforces fragmentation in the conflict and complicates resolution" (2009, 6).

The expectation is thus that the involvement of multiple third parties in mediation efforts heightens the attenuation effect in which long-term stability becomes more precarious. Coordination and collective action problems become starker in such situations, leading to a faster decline in third-party influence during implementation.[34] Also, the prior involvement of multiple third parties could increase the uncertainty around the future incentives for peace and the costs of conflict. The former belligerents will be left to guess which of the third parties may again become involved should the situation deteriorate. The heightened uncertainty, in turn, can make the failure of renewed bargaining more likely.

> Hypothesis 5.6 *The trade-off between short-term peace and long-term stability in mediation outcomes is starker when multiple third parties serve as mediators.*

These hypotheses about the characteristics of the third parties can be tested empirically using research designs similar to those considered for my earlier hypotheses. Variables that capture the deployment of peacekeepers after a crisis, the involvement of an IGO as the principal mediator, and the occurrence of multiparty mediation are used to examine Hypotheses 5.4, 5.5, and 5.6.[35] Note that a slightly different approach has been taken with the ICOW data to assess the question of what properties of mediation are more conducive to the attainment of long-term stability. Using the ICOW data, models of what affects the propensity for MIDs within ten years after an agreement are run on the sample of cases that experienced mediation so that we can directly observe what characteristics are better able to shape long-term mediation success.[36]

---

34. For an empirical analysis of the ineffectiveness of multiparty mediation in reaching conflict settlements, see Beber (2010b). We might wonder why multiple third parties would become involved in a situation. A supply-side explanation suggests that multiple third parties may benefit from being involved in shaping conflict outcomes, which leads to multiple third parties pushing to be involved. A demand-side explanation suggests that multiple third parties may be necessary to bring in multiple sources of information and leverage, or to counteract any perceived biases, so that each side can have a third party at the table that more closely represents its interests—consiglieres of sorts. Crocker notes that turning to multiparty mediation creates a situation that is beneficial to short-term outcomes in which "the lead mediator gains the benefit of the partners' insights, relationships, credibility, resources, diplomatic 'reach,' and political 'balance.' Broadening, when successful, isolates the spoilers and 'rejectionists' common to most conflict situations" (1999, 230). See also Böhmelt (2010b).

35. The effect of peacekeeping on MID occurrence, relevant to Hypothesis 5.4, is not tested using the ICOW data because there were so few cases of peacekeeping during the many low-level ICOW disputes.

36. The reference category for the ICOW data is thus a baseline type of mediation, whereas the reference category for the ICB data is nonmediation. A split-sample approach is used with the ICOW data to see more easily the conditioning effects of the relevant variables because mediation itself does not have a statistically significant relationship with the occurrence of a MID within ten years after an agreement.

Characteristics of the Bargaining Environment: Credible Commitments

Heterogeneity in bargaining environments can also help explain some variation in how much third parties exacerbate long-term instability. In particular, environments without much ex ante potential for future renegotiation are safer for mediation. When the issue cannot be reneged on after an agreement is reached, mediation cannot feasibly cause a weaker peace in the long run. Whereas military disengagement or territorial concessions might be promised and then taken back in the future, other issues in a conflict do not offer much possibility of future renegotiation or defection. For instance, when an intermediary helps combatants exchange prisoners, once the swap occurs, there is little risk of the prisoners being taken again. Or when mediation helps the actors simply achieve a transfer of funds or goods, the actors are not likely to find it possible to recover what was transferred. Mediation in the absence of a commitment problem is thus less vulnerable to creating long-term instability.[37]

Also related to commitment problems in the bargaining environment, and an issue that often arises in mediated peace processes, is the potential for actors not at the negotiation table to disrupt implementation. When stakeholders are excluded from important peace initiatives they often actively try to spoil the resulting settlements (see chap. 6). Having all the relevant parties at the bargaining table thus facilitates the reduction of a commitment problem, but this also makes bargaining cumbersome during the negotiation phase.[38] To keep the discussions tractable, mediators often choose to restrict the number of parties at the table, but this can cause another trade-off between short-term peace and long-term stability—having fewer parties increases the ease of reaching an agreement but also increases the spoiler problem. Regarding this trade-off, Joel Wit, Daniel Poneman, and Robert Gallucci write, "although reducing the number of parties in direct negotiations can facilitate reaching a deal, it can complicate implementation to the degree that the arrangement does not adequately address the concerns of the governments whose cooperation is essential to success" (2004, 401). An ideal bargaining environment that minimizes the long-term mediation risks is thus one in which there are only a few key stakeholders and each is given a seat at the bargaining table.

---

37. Note, however, that the absence of a time inconsistency problem for one issue might not lead to long-term peace if there are multiple issues being contested. For example, the Algerian mediation to free the U.S. hostages in Iran did well in settling permanently the Iran hostage crisis, but it did not address the many other issues of contention between the two states that led to later tension.

38. On the problem of multiple parties in conflict bargaining, see Cunningham (2006).

Note that the absence of a potential commitment problem makes the nego-tiation phase more difficult even as it assures implementation. When actors are confronted with the notion of giving up a good or a policy position permanently, with virtually no opportunity to get it back, they will be much more reluctant to make such a concession in the first place.[39] Their possession of that good or policy position is a key source of leverage, and once they give it up there is no more quid pro quo, no more ability to extract reciprocal concessions. The parties will thus want to milk their returns as much as possible before finalizing a deal and entering into the implementation phase. As a result, mediators with leverage might be most necessary in such situations.

It is difficult to explore systematically such ideal-type situations in which there is an absence of a commitment problem. As a result, hypothesis tests are not conducted here; nevertheless, the logical bases are straightforward. The case studies in this chapter and the next explore some of the dynamics related to the conditioning effects of the bargaining environment. I leave the full testing of these expectations, especially using experimental research designs, to future research.

Results

The findings generally support the hypotheses regarding the conditioning of the dilemma. Starting with the results from the models using the ICB data, in ex-amining Hypothesis 5.2 the findings show that manipulative mediation indeed has a statistically and substantively significant nonproportional effect on the risk of crisis recurrence. Soon after crisis termination, arrangements reached under manipulative mediation are more stable than unmediated cases. As time passes, the reverse is true. Facilitative mediation and formulative mediation, in contrast, do not appear to significantly increase the propensity for crisis recurrence in the long run, but their impact in the short run is also diminished. Mediation without leverage does not much impede long-term settlement, but it also is less able to strengthen peace in the short run.

One way to view these relationships is to compare the relative risks of crisis recurrence one year and ten years after a crisis for different types of mediation.[40] These are presented in figure 5.2, which displays the recurrence risks one year

---

39. For formal treatment of this argument, see Fearon (1998).

40. These values are calculated from the estimated Cox models by taking the hazard ratios at each time and subtracting 1. Multiplying the result by 100 gives the percentage change in the risk of recurrence.

after crisis termination, and figure 5.3, which displays the recurrence risks at ten years after crisis termination. The solid bars are the relationships that are statistically significant, whereas the empty bars lack statistical significance. As in figure 5.1, we can see the short- and long-term trade-off caused by mediation; the risk of peace failure one year after crisis termination decreases by over half with mediation, whereas the risk of failure after ten years increases by 187 percent.

When manipulation (leverage) is used, the risk of crisis recurrence at one year after a crisis is even less than with general mediation, with a decline of more than 68 percent. The substantial trade-off that manipulative mediation creates with regard to long-term peace, then, is seen in how the risk of failure at ten years after a crisis ends is nearly four times (297 percent) greater than the risk without mediation. Again, this magnitude is greater than that for general mediation. Manipulative mediation thus generates a greater potential for both short-term peace and more fragile long-term relations than general mediation.

Note that it is not simply the case that heavy-handed manipulative mediation is inadvisable because it generates such long-term instability. The choice of a manipulative strategy appears to be a classic risk-reward trade-off. Less intrusive mediation may lead to less risk for long-term instability, but there is also less reward in the short run. The other styles of mediation, namely facilitation

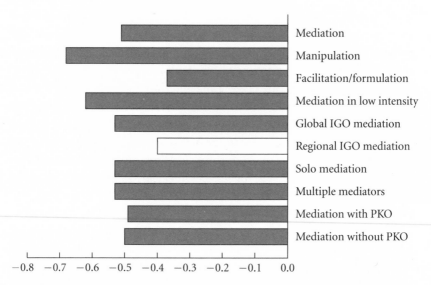

FIGURE 5.2 Relative risks of crisis recurrance at 1 year after crisis termination. Values are relative changes in the risk of crisis recurrence when the treatment is present. Shaded bars are statistically significant ($p < 0.05$, one-tailed test). IGO, intergovernmental organization; PKO, peacekeeping operation.

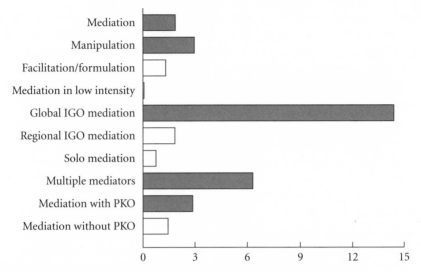

FIGURE 5.3   Relative risks of crisis recurrence at 10 years after crisis termination. Values are relative changes in the risk of crisis recurrence when the treatment is present. Shaded bars are statistically significant ($p < 0.05$, one-tailed test). IGO, intergovernmental organization; PKO, peacekeeping operation.

and formulation, still have a statistically significant effect in the short run, but the drop-off in the risk of recurrence at one year is only 37 percent. The effect of facilitative or formulative tactics on the risk of recurrence at ten years is not statistically significant, which means that there is very little downside to these tactics. Again, the dilemma arises in choosing between a mediation style that typically pays off very well in the short run at the expense of long-run instability and a mediation style that has less risk of long-term failure but less promise of short-term success.

We also see support for Hypothesis 5.3. At low levels of violence and difficulty, mediation decreases the propensity for crisis recurrence by over 62 percent in the short term, and it does not significantly increase the risk in the long run. As a result, mediation appears less risky in the less intense crises because crisis dyads that experience mediation are less likely to relapse soon after crisis termination and this peaceful dividend does not tend to diminish. The results confirm that patience, as when desperation is low while conflict is light, diminishes the stark trade-off in mediation and allows actors to find a more self-enforcing arrangement with outside assistance.

Inconsistent with Hypothesis 5.4, but not wholly unexpected given our discussion, the evidence suggests that peacekeeping is not a great solution to the mediation dilemma. With or without peacekeeping, mediation leads to a short-term drop in the propensity for recurrence. In the long run, the deployment of peacekeeping after mediation is actually associated with a greater risk of crisis recurrence, whereas the absence of peacekeeping after mediation does not lead to as much of an increase.[41] Thus, the trade-off between short-term peace and long-term stability appears to hold even in the presence of peacekeepers. Because peacekeepers tend to be deployed to the places with a greater potential for relapse, it is possible that there are additional factors, not controlled for in the models, which diminish the observed ability of peacekeeping to bolster peace after mediation.[42] At the same time, there are reasons why we might expect peacekeeping to not ameliorate the long-term instability of mediation. Peacekeepers tend to decrease the incentives of the negotiating parties to deal fully with the remaining contentious issues and can encourage stalemated cease-fires that never fully resolve the conflict. So, even with sustained peacekeeping, mediated settlements can be rather shallow. Moreover, peacekeeping missions can involve a complex array of actors that introduce coordination and collective action problems, thereby making it difficult to maintain the incentives present during mediation. On this last point, Ban Ki-moon (2009) highlights in his special report to the UN Security Council that it is often difficult for third parties to transition from peacemaker to peacekeeper.

The nature of the third parties that frequently engage in peacekeeping—namely IGOs—also makes consistent engagement less sustainable because of the constant need for coordination among member states, contributing countries, and organizational bodies. The collective action and coordination problems that exist within an organization such as the UN, with universal membership, a need for consensus among the permanent five members of the Security Council, and an autonomous Office of the Secretary-General, are immense. It is thus difficult for the UN to sustain the involvement necessary to avoid creating an ephemeral environment for peace when it mediates, and this helps explain why global IGO mediation efforts are especially associated with long-term instability. When the UN (or League of Nations) is the primary mediator, the risk of crisis recurrence after ten years increases by a remarkable 1,441 percent. We must interpret this finding with some degree of caution because the UN often chooses to intervene

---

41. The difference between the long-term chances of recurrence with and without peacekeeping after mediation is statistically insignificant.

42. See especially Fortna (2008); Gilligan and Stedman (2003); Gilligan and Sergenti (2008). The bivariate probit models used to check for potential selection effects endogenize mediation but not both mediation and peacekeeping.

in particularly nasty conflicts with a protracted history of recurrence, such as those in the Middle East and in Cyprus. That being said, it is doubtful that selection effects are completely driving this finding because global IGOs do quite well in securing short-term peace—which is counter to what we would expect if they simply got the most difficult conflicts—and regional IGOs are not associated with much of a decline in long-term stability.

The evidence also supports the expectation that mediation by multiple third parties further worsens the long-term stability of peace. Mediation by a single third party produces short-term dividends that persist. That is, mediated crises have a decreased risk of recurrence at one year and do not have a significantly increased risk at ten years when there is a single mediation process in play.[43] When there are multiple mediation processes from different third parties not coordinating with each other, we observe the now familiar effect of short-term peace and long-term instability. The risk of recurrence at ten years after a crisis is more than seven times (632 percent) greater with multiple mediators than without any mediation. This is an important finding because over half (56 percent) of the mediated crises in the data experienced multiparty mediation of some form. An important example of multiple mediation attempts leading to only a short-term peace is the Zaire Civil War, which occurred from 1996 to 1997 and also featured conflict between Zaire and Rwanda. The conflict experienced multiple instances of mediation from the UN, the United States, and South Africa, as well as significant diplomatic involvement from many other international actors. Although the international pressure contributed to Mobutu Sese Seko's departure and the end of the civil war, it was unable to address many of the other security concerns in the region, particularly the presence of Hutu militias in the east. As a result, conflict renewed just over a year later when Rwanda, seeking to confront the Hutu militias, helped trigger a massive regional war that lasted until 2002.

As previously noted, the ICOW data can be used to validate further some of the hypothesized expectations by analyzing what affects the absence of a MID within ten years of an agreement. Figure 5.4 presents the relative risks of the occurrence of a MID within ten years of an agreement for different mediation groups.

The first thing we note in this figure is that mediation does not have a statistically significant effect on long-term stability. When coupled with the finding in the previous chapter that mediation increases the likelihood of concessions and

---

43. A single mediation process does not mean that it lasted only one round of talks but, rather, that there was one party or tight group of parties that was responsible for the mediation throughout a crisis.

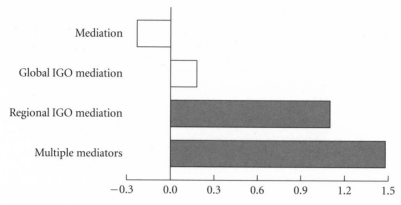

FIGURE 5.4 Relative risks of MID occurrence within 10 years. Values are relative changes in the predicted probability of a MID occurring within 10 years of the agreement. Shaded bars are statistically significant ($p < 0.05$, one-tailed test). IGO, intergovernmental organization; MID, militarized interstate dispute.

full settlement of issues within two years, we see further evidence of the familiar attenuation effect of mediation. For Hypothesis 5.3, as previously mentioned, the ICOW data have so few disputes with violence that it is impossible to fully gauge the effectiveness of mediation in high-intensity disputes. There are sixteen cases in the ICOW data that experienced fatalities during the year of the agreement. Of these, only three agreements resulted from mediation—Bolivia and Paraguay in 1936 during their Chaco Boreal dispute, Ecuador and Peru in 1938 during their Oriente-Mainas dispute, and Honduras and El Salvador in 1969 during their Bolsones dispute—and none of those resulted in lasting peace; all three experienced a MID within ten years. This, at least, provides some suggestive evidence in support of the hypothesis that mediation does less well in securing long-term stability when intensity is high.

Results using the ICOW data also support Hypothesis 5.5 because both global and regional IGO mediators have positive relationships with the long-term propensity for militarized conflict after a mediated agreement and the latter is statistically significant. Note that these results slightly differ from the analysis using the ICB data, which found a significant relationship for global IGO mediation but not for regional IGO mediation. This may suggest a difference between the low-level disputes typically found in the ICOW data and the more militarized ICB crises; perhaps regional third parties are more likely to meddle in the former while international third parties are more likely to meddle in the latter. Finally, we again see, in support of Hypothesis 5.6, that multiple mediators can be quite destabilizing for long-term peace. When multiple third parties help bring about a mediated agreement, the estimated probability of a MID within ten years increases by more than 147 percent compared to agreements that involved a single mediator.

In sum, it appears that context plays a crucial role in shaping the mediation dilemma. We observe a few factors that exacerbate the trade-off between the short- and long-term benefits. Mediation with leverage creates an especially stark trade-off, but there do not appear to be clear benefits of pursuing less intrusive styles of intervention because they do not produce the same short-term rewards. Mediation by intergovernmental organizations also appears especially prone to long-term destabilization. More positively, we do see evidence that the dilemma is minimized, so that mediation produces positive peaceful dividends that persist, when the severity of conflict is low and the number of mediators is small. When actors are not desperate for peace, they are less prone to take the first available settlement and can wait for an arrangement that is more likely to be self-sustaining and hence durable. When third parties do not face collective action and coordination problems, they are more likely to be able to maintain their commitments and are less likely to obfuscate the bargaining environment.

Illustrative Cases

In returning to the case studies, the approach taken here deviates from previous chapters in one key respect. Each of the cases involves the occurrence of mediation and the realization of short-term peace, so the dependent variables have not varied across these cases in the earlier chapters. My purpose in selecting these cases was so that, in this chapter, we can see a variety of outcomes related to long-term effectiveness without having to change the underlying parameters of mediation occurring and leading to short-term benefits. We can now see how specific contextual factors, especially the extent to which leverage is used, change the ability for mediation to achieve long-term peace. In this way, we can gain additional insight into how mediation can be most appropriately applied and when mediation participants must be the most cautious.

Kissinger's and Carter's efforts in the Middle East provide a useful contrast between the ultimate outcome pertaining to Egyptian-Israeli relations and the outcome pertaining to a more comprehensive peace that includes the Palestinian question. Although the U.S. mediators used leverage throughout in pushing forward both agendas, their influence was sustainable in regards to the Egyptian-Israeli peace and not sustainable in regards to the more comprehensive peace. That is, the U.S. effort in regard to the interstate peace was atypical—we actually observe a long-term commitment to leveraged involvement and sustained engagement in this case. At the same time, U.S. involvement relating to the comprehensive peace exhibited the more typical pattern of diminishing influence. This helps explain, even beyond the fact that a comprehensive peace has always been more difficult to achieve, why mediation produced a stable peace between Egypt and Israel but failed in fully implementing the Framework for Peace in the Middle East.

Less nuanced are the cases of Carter's involvement in the DPRK and Roosevelt's involvement in the Russo-Japanese War. In the former case, the Agreed Framework that Carter helped reach through the use of international media pressure, and probably in the midst of insincere DPRK motives, ultimately collapsed eight years later. In the latter case, Roosevelt was restrained in applying leverage to the negotiators at Portsmouth, and as a result, a relatively self-enforcing—if not a perfectly warm—peace emerged between Russia and Japan.

Kissinger and Carter in the Middle East

Henry Kissinger's and Jimmy Carter's mediation initiatives in the Middle East produced a remarkably stable peace between Egypt and Israel; that is, no major violence has occurred between these two protagonists since 1973.[44] At the same time, the comprehensive-oriented Framework for Peace in the Middle East that was part of the Camp David Accords failed to realize much progress on even some of its more modest provisions. A key variable considered in comparing the Egyptian-Israeli peace to the comprehensive peace is the degree to which U.S. leverage remained in effect after the signing of the Camp David Accords. With regard to the Egypt-Israel component, the United States was able to keep the pressure from waning—right through to the reaching of the Egyptian-Israeli peace treaty and well after. It did this directly, through the provision of aid and monitoring resources. It also helped maintain the incentives for lasting interstate peace indirectly, by removing some of the sources of endemic insecurity and enabling both sides to depend less on U.S. involvement. But with regard to the framework for a comprehensive peace, the United States did not follow through on pressuring the actors to implement what they had agreed and was unable to get each side to buy sufficiently into issue settlement.

Given that mediation tends to be associated with less stable long-term peace arrangements, my discussion here considers what was so special about the Egypt-

---

44. The dispute over Taba that persisted until 1989 does suggest that the 1979 treaty did not resolve all the issues on the Sinai, but it is telling that the Taba dispute was successfully resolved in arbitration and did not result in further armed conflict.

Israel peace that allowed U.S. influence to persist and contribute to a fairly stable relationship between former adversaries. Four factors are considered: U.S. geostrategic interests in that dyadic peace, a favorable bargaining environment, U.S. monopolization of the mediator role, and the step-by-step approach. Although the failure of the United States to see through execution of a more comprehensive peace is less surprising, especially in light of our empirical findings and the difficulty of the issues involved, it is still worth considering what contributed to implementation failure. In this regard, I posit that the U.S. leadership faced fewer foreign and domestic political incentives to continue pressing on the Palestinian question, that Carter's committed efforts could not be sustained by him or by his successors, and that progress on the Egypt-Israel peace necessarily undermined some of the potential for progress on the comprehensive peace.

THE EGYPTIAN-ISRAELI PEACE

As we have seen in chapter 4, Kissinger and Carter used a substantial amount of leverage to reach the disengagement agreements, the Camp David Accords, and the Egyptian-Israeli peace treaty. Whereas temporary leverage is expected to foster only a fleeting and incomplete peace between adversaries, the perpetual application of third-party influence should not worsen time-inconsistency problems. We see this borne out specifically with regard to the Egyptian-Israeli peace, in which the United States was able to maintain sufficient leverage indefinitely and even addressed a number of underlying security concerns so that less emphasis on leverage was needed over time to keep the peace stable in the long run.

The U.S. commitment to maintaining the incentives for peace between Israel and Egypt can be seen especially in the period immediately following the signing of the Camp David Accords. The process of getting from Camp David to the Egyptian-Israeli peace treaty was much more difficult than expected because there were a number of issues related to sequencing and timing that contributed to an initial collapse in implementation of the framework for the treaty. Israel wanted the exchange of ambassadors to occur before its withdrawal from the Sinai, both Israel and Egypt desired firmer U.S. financial and military commitments, Israel wanted guarantees that it would not be adversely affected by turning over the oilfields and airfields in the Sinai, and Egypt wanted a timetable for ending Israeli military rule in Gaza and the West Bank.[45] Instead of exiting on a high note at Camp David and abandoning the peace process, Carter understood the importance of a sustainable peace and thus expended substantial effort and political capital to act as midwife to the 1979 treaty in the midst of these linger-

---

45. See Brzezinski (1985, 281); Stein (1999, 257).

ing issues. In additional talks at Blair House in Washington, Camp David, and in the Middle East, and through the provision of additional guarantees, Carter was relentless in his efforts to get to the final deal.[46] Moreover, even after the treaty was signed, the United States did not abandon its commitment to peace between Israel and Egypt. That commitment to maintaining the security of Israel and Egypt is still evident through the ongoing provision of aid that makes Israel and Egypt two of the largest beneficiaries of U.S. military assistance.

Four factors explain why U.S. influence did not attenuate and create an inhospitable environment for perpetual peace between Egypt and Israel: ongoing U.S. security concerns in the region, a favorable bargaining environment, the emergence of Kissinger and Carter as the sole intermediaries, and the gradual step-by-step approach. These factors, with greater weight on the first two, have allowed peace, even if only a cold peace, to endure between Egypt and Israel for over thirty-five years. They thus speak to why Kissinger's and Carter's efforts in reaching an interstate peace proved exceptional, allowing a third party to sustain its influence and enable the belligerents to avoid renewed conflict.

The first factor explaining why the United States maintained its involvement after attaining the breakthrough interstate agreements relates to the fundamental U.S. security concerns in the Middle East. Stability in the region and the security of Israel strongly affect U.S. interests, which means that the United States could credibly guarantee to keep up whatever pressure was necessary to maintain peace between Egypt and Israel. The 1973 war and the wars that preceded it demonstrated that the conflicts between Israel and its Arab neighbors posed a risk of becoming a flashpoint for superpower conflict. The United States thus had a strong interest in preventing another regional war that could bring the United States and the USSR closer to armed confrontation. Note that this is in contrast to the conflict between Israel and the Palestinians, which, as long as it could be partially separated from the conflict between Israel and its Arab neighbors, has never posed the possibility of drawing in superpower military intervention. The United States also had a continual incentive to uphold its commitments to securing Israeli oil supplies and to supporting the monitoring mission in the Sinai because of the ongoing importance, for both geostrategic and domestic political reasons, of promoting Israeli security.[47]

---

46. On Carter's post–Camp David efforts, see Brzezinski (1985, 273–88); Quandt (1986, 259–309).

47. Moshe Dayan, as Israeli foreign minister, at one point asked Vance what would happen after fifteen years, the period in which the United States had promised to guarantee the Israeli oil supply. That Vance jokingly rejoined, "if only someone would guarantee oil supplies to the United States for fifteen years!" and assured Dayan that this would not be an issue indicates the level of confidence that Vance had in the U.S. commitment to Israeli security (Dayan 1981, 277).

A favorable bargaining environment, manipulated in part by Kissinger and Carter, also allowed the influence of their leverage to last by minimizing the structural sources of commitment problems. As discussed, a bargaining environment in which neither side has an incentive to renege fosters the ability for mediation to have both short- and long-term benefits. This was not tested empirically, but we can see some evidence of this logic here. Once Israel withdrew from the Sinai, it would have been quite difficult for it to take it back if it had wanted to, especially given the presence of international peacekeepers and monitors. More strongly, once Israel dismantled the settlements in the Sinai, it could not have conceivably rebuilt them on Egyptian soil. As a result, Egypt had little reason to fear that Israel would renege on the bulk of its commitments in the Egyptian-Israeli peace treaty. For this reason, Carter adamantly insisted, even after agreement had been secured on virtually all other issues, that Israel dismantle those settlements in the Sinai.[48] This involved extensive U.S. leverage, but any decrease in U.S. involvement afterward would not have led to Israeli backsliding on this issue simply because of how difficult it would have been to do so once a complete withdrawal had been implemented.

Another factor related to the favorable bargaining environment pertains to the potential for, or lack of, insincere motives that would lead to only a temporary peace. In the Egyptian-Israeli case, it is reasonable to expect that both sides had sincere motives and were not using mediation merely as a stalling tactic or to manipulate various audiences. Recalling his optimism during the Sinai I negotiations, Kissinger presents the logic for why he expected both sides to be sincere: "And once a negotiation is thus reduced to details, it has a high probability of success—unless one party has consciously decided to make a show of flexibility simply to put itself in a better light for a deliberate breakup of the talks. Egypt was precluded from such a course by the plight of the Third Army, Israel by the fear of diplomatic isolation" (1982, 802). Ezer Weizman also notes that even though the Israeli leadership initially feared that Sadat had sought disengagement only as a prelude to renewed conflict, there were actually strong signals that Sadat had a more permanent peace in mind. "We had not," Weizman writes, "taken sufficient notice of what [the disengagement agreements] signified: Egypt's willingness to separate her forces from Israel's and create a buffer zone; her willingness to bring in the United States through Kissinger rather than the UN. If you kick out the Russians and bring in the Americans, you're not preparing for war" (1981, 19).[49] In his memoirs, Yitzhak Rabin (1979, 316) also contends that Sadat could only

---

48. See Weizman (1981, 371).
49. For a description of the Israeli suspicion that Sadat was going to use the Camp David process for insincere motives, see Weizman (1981, 341).

move forward in his quest for peace after the disengagement agreements, especially after having burned his bridges with the Soviets.

At the same time, and perhaps ironically because of their monopolization of the peace process, Kissinger and Carter helped structure the bargaining environment such that the peace was less dependent on outside support. Not only did the United States keep up its leverage after Camp David, but it also fostered the development of a long-term peace by helping reduce the Israeli sense of vulnerability to Egyptian defection through its provision of air bases in the Negev. The airfields were important in contributing to long-term peace because, once built with U.S. help, they would remain even if U.S. support proved to be mercurial. They were pieces of leverage that the United States helped put in place that would keep their influence even without continual U.S. effort in the future. On the ability for the treaty to set Israel and Egypt on a firm foundation for lasting relations, Moshe Dayan writes,

> The Egypt-Israel peace treaty . . . was not a pastoral idyll full of sweetness and sunshine and repose in lush meadows. It was not the fulfilment of Isaiah's end-of-days vision when swords would be beaten into ploughshares, and nation would not lift up sword against nation any more. This was a peace treaty which contained military clauses, a treaty which called for the construction of air bases, and held guarantees for the strengthening of Israel's armed forces. It was also a political treaty. But above all it was a realistic peace treaty, set in the context of current realities, and designed to bring about relations between two neighboring countries, Egypt and Israel, as normal as those between any two particular countries in the world. (1981, 282)

A third factor, but perhaps less important than the previous two, accounting for why the U.S. push for interstate peace persisted was the domination of the negotiations by Kissinger and Carter such that other potential mediators were left on the sidelines and problems of coordination and collective action were minimized. Kissinger was more intentional about this than Carter, as seen in how Kissinger used the Geneva Conference to actually minimize Soviet involvement,[50] whereas Carter's early push for a return to the Geneva Conference with full Soviet involvement nearly scuttled the entire peace process.[51] Carter's eventual

---

50. See Kissinger (1982, 749–50, 755, 843); Miller (2008, 131). See also Stein (1999, 146).

51. Brzezinski (1985, 87) recalls, however, that the motivation to reconvene the Geneva Conference was similar to that of Kissinger, namely to provide legitimacy for the deals that would be reached later. Carter's push for Geneva was ultimately abandoned because disagreement persisted regarding Soviet involvement and how the Palestinian Arabs would be represented, if at all (Stein 1999, 188, 192, 205; Weizman 1981, 241).

monopolization of the role of intermediary was more of a consequence of his remarkable determination for peace that left little room for other third parties to be involved than the type of strategic calculation that characterized Kissinger's manipulation of the bargaining environment. In either case, the U.S. role was predominant and, consistent with the argument and empirical finding that solo mediators do much better in securing long-term outcomes, this helped simplify the follow-up process.

The fourth factor was Kissinger's step-by-step diplomacy, which provided the framework for continual U.S. involvement and allowed peace to build.[52] Even though Richard Nixon advocated an approach by which the United States would impose a comprehensive peace, Kissinger saw the danger in that approach and strongly contended that a comprehensive approach would not succeed.[53] Instead of attempting one grand effort to deal with all parts of the Arab-Israeli conflict in a single stroke, Kissinger, and to a lesser extent Carter, put in place a framework by which each step would lay the foundation for the next. In this way, the purpose for perpetual third-party involvement could be intentional and clearly defined. In addition, the step-by-step approach reduced the sense of artificiality in U.S. involvement, in that it allowed the United States the opportunity to become a full partner in the peace efforts. The United States would not cut and run after, say, the disengagement agreements were reached because so much had already been invested in the process and progress was still to be made. It is interesting to note that although Carter formally abandoned the step-by-step approach, his efforts with regard to the Egyptian-Israeli peace resembled those of Kissinger; that is, he first achieved a settlement for a framework for a peace treaty at Camp David and then followed up with negotiations to reach the treaty. Carter's involvement thus also built over time, further consolidating U.S. commitments.[54]

---

52. Some have criticized the step-by-step disengagement for making it more difficult to reach a full and comprehensive peace in the Middle East (Telhami 1990). My analysis supports such a contention, but the point here is that the step-by-step approach facilitated a durable peace specific to Egyptian-Israeli relations. See also Ben-Ami (2005, 152–53).

53. See Miller (2008, 132); Isaacson (1992, 551).

54. One criticism of such a step-by-step process is that it only puts off necessary substantive decisions to the future. Echoing this criticism, William Quandt writes, "Step-by-step diplomacy therefore remained a tactic for buying more time, a tactic cut off from a larger political concept of peace in the Middle East" (2001, 156). See also Rabin (1979, 242, 275). We should recognize, however, that the process did have more political substance than some other alternatives that were considered. For example, early in the disengagement talks, Sadat considered pursuing an agreement solely pertaining to the separation of forces, and Kissinger convinced him that a process of step-by-step diplomacy that included some political dimensions would be superior (Stein 1999, 114).

THE COMPREHENSIVE PEACE

In contrast to the enduring stability of relations between Egypt and Israel, the progress made at Camp David regarding the framework for a more comprehensive Middle East peace quickly faltered after the signing of the accords. Even though the full resolution of the Arab-Israeli conflict has always been a long shot, the Camp David signatories failed to implement some of the more practical and realistic goals of the Framework for Peace in the Middle East, including the holding of elections for the Palestinian self-governing authority; the negotiation of the details of a transitional arrangement among Israel, Egypt, and Jordan; and the withdrawal of the Israeli military government.[55] Although reaching an agreement on the framework in the first place was a substantial feat—and remains an important source of hope for future progress—it also represents the typical mediation outcome of a settlement that is not self-enforcing and that falls apart without constant third-party handholding.

The demise of the Framework for Peace began almost immediately, during the interim period between the signing of the accords and the signing of the Egyptian-Israeli treaty. Although Begin and Sadat ostensibly had found the accords reasonable in the confines of Camp David, protected from the international press and under the auspices of Carter's leadership, they were soon pressed to push for better deals by domestic and international audiences on both sides who felt that too much had been given away by their respective parties.[56] In response to these changing environments, a number of "differences of interpretation"— chief among them the length of the moratorium on settlements and the meaning of the autonomy that Begin promised the Palestinians—emerged as the parties felt compelled to backtrack.[57] After the signing of the Egyptian-Israeli peace treaty, any of the remaining positive momentum on autonomy talks and on the final status of the occupied territories halted. Begin was especially reluctant to move forward with the established framework, which spurred dissent within his cabinet. Moshe Dayan resigned after becoming dissatisfied with the way that Begin's position on autonomy had changed after Camp David.[58] Ezer Weizman also resigned after becoming frustrated with Begin's increasing intransigence, noting that "no sooner had the treaty been signed than Begin gave up promoting the peace process" (1981, 384). Whether or not Begin ever intended to fulfill all his

---

55. See Vance (1983, 233–55).

56. On the audience pressures immediately after Camp David, see Carter (1982, 405); Vance (1983, 229, 237–38, 242); Quandt (1986, 261–64; 2001, 206–18); Weizman (1981, 380–84); Dayan (1981, 191–98); Miller (2008, 180); Shlaim (2000, 375–78); Stein (1999, 254).

57. On the issues of settlements and autonomy, see Vance (1983, 225–38); Dayan (1981, 186–88); Quandt (1986, 261–64; 2001, 206–18); Weizman (1981, 383–84); Stein (1999, 255–56).

58. See Dayan (1981, 303–20) for his explanation of why he resigned.

commitments, the fact remains that he and Sadat failed to implement much of what they had promised one another.

In the midst of the backsliding, and in part at the root of the backsliding, the U.S. commitment to the comprehensive peace faltered. According to Cyrus Vance, the withdrawal of involvement by the third party that had brokered the initial compromises doomed the implementing of the Framework for Peace:

> At most only the same level and intensity of leadership on all three sides that had characterized the peace process leading to Camp David and the Egyptian-Israeli peace treaty could have made the autonomy talks succeed in that period of time, and even that might not have succeeded. The odds that Israel and Egypt, without constant top-level U.S. participation, could negotiate an autonomy arrangement were extremely poor. (1983, 254)[59]

This case, much more than the Israel-Egypt interstate peace, is thus an example of the expected third-party activity that follows a mediated settlement.

The U.S. commitment to the implementation of the Framework for Peace in the Middle East waned—even though its efforts toward the achievement of peace between Israel and Egypt lasted—for three reasons. First, U.S. policymakers faced different foreign and domestic incentives to push for interstate peace between Israel and its Arab neighbors than they faced to push for a more comprehensive two-state solution to the Palestinian question. Pertaining to foreign incentives, the conflict between Israel and the Palestinian Arabs did not carry the same systemic consequences as the interstate conflicts in the region. Without ignoring the severity of the human security situation that has characterized the Palestinian question for decades or the importance of that issue to the broader Arab-Israeli conflict, the fact remains that the conflict between the Israeli government and the Palestinians in the occupied territories did not pose an existential threat to the state of Israel and did not carry the potential to create a Soviet and U.S. confrontation if left unresolved. The prospect of an endemic war between Israel and its Arab neighbors, in contrast, carried such threats, particularly during the Cold War. So, in terms of achieving its own foreign policy goals, the United States was much more interested in reaching a durable agreement between Israel and Egypt than in resolving the Palestinian question.

If a foreign policy perspective leads us to expect that an interstate peace was more important than a more comprehensive peace, a domestic politics perspective similarly leads us to expect that the United States had an incentive to be

---

59. See also Quandt (1986, 289–90).

gentler, even restrained, in pushing Israel toward a lasting settlement with the Palestinians. It is well known that U.S. leaders must consider strong pro-Israeli political voices when deciding Middle East policy.[60] Issues such as the status of the West Bank (Judea and Samaria) and East Jerusalem have been much more salient than the status of the Sinai to the pro-Israeli community in the U.S., which means that domestic politics have limited the ability of the United States to constantly pressure Israel to take the steps necessary to fully resolve the Palestinian question. Much more, the concessions needed to reach a comprehensive peace are much deeper than they were for Israel to reach accords with Egypt and later Jordan, so the resistance among U.S. pro-Israeli groups to sustained U.S. pressure toward resolving the Palestinian question has been expectedly fiercer.

A second reason why U.S. pressure waned is that Carter's devout and tireless commitment to Arab-Israeli peace, which characterized U.S. foreign policy during his first two years in office, simply could not be sustained. The administration could not maintain the same level of intensity in moving the process forward because of other emerging priorities. Other issues, principal among them the Iranian Revolution and subsequent hostage crisis, negotiations with the Soviets on the Strategic Arms Limitation Talks (SALT) treaty, the Soviet incursion into Afghanistan, the health of the U.S. economy, and the 1980 elections became higher priorities once the landmark agreements had been achieved.[61] Moreover, Carter's zeal did not carry over into future administrations, and any remaining momentum for a comprehensive peace died during the Ronald Reagan years.[62] More specifically, because Carter was more willing to stand firm against pro-Israeli domestic opposition, U.S. pressure on Israel diminished after Carter left office.[63] In these ways, the preferences of the third party shifted and the state of the relations between Arabs and Israelis became further removed from the landscape in which the Camp David Accords had been reached with abundant U.S. leverage and guarantees. What was true of the incentives for a comprehensive peace in 1978 was inconsistent with the incentives by 1981.

A third explanation for the drop in the U.S. commitment to a comprehensive peace is connected to its efforts on the Egyptian-Israeli treaty. Because enduring peace between Israel and Egypt was so highly desirable, the Carter administration ensured that progress toward that goal was not sidetracked by efforts to

---

60. See especially Mearsheimer and Walt (2007); Miller (2008). See also Horne (2009, 237, 260).

61. On the importance of Iran, see Vance (1983, 241–42); Quandt (2001, 223). On the importance of the U.S. election cycle, see Quandt (1986, 260–61, 316; 2001, 207, 223). See also Brzezinski (1985, 278–79).

62. See Stein (1999, 263); Miller (2008, 247–49).

63. On Carter's willingness to defy pro-Israeli political pressure, see Miller (2008, 184–88); Ben-Ami (2005, 167).

resolve the more difficult issues related to the Palestinians and the occupied territories. Especially during the interim period between the signing of the Camp David Accords and the signing of the Egypt-Israel peace treaty, Carter had to overlook setbacks to the implementation of the framework for a comprehensive peace to keep the momentum strong for the interstate peace.[64] A consequence of pushing forward on peace between Egypt and Israel before much progress had been realized on the comprehensive peace was that the incentives for further progress on the latter diminished as tensions in the Sinai defused and aid to Israel and Egypt increased. Much of the pressure for a comprehensive peace was tied to the threat of severe war between Israel and its neighbors, but that threat abated with the disengagement process and the signing of the Egyptian-Israeli peace treaty, which lacked strong linkage to progress on the other issues. Israel chiefly desired recognition and a firm declaration of peace with its most powerful Arab neighbor, as well as increased assistance from the United States, and once it achieved those goals it had little reason to proceed with the Framework for Peace in the Middle East. Whatever implied linkage had existed between the two frameworks disappeared.

Zbigniew Brzezinski speaks directly to how the mediation process yielded short-term gains and long-term struggles for a comprehensive peace and stresses the importance of the fading linkage in jeopardizing the ability to make further progress: "Camp David had worked because Carter had been able to keep both parties under his control; neither dared to assume the responsibilities of failure. The agreements had offered something beneficial to both. The problem by the winter was that Carter had lost control of the negotiations. Camp David had created the impression that a separate peace between Egypt and Israel was acceptable" (1985, 277). William Quandt similarly stresses how the early achievement of the resolution between Israel and Egypt compromised the pursuit of a more comprehensive peace:

> Once Egypt and Israel were at peace, Begin had few remaining incentives to deal constructively with the Palestinian question. Sadat did feel strongly about the need for linkage, and for many months he had tried to establish some explicit connection between what would happen in bilateral Egyptian-Israeli relations and the Palestinian negotiations. But when put under pressure by Carter, in the face of Begin's intransigence, and when confronted with hostility from other Arab leaders, Sadat resigned himself to accepting the separate agreement that he had

---

64. See Carter (1982, 404–25); Vance (1983, 233–55); Brzezinski (1985, 273–88).

hoped to avoid when he first set off for Jerusalem in November 1977. (2001, 242)

Indeed, a common criticism of the Camp David Accords and the 1979 peace treaty is that the Egypt-Israel agreement can be considered a separate peace, with little linkage between the frameworks. According to Vance (1983, 226), Carter admitted to Sadat that he would have preferred stronger linkage between the agreement on peace between Israel and Egypt and the agreement establishing a framework to address the remaining issues. Brzezinski similarly laments that, even though the accords were a remarkable achievement, "the issue of linkage between an Egyptian-Israeli settlement and the West Bank-Gaza negotiations, which had been flagged from the outset of Camp David as the single most important issue, was not resolved, largely because Carter in the end acquiesced to Begin's vaguer formulas" (1985, 273).[65] "Separate peace," however, can be a loaded term. The point here is not to diminish the accomplishments or the sincerity of the Framework for Peace in the Middle East.[66] Nor is it to place most of the responsibility for the separateness of the peace on the Carter administration; the Sinai II agreement and auxiliary memos clearly divorced disengagement from a comprehensive solution as well, setting the stage for what was to come.[67] In this regard, some have criticized Kissinger for missing the opportunity to use the 1973 war as momentum for lasting progress on much more than Egyptian-Israeli disengagement.[68]

Instead, the point here is that the two agreements that were part of the Camp David Accords had only a weak linkage between them and, as events unfolded, they did in reality become separate when the Framework for the Conclusion of a Peace Treaty between Egypt and Israel was realized and the Framework for Peace in the Middle East was not. Carter's push for a solution on the interstate dimension and insistence that an agreement be reached at Camp David may have increased the ability of the sides to reach a deal, but in doing so it created incentives for the parties to "satisfice" and feel more content with an imperfect agreement. Because of the high political stakes of failure for all involved, an agreement became desirable as an end in itself and it became easier to look past the deep flaws in the Camp David Accords, including the weak linkage between

---

65. See also Vance (1983, 234, 239, 249); Dayan (1981, 244); Weizman (1981, 375); Stein (1999, 254).

66. For a defense against the view that the Framework for Peace in the Middle East was merely a front to establish a peace between Israel and Egypt, see Vance (1983, 229, 253). See also Ben-Ami (2005, 169–71).

67. On the separateness of the Sinai II agreement, see Ben-Ami (2005, 153); Shlaim (2000, 340).

68. See, for example, Telhami (1990, 68).

the two frameworks and virtually no enforcement mechanisms for progress on the Framework for Peace. On this, Ezer Weizman notes, "The desire on the part of all three participants—Israel, Egypt, and the United States—to bring the conference to a successful conclusion had resulted in a number of important issues being swept under the carpet" (1981, 379). Yitzhak Rabin uses the same imagery when he observes that the Camp David Accords were meant to begin a graduated process in which Israel and Egypt would first establish peaceful relations, meanwhile "sweeping the more difficult issues under the carpet to be dealt with at a later date" (1979, 328).

In support of the notion that trade-offs often exist in mediation initiatives between what is immediately attainable and more full future resolution, it is worth noting that the Carter administration anticipated the risks taken in pushing for the Egyptian-Israeli deal before substantial progress could be made on implementing the more comprehensive framework. For instance, Vance (1983, 233–34) recalls that the administration correctly foresaw that the successful conclusion of a peace treaty between Egypt and Israel would be in tension with a comprehensive peace. Throughout the negotiating process, Carter suspected that the Israeli leadership preferred a separate peace and tried to defend against that outcome. In this regard, Brzezinski noted in his journal soon after the Camp David Accords were signed that he and Carter had agreed that "through his statements and public posture, Begin is trying to create the impression that the only accord that really counts is the Israeli-Egyptian agreement. If he can get away with it, he will obtain a separate treaty and then the whole structure of peace in the Middle East will crumble as the Saudis and Jordanians react negatively" (Brzezinski 1985, 275).[69] Vance (1983, 206) also explicitly warned Dayan that the United States could not support Israel in its bid for a separate peace.

This all points to the conclusion that the potential of brokering a settlement with only weak linkage was a true dilemma for Carter and his diplomatic team and that they were not ignorant of the long-term potential ramifications of their decisions. Optimizing the chance of substantial progress on normalizing relations between Egypt and Israel meant reducing the chance of a full commitment to a broader settlement. They knew that, had they chosen instead to push only for a comprehensive settlement and to rule out any notion of a separate peace, this would risk missing out on the window of opportunity for securing an immediate end to Israeli-Egyptian hostilities. Forced with a difficult choice and without a magic bullet, Carter, as well as Kissinger before him, chose not to let the myriad obstacles to a comprehensive peace hold hostage the Egypt-Israel angle, even if

---

69. See also Vance (1983, 181, 206–7); Brzezinski (1985, 235, 275–76).

this added to the already immense difficulty of pursuing a comprehensive settlement in the Middle East.

Carter in North Korea

Carter's mediation in the DPRK also demonstrates the struggles of mediation in the long run, especially when there are probably insincere motives in play. The Agreed Framework that Carter's efforts helped establish did not by any means create a permanent settlement either on tensions on the Korean peninsula or on the nuclear question. In fact, it was always intended to be the first step of many toward resolving the nuclear issue.[70] Once established, the Agreed Framework lasted for eight years, but it eventually failed in a resounding fashion. With assistance from A.Q. Khan's network, the DPRK pursued an undeclared uranium enrichment program and, when called on it, became in January 2003 the first state ever to leave the Nuclear Non-Proliferation Treaty, resumed its plutonium program, and ultimately conducted a nuclear test in 2006. The international community, in no small part because it doubted the probity of the DPRK commitments, never provided the promised light-water reactors and eventually strengthened the sanctions against the DPRK.

The eight years of nuclear freeze were important because they were years in which the DPRK could not build any nuclear weapons from its plutonium sealed at Yongbyon, but they constituted only a temporary lull in hostilities. The mediation dilemma presented itself in 1994—the Clinton administration could have pursued, as it did, a temporary peace through Carter's efforts and avert a grave crisis, or it could have gone down the path of stronger sanctions and potential military action to derail the DPRK weapons program more permanently. Carter's efforts certainly reaped immediate peaceful dividends, and the risk of a nonpermanent settlement was one that the Clinton administration found worth taking.

The Agreed Framework is a classic case of an agreement that is not a permanent, self-enforcing resolution of the fundamental source of disagreement. Both sides had intended from the start to replace it with a bargain that provided greater benefits—the DPRK hoped to achieve security guarantees and ever-greater flows of resources from the developed world; the United States hoped to achieve the verifiable abandonment of the DPRK weapons program. They reached the agreement because of the incentives of the threat of imminent conflict and the pressure from domestic and international audiences that Carter ably manipulated.

---

70. See Troester (1996, 82–83).

But these incentives were fleeting and could not endure as time passed. The domestic political landscapes changed greatly after June 1994 when Carter helped broker the Agreed Framework, first with the death of Kim Il Sung and then with the U.S. election of George W. Bush, whose administration pushed for a more permanent and verifiable termination of the DPRK nuclear program soon after taking office.[71] The international political environment shifted as well during this time. Joel Wit, Daniel Poneman, and Robert Gallucci write that "once the 1994 crisis had passed the international mood quickly shifted from galvanized anxiety to lethargic apathy, leaving the administration struggling in vain to raise significant funding for KEDO from countries beyond South Korea and Japan" (2004, 373). The lack of international support, in addition to the suspected perfidy of the DPRK regime, contributed to the inability to implement the Agreed Framework and to its eventual abandonment in 2002.

Insincere motives also lay at the heart of the escalation of tensions in 2002. Kim Il Sung had strong incentives to just delay settlement. The longer he could avoid adopting new full nuclear safeguards, the more he could move on with other aspects of his nuclear program and gain even more bargaining leverage in the future. Continuing negotiations through mediation, and ultimately the nuclear freeze, kept the risk of war low while allowing the DPRK to secure its program and pursue an alternative path to acquiring nuclear weapons. Although the plutonium path remained temporarily closed with IAEA safeguards in place at Yongbyon, the absence of full safeguards at undeclared sites allowed the DPRK to pursue the uranium option, which, in summer 2002, the U.S. intelligence community concluded had moved beyond the experimental level (Funabashi 2007, 95).[72] Also, delaying major retreats from its nuclear program allowed the DPRK to wait for circumstances to change such that war was less likely when the weapons program eventually resumed at full pace. By 2002, the risk of war over the DPRK nuclear program had diminished because U.S. troops were mobilizing for the invasion of Iraq and relations had thawed with the ROK. In essence, Carter's mediation, the resulting additional round of talks, and ultimately the Agreed Framework bought the DPRK time free from the threat of war and sanctions, during which it could pursue another route for its nuclear weapons program and after which it could easily resume its previous path with much less cost.

Without documented evidence that Kim Il Sung's government never intended to compromise on changing the course of its nuclear program and only wanted

---

71. See Funabashi (2007, 109, 152).

72. Intelligence reports of a DPRK uranium enrichment program had started in 1998, but this did not receive the attention of top administration officials until 2002. See also Funabashi (2007, 119–25).

to buy time, we will never know for certain whether devious motives were in play. But given the behavior of the DPRK after 1994, this conclusion appears reasonable. Since the collapse of the Agreed Framework, without any safeguards in place to inhibit progress on both its plutonium and uranium programs, the DPRK has continually bought time using the series of six-party (the DPRK, the ROK, China, Russia, Japan, and the United States) talks.[73] The approach of returning to negotiations when the international pressure increases, all the while moving forward with its weapons program, appears to be a consistent DPRK strategy over the last two decades.

Finally, this case provides additional insight when we consider that the easing of tensions following Carter's mediation almost faltered even before the Agreed Framework could be negotiated. Two complications between Carter's visit and the signing of the Agreed Framework arose that demonstrate the difficulty of mediation having a lasting effect. First, Carter had negotiated an agreement with Kim Il Sung, who passed away before the framework could be settled. Regime change can create a strong time-inconsistency problem if the incentives provided by the third party do not carry over to the successor. Especially because some of the positive inducements for compromise that Carter had provided related to intangible benefits such as prestige and respect, there was some question of whether Kim Jong Il would abide by his father's pledge.[74] Second, the ROK was left out of much of the negotiations, but its support was necessary for the Agreed Framework to work. The U.S. negotiating team thus had the delicate task of selling the proposed settlement to the ROK and enticing it to substantially fund KEDO.[75] Had the ROK been a principal member of the negotiations, it is likely that more progress would have been made on providing the light-water reactors. This speaks to the difficulty of having multiple stakeholders in a conflict; restricting the parties at the negotiating table increases the potential for some sort of settlement but also makes the commitment problem during implementation direr.

Roosevelt at Portsmouth

Theodore Roosevelt's involvement in ending the Russo-Japanese War offers lessons about possible positive long-term effects of mediation. The peace achieved

---

73. Wit, Poneman, and Galucci (2004, 402) similarly discuss the potential for the DPRK to manipulate the diplomatic initiatives, especially the multilateral six-party format, to give it more time to consolidate its weapons program.

74. On the uncertainty related to the DPRK regime transition, see Wit, Poneman, and Galucci (2004, 255–65).

75. On tensions between the United States and ROK during the negotiations about the Agreed Framework, see Wit, Poneman, and Galucci (2004, 265, 295, 321).

between Japan and Russia at Portsmouth laid the foundation for relative peaceful coexistence in northeast Asia. The Egyptian-Israeli Peace Treaty demonstrates that leverage sustained indefinitely can foster stable peace in the long run. In contrast, this example demonstrates that long-term peace also can be attainable if leverage is used sparingly so that there is no need for the third party to maintain its influence over time. Even though Roosevelt's involvement in the Russo-Japanese War is mostly a success story, we cannot universally apply it as a model for mediation because the favorable bargaining environment in which Roosevelt operated is not typical. That being said, the example does demonstrate that limiting the amount of leverage when more is not needed for progress can contribute to a self-enforcing peace. It is also worth considering an important facet of the Treaty of Portsmouth that contributed to future regional instability. The Treaty of Portsmouth excluded Chinese input and did not permanently delineate rights in Manchuria, which may have allowed for flexibility in the Russian and Japanese foreign policy positions with regards to that region; however, it also put Japan on a collision course with China and the United States that directly led to the Second Sino-Japanese War and, perhaps more indirectly, to the Pacific War with the United States during World War II.

It is notable that Russia and Japan maintained a relative peace from 1905 until 1938, although Japan did participate in the allied intervention during the Bolshevik Revolution. The peace achieved at Portsmouth was arguably quite robust.[76] In the decade after the treaty, Japanese and Russian ties actually strengthened; they concluded a number of additional agreements in 1907, including an entente that was later strengthened in 1910. It is also striking that the peace agreement between Russia and Japan endured major political shifts in both countries, a world war in which the two countries were allies, and the Japanese invasion of Manchuria. Norman Saul writes, "While both countries felt let down from their expectations in the war, they soon formed a quasi bond and alliance that would basically keep the Far East out of World War I and supply lines to Russia open across the North Pacific through 1919 and crucially during World War II" (2005, 507). In other words, there were many opportunities for major conflicts to reemerge in the years after Portsmouth; instead, we observe, for the most part, restraint.

A number of factors were responsible for peace between Japan and Russia, but chief among them was their reaching a self-sustainable understanding of acceptable bargaining positions at Portsmouth.[77] As we have seen in chapter 4, Roosevelt allowed the bulk of the negotiations to proceed without much personal

---

76. This point is made by Yokote (2008); Berton (2007).

77. Lukoianov notes that both Russia and Japan "were to a certain extent interested not only in concluding peace but in establishing a state of affairs in the Far East that neither side would have cause to reexamine later" (2008, 54). See also Togo (2008).

involvement. After making some initial recommendations to both delegations before the talks began, he then retreated to his vacation home in New York and allowed the participants to get as far as they could bilaterally. When those negotiations reached the point of near-breakdown, Roosevelt then returned to Portsmouth and provided the necessary nudges and suggestions needed to clear the last few remaining hurdles. In this way, Roosevelt's key to success was to simply get out of the way when the disputants were able to make progress on their own and then to provide calculated assistance when needed.

The sides were thus able to reach a more natural agreement on the items of Japanese control of Korea, Japanese rights on the Liaodong peninsula and over the South Manchuria railway, and Chinese rights in Manchuria. Moreover, when Roosevelt did become more involved with respect to the issues of Sakhalin and indemnity, his role mostly consisted of making proposals and building support in the international community, hardly heavy-handed intrusions into the bargaining environment. There was therefore little need for follow-up involvement by Roosevelt or for the United States in general because the incentives for peace were not dependent on the mediator and the course of the war had not been interrupted prematurely. Of course, Roosevelt's ability to succeed without the application of much leverage resulted mostly from a particularly manageable bargaining environment in which both sides were eager to end the war and were primarily negotiating over details. So, although this case illustrates a key implication of the theoretical framework about the crucial role of leverage in shaping the long-term effects of mediation, it is not typical and thus is limited in serving as a general model for how mediation should be done.

The treaty itself also provided a suitable framework to work out the balance of power in the region. In this respect, the sides understood the need for flexibility in moving forward and used vague language with regard to access to Manchuria to resist Chinese attempts to reassert full sovereignty.[78] The benefit of this flexibility can be seen in how Russia peacefully negotiated further accords with Japan, without need of third-party assistance, clarifying their respective spheres of influence in Manchuria in 1907, 1910, and 1912.[79] The ease of negotiations after Portsmouth was also indicative of the fact that Russia finally took Japan seriously as a regional power; its failure to do so earlier contributed to the onset of the war in the first place.

---

78. On the vague language concerning Manchuria, see Yokote (2008). On the importance of the treaty in providing a flexible framework, see Berton (2007, 79).

79. On these agreements, see Schimmelpenninck van der Oye (2008, 21–23); Berton (2007, 79–81); Esthus (1988, 195–203).

Whereas peace between Russia and Japan endured in northeast Asia following the treaty, relations between Japan and the United States and between Japan and China worsened for reasons related to the terms of the treaty. Labeling Roosevelt's mediation at Portsmouth a success story must carry this important caveat. Ironically in light of the riots in Tokyo, the Treaty of Portsmouth implicitly recognized Japan as the victor despite the weakening state of the Japanese military and economy. As a result, the outcome of the Russo-Japanese War emboldened Japan as a regional power, which contributed to its more expansionist policy in northeast Asia and a desire to seek greater independence from the United States (White 1964, 310, 343; Bradley 2009, 5). In fact, soon after Portsmouth, we observe tensions between Tokyo and Washington as the United States, especially under the new Howard Taft administration, became frustrated that Japan was not abiding by the U.S. "open door" policy, in which all powers would have equal opportunity to trade in Manchuria and in which the territorial integrity of China would be maintained. The vague language pertaining to Manchuria in the treaty made it especially difficult to pin down Japanese commitments.

An additional facet of the Portsmouth negotiations that potentially contributed to later conflict—although not between Japan and Russia—was the absence of China from the negotiations even though Russia and Japan were negotiating over access to parts of China.[80] China had requested that it be included in the peace process, but Roosevelt refused.[81] China was so weak at the time that Japan simply imposed the conditions negotiated at Portsmouth on the Chinese leadership (Yokote 2008; White 1964, 263). But Chinese acquiescence was only temporary and resentment toward such ill treatment by the Japanese gave rise to Chinese nationalism, which put the two countries on a collision course over Manchuria and led to war in the 1930s.[82] Had China been a participant at Portsmouth, perhaps a framework could have been established clarifying the rights of each actor in Manchuria and laying the foundation for future coordination as both nations strengthened in the twentieth century.[83] Of course, this would have greatly complicated the negotiations and probably would have led to their failure, which is why China was excluded in the first place. As such, we see an

---

80. Representatives from Korea were absent too, but Japanese dominance in Korea was so complete that Korean input would have been meaningless.

81. See Hirakawa (2007, 545). For the formal request and refusal, see *Papers Relating to the Foreign Relations of the United States* (1906, 817).

82. On the long-term implications to peace between Japan and China, see Teramoto (2008); Yokote (2008).

83. Togo (2008, 173) considers such a counterfactual to be a potential lost opportunity but also fairly idealistic.

additional example of how peace processes typically involve a trade-off between establishing an arrangement, however imperfect, in the present and creating an arrangement that endures.

In this chapter, I have explored why mediators are often constrained from having more of a lasting impact on peace stability than they do. As well as it performs in the short run, mediation is simply not well suited to create long-term peaceful benefits. Mediation might inhibit the long-term resolution of a conflict via a number of different mechanisms. First, and potentially most important, intermediaries can push for agreements that are simply not viable in the absence of third-party pressure. Second, third-party intervention can interfere with the natural learning processes that are necessary for the successful renegotiation of the terms. Third, mediation can be used by combatants for objectives other than peace; that is, they can go through the motions of pausing hostilities and entering mediation, only to renew conflict when they are in relatively stronger military and political positions. In the absence of the continual third-party assistance that was necessary to expedite the end of a crisis episode in the first place, protagonists will have a higher tendency to become dissatisfied with their end of the bargain and will also find the renegotiation of that bargain more difficult.

The empirical record confirms this logic. Pairs of states that have been in a crisis are less likely to relapse within the first few years of peace when they have experienced mediation. But they are also more likely than dyads that did not experience mediation to return to conflict after four or five years of peace. Over time, the incentives of third-party mediators to remain involved as peace advocates fade and the lack of a self-enforcing peace is exposed.

This effect is magnified when the third parties use heavy-handed mediation tactics because the trade-off between short-term peace and long-term stability appears proportional to the amount of leverage the mediators bring to bear. The more important to the attainment of a settlement third-party influence becomes, the more fragile the settlement results as the external influence diminishes and leaves behind a bargaining environment that is much different from the one in which the settlement was birthed. In contrast, the absence of third-party leverage limits the prospects for making an immediate agreement but improves the chances that any agreement that is established will remain mutually satisfying in the long run.

Mediation initiatives by multiple third parties and IGOs are also especially likely to contribute to a sharp drop in the long-term durability of peace because of collective action and coordination problems. In addition, peacekeeping deployments do not appear to resolve the link between mediation and unsustainable settlements. On the other hand, mediation the occurs during periods of low-intensity conflict does enable the parties to find more durable agreements. In such situations, patient actors can use the involvement of a mediator to their advantage while also waiting for an agreement that is likely to be self-enforcing. The absence of credible commitment problems, finally, allows mediation to produce more stable settlements because the risk of backtracking by the actors is minimal.

Insight from the case studies confirms these conclusions while also adding nuance. Carter's efforts in the DPRK in 1994 most clearly demonstrate the difficulty for third parties of using leverage to achieve an agreement that becomes fully implemented in the long run. The difficulty is even starker when belligerents have insincere motivations for going along with mediation, as the DPRK regime probably had and continues to have. Kissinger's and Carter's efforts to achieve progress on a comprehensive peace in the Middle East also demonstrate well the trade-off between the short-term and long-term effects of mediation. Although the Framework for Peace in the Middle East was a landmark agreement, its implementation faltered in the absence of sustained U.S. pressure in that regard.

Two of the cases also demonstrate the potential for the trade-off to be minimized. The Egyptian-Israeli peace mediated by Kissinger and Carter endured well after the achievement of the disengagement agreements and the peace treaty. In this case, the long-term risks of mediation were for the most part avoided because the United States maintained its influence on Egypt and Israel through either constant pressure or through helping shape the bargaining environment so that it was not so dependent on sustained outside pressure. Leverage itself is thus not bad for a self-enforcing peace as long as the impact of that leverage does not wane and leave the actors with a time-inconsistency problem. Finally, Roosevelt's involvement in the Russo-Japanese War demonstrates that long-term peace can be reached through mediation when the mediator does not rely much on leverage yet is still able to broker a settlement.

MEDIATION IN INTRASTATE CONFLICTS

"Really," Odette said, "it was UNAMIR [United Nations Assistance Mission for Rwanda] that tricked us into staying. We saw all these blue helmets, and we talked with Dallaire"—Major General Roméo Dallaire, the Canadian in command of the UN force. "We thought even if Hutus start to attack us the three thousand men of UNAMIR should be enough. Dallaire gave us his phone number and his radio number, and said, 'If anything happens you call me immediately.' So we trusted them."

—A survivor of the Rwanda genocide, as told by Philip Gourevitch (1998, 102)

The U.N. Mission, and those Rwandans it was intended to secure, fell victim to an inflated optimism to which I contributed, thereby creating expectations that the U.N. did not have the capacity to fulfill.

—General Roméo Dallaire, quoted in Khadiagala (2002, 490)

Intrastate conflicts are, in the twenty-first century, more prevalent and more deadly than their interstate counterparts. Both the quantitative and qualitative analyses thus far have focused exclusively on interstate crises and disputes even though the theoretical underpinnings of the mediation dilemma are not specific to either interstate or intrastate peace processes.[1] Recall that we have arrived at a theoretical understanding of the trade-off between the short- and long-term effects of mediation by characterizing a bargaining environment in which actors are in disagreement and in which third parties can help the combatants reach a settlement but in so doing can also disrupt the ability for the resulting peace to be self-enforcing. Because we have made no assumptions about whether the

---

1. Although most of the literature on mediation in general has focused on interstate conflict, some recent studies have considered how mediation plays out specifically in civil wars (Regan and Aydin 2006; Greig and Regan 2008; Gurses, Rost and McLeod 2008; Melin and Svensson 2009; Sisk 2008; Svensson 2007a, 2007b).

disputing actors are states or insurgents, we can also expect this trade-off to exist for mediation initiatives in intrastate conflicts. Existing analyses in the literature provide some confirmation that, indeed, third-party conflict managers in civil wars can hinder the realization of long-term stability.[2] But this does not mean that the bargaining environments in intrastate conflicts are exactly the same as the bargaining environments in more conventional interstate contests. Here I explore, primarily through illustrative case studies, some of the special character-istics of intrastate conflict that need to be taken into account when considering the mediation dilemma.

There are at least four reasons why the long-term risks inherent in mediation can be even more pronounced in intrastate conflicts than in interstate ones. First, vulnerabilities to commitment problems are greater because of the need for the disputants to coexist following the conflict, which means that long-term trust will be more difficult to establish and easier to disrupt. Second, external involve-ment in civil conflicts can decrease the co-dependence between the governed and the governors necessary for stable domestic rule. Third, mediation is likely to make the problem of spoilers worse when there is a fractured polity because the third party can confer political legitimacy on certain actors while threatening the ability for other, excluded actors to represent their supporters. Fourth, the pur-suit of mediation for insincere motives is more likely in environments in which insurgencies depend on local recruitment and actors can benefit from stirring up nationalism. I explore each of these factors in turn through brief analyses of four additional case studies. I conclude the chapter on a more optimistic note by considering the case of peace in Aceh, in which the bargaining environment and resulting mediation initiative seem to have been conducive to both short-term and long-term success because these additional issues were avoided.

Increasing Vulnerability to Defection: Rwanda

As shown in the previous chapter, mediation can decrease the stability of post-conflict peace because the combatants become prone to renegotiation and sub-sequent bargaining failure after the influence of the third party wanes. This effect

---

2. Stedman and Rothchild (1996) and Stedman (2002), for example, discuss a number of ways in which third parties without a sufficiently long time horizon can disrupt the implementation of intrastate peace processes. The findings of Gurses, Rost, and McLeod (2008) confirm that the trade-off is present in intrastate conflicts, in that mediated agreements and great power mediation increase the fragility of peace after civil wars. The conclusions in Roeder and Rothchild (2005) also touch on a related trade-off in which power-sharing arrangements in ethnically divided societies often serve as a quick fix while making conflict more protracted in the long run.

should be even more pronounced in intrastate conflicts, in which the vulnerabilities to such failed implementation can be much greater. When combatants in a civil war achieve some sort of settlement, they have to coexist within the same system of governance. After disarming and submitting to the authority of the state, former combatants become vulnerable to the potential for competing factions to use the coercive capacities of the state to harm, exclude, and potentially even eliminate them.[3] If one side is left with greater control of the state than the other or otherwise is able to remain armed, it will find it difficult to commit credibly to not renegotiate or violate the terms of peace while trying to extract more from its defenseless opponent.[4] The level of vulnerability is less pronounced in interstate conflicts, in which reneging on a peace pledge simply leads to a return to hostilities between actors that still have the ability to defend themselves.

Amid a heightened sensitivity to commitment problems, mediation in intrastate conflicts can lead to even greater instability.[5] Both the frequency and severity of conflict recurrence may rise in the long run following a mediation attempt. With regard to frequency, former combatants that feel vulnerable after an intrastate conflict are more suspicious of opponent defection and thus will be readier to abandon a fragile peace that they suspect is not self-enforcing. With regard to severity, third-party security guarantees offered during mediation but not completely implemented can create windows of vulnerability as one side begins to demobilize and the other seizes the opportunity to decimate its opponent.

The Rwandan genocide presents a stark example of the potential long-term instability that third parties can foster by aggravating vulnerabilities to defection.[6] On August 4, 1993, Rwandan President Juvénal Habyarimana and Alexis Kanyarengwe, Rwandan Patriotic Front (RPF) chairman, signed the Arusha Accords in Tanzania. In a matter of months, the agreement that was supposed to

---

3. This is the security dilemma that Snyder and Jervis (1999) discuss as the key driver of civil wars. Walter (1997) terms this problem the "critical barrier" to civil war settlement. Note that we are assuming that partitioning did not occur. For a study of how partitioning may be a solution to the commitment problem in civil war, see Chapman and Roeder (2007). For now, partitioning is relatively rare, so the view that after the resolution of a civil war factions need to coexist in some way still holds.

4. Diarmament can be considerd as a massive power shift, and Powell (2006) argues that such power shifts are important causes of commitment problems.

5. Snyder and Jervis (1999) discuss how foreign intervention in civil war sometimes has the potential to resolve security dilemmas endemic in intrastate conflict but also has the potential to make them even worse. Woodward (1999) similarly demonstrates that the heavy-handed third-party intervention in Bosnia that led to the Dayton Accords actually exacerbated the security dilemma.

6. Although the Rwanda case is considered as an example of intrastate conflict, it is worth noting there were significant international dimensions to the conflict because the Rwandan Patriotic Front had firm roots in Uganda (Davenport and Stam 2009). Rwanda is included as an intrastate conflict here because it involved a contest between a sovereign government and a nonstate rebel group fighting for control of the country.

end a violent three-year civil war between predominantly Hutu and Tutsi factions dissolved into a brutal genocide that left over 1 million Rwandans dead.[7] Meanwhile, the international community that was supposed to monitor and enforce the agreement failed to take sufficient action; the UN peacekeeping mission, UNAMIR, was slow to deploy, weaker than expected, unresponsive to the escalating tensions, and quick to abandon the country when hostilities rose.[8]

The talks leading to the Arusha Accords commenced in 1993 after the mounting costs of hostilities increased the eagerness of the combatants to seek peace.[9] The negotiations involved substantial international pressure and assistance, including regional actors such as Tanzania, Uganda, Zaire, Burundi, and the Organization of African Unity (OAU); the Western powers Belgium, France, Germany, and the United States; and the UN.[10] Although international involvement proved instrumental in starting and shaping the peace process, it also was responsible for the resulting document, which was not self-enforcing in the absence of the promised international peacekeeping commitment and in the exclusion of Hutu nationalists.[11] That is, international pressure generated a power-sharing agreement that made both parties vulnerable unless there was a substantial peacekeeping force and that created an incentive for spoilers to subvert the resulting peace. We can particularly get a sense for the vulnerability that the negotiated agreement created when we consider that it called for elections to be held after the transitional period, which would have left the minority Tutsi population at risk of losing all meaningful representation in the government.[12] With the deployment of UNAMIR, the necessary UN peacekeeping force, being delayed and weaker than expected in both size and mandate, the sides failed to implement the accords and the Hutu militias attempted to resolve the security dilemma by eliminating the opposition. Alan Kuperman writes, "While conflict management gurus have in recent years emphasized the need for mediators to utilize leverage—such as aid,

---

7. Davenport and Stam (2009), as part of their GenoDynamics project, provide a reexamination of the content and extent of the violence and conclude that the conventional genocide story is too simplistic. My focus here is on explaining the onset of the violence, which primarily involved Hutu militias killing Tutsis, and not the later violence in which both Hutus and Tutsis were killed in large numbers.

8. See Khadiagala (2002, 482–90).

9. Khadiagala (2002, 467) reports that the costs of the war accounted for 70 percent of Rwandan government expenses in 1993.

10. For overviews of the role of third parties in the Arusha peace process, see Stettenheim (2002); Khadiagala (2002, 470–76).

11. For extensive discussions of variants of these points, see Kuperman (1996; 2001, 110). Note that the argument here is partly, but not completely, about failing to get the terms right at Arusha. The flawed security guarantees were a direct product of the international involvement, so that involvement was really at the heart of the long-term issues.

12. Stam (2008) stresses the importance of the looming elections in contributing to the vulnerabilities at the root of the violence.

trade, sanctions and embargoes—the Rwandan experience demonstrates that such leverage is a double-edged sword, equally capable of driving contending parties to the most extreme measures" (1996, 221).

The mediation of the Arusha agreement primarily contributed to greater vulnerability through the application of leverage, which led to a strong dependence on fickle third-party guarantees. The third parties used substantial economic and political pressure, especially on the Habyarimana regime, to promote compromise. While negotiations were taking place in 1993, the United States, International Monetary Fund (IMF), World Bank, European Union, and Belgium all either withdrew or threatened to withdraw tens of millions of dollars in aid and assistance (Kuperman 1996, 227).[13] They also promised enforcement resources to keep the parties honest.[14] And this was on top of the French military deployment intended to prevent an RPF victory, create a sense of stalemate, and get the combatants to Arusha in the first place. In other words, the third parties rather heavy-handedly increased the attractiveness of compromise during the negotiations.

Because the primary incentives of the belligerents to compromise came from external pressure, not maintaining that pressure created dissatisfaction with the accords and vulnerability to any resulting defection. That is, without the sustained outside pressure the Hutu nationalist elites, whose power was threatened by the Arusha agreement, lacked sufficient incentives to abide by what Habyarimana had promised. They ultimately seized the opportunity, again created by the absence of a substantial peacekeeping force, to exterminate the opposition, especially the vulnerable Tutsis in Kigali, which was far away from the protection of RPF forces.[15] An additional factor contributing to the vulnerability in Rwanda was the fact that UN observers (United Nations Observer Mission Uganda-Rwanda, UNOMUR) were in place on the border of Uganda and Rwanda attempting to prevent the RPF from entering Rwanda but, thereby, keeping the Tutsis at risk of a first-strike attack.

As discussed in the previous chapter, one of the reasons why many third parties are not able to act strongly in an enforcement capacity is the problem of collective action and coordination among multiple involved third parties. With the UN taking the lead on the peacekeeping efforts, the OAU and Tanzania did not involve themselves much in post-conflict enforcement. Meanwhile, no state wanted to bear the brunt of the UN peacekeeping costs, given the absence of interest by the international community and the incentives to free ride.[16] This helps

---

13. See also Khadiagala (2002, 475–76).

14. Khadiagala (2002, 471, 479–80) posits that the third parties at Arusha fostered an exaggerated sense of the commitment of the international community to remaining engaged afterward.

15. See Khadiagala (2002, 487); Kuperman (1996).

16. See Khadiagala (2002, 481, 489–90).

explain why the United States contributed hardly anything and why Belgium withdrew, instead of augmenting, its forces after ten of its troops were brutally murdered in the early stages of the genocide. In addition, the diverse organs and bodies of the UN found it difficult to coordinate on what the appropriate level of involvement should be to prevent and respond to the hostilities.[17] Buckpassing and confusion thus prevailed.

In addition to the problem of fleeting third-party leverage, some have argued that the mediators helped sow the seeds of genocide by excluding the more radical Hutu groups, namely the Coalition for the Defence of the Republic (CDR), and thereby giving them an incentive to spoil an agreement that, if implemented, would weaken their political power.[18] Note that it is not clear that the Arusha negotiations actually created spoilers that would not otherwise have existed. The CDR was not so much excluded by the third parties; we might say more accurately that it excluded itself from any negotiations that considered power sharing.[19] That being said, it is clear that the radical Hutu elites felt threatened by the compromises that Habyarimana made under pressure by international actors and had a heightened interest in seizing any opportunities to renew hostilities. The heavy-handed nature of the international efforts at Arusha thus forced compromises that severely threatened the more radical elites, who then took action to thwart the peace and to eliminate the opposition.

The Rwandan case demonstrates that both heavy-handed and hesitant intervention, especially when the former precedes the latter, can have serious negative consequences for peaceful relationships among combatants. Although each could have been counterproductive alone, in Rwanda the international community committed both the sin of impatiently leveraging the combatants into an agreement and the sin of not acting strongly enough when conflict spiraled out of control. Such a mixture, combined with the vulnerabilities felt by opposing ethnic groups needing to coexist, provided the kindling for genocide.

Interfering with the Social Contract: Haiti

All rulers must have some minimal level of assent from those who are ruled. That assent might be mostly voluntary, as in representative democracies, or mostly coerced, as in authoritarian regimes. When the assent is voluntary, the rulers must

---

17. For a detailed account of how the bureaucratic culture of the UN made a concerted response difficult, see Barnett (2002).

18. See Kuperman (1996, 222, 230; 2001, 110); Khadiagala (2002, 463).

19. For a variant of this argument, see Khadiagala (2002, 491–92).

provide a sufficient amount of public goods to retain the needed support. When the assent is coerced, the rulers must provide a sufficient amount of private goods to the military and economic elites to continue the means of oppression. Either way, every leader is in some way beholden to the desires of a domestic audience, or selectorate, which is responsible for the leader's ability to remain in power.[20] According to this logic, a contract of sorts exists between the rulers and their selectorates such that the rulers provide public or private goods in exchange for the ability to rule. A stable, self-enforcing polity is one in which that contract is strong and mutual dependence exists between the leader and the relevant domestic audience.[21]

When third parties become involved in the resolution of intrastate conflicts, they have the potential to weaken the social contract on which the exercise of power depends. When leaders can rely on the support of outside actors to keep them in power—by receiving subsidized public or private goods, especially security forces—they have less incentive to find their own means of providing for the needs and wants of their domestic audiences. They become less accountable. When such third-party support is retracted from a leader, instability results as the leader's foundation of support crumbles. In this way, mediators in civil wars will struggle to both secure the resumption of governance in the short run and ensure stable governance in the long run. Third-party leverage typically helps produce the short-run objective, but it also leads to less stable domestic institutions in the long run when the third-party leverage eventually wanes. U.S. involvement in Haiti provides an example of this dynamic.

From the time of Jean-Bertrand Aristide's exile to the United States in 1991 until 1994, the United States, the UN, and the OAS attempted to negotiate the peaceful return of President Aristide and the abdication of power by General Raoul Cedras, the leader of the junta. The United States was primarily motivated by humanitarian concerns, the desire to preserve democracy in Latin America and the Caribbean, and the growing number of Haitian refugees trying to reach the United States.[22] Employing tough sanctions, including a UN-authorized embargo, and promising aid, the intermediaries successfully brokered the Governor's Island Agreement and the New York Pact in mid-1993.[23] But implementation of

---

20. For more on selectorate theory, see Bueno de Mesquita et al. (2003).

21. North and Weingast (1989) consider the importance of self-enforcing relationships between the rulers and the ruled in contributing to both political and economic stability.

22. See Clinton (2004, 616); Pezzullo (2006, 275). Carter (2007, 49) was also motivated by humanitarian concerns.

23. For an account of these negotiations, which involved substantial leverage, including both tangible carrots and sticks and intangible threats of blame, toward both Aristide and Cedras, see Pezzullo (2006, 86–106, 119–31).

the agreements failed when the junta refused to completely yield its powers. The Clinton administration eventually resolved to invade Haiti in September 1994, with authorization from the UN Security Council, to restore Aristide. Literally hours before U.S.-led forces commenced the assault, Jimmy Carter, Sam Nunn, and Colin Powell (CNP) successfully mediated the terms under which the junta would peacefully exit the country.[24]

Aristide had promised liberal political and economic reforms but, instead, upon his return he concentrated more power in the executive office and allowed the country to fall even further into ruin.[25] Aristide did cede power to his handpicked successor, Réne Préval, in 1996, but he continued to dominate Haitian politics and returned to formal power in 2001. Because of his egregious human-rights abuses and corruption, as well as the persistent Haitian refugee problems and poverty, the United States eventually reversed course completely and removed Aristide from power in 2004.

The third-party efforts to restore Aristide to power during his time in exile are a fairly extreme example of heavy-handed mediation in the domestic affairs of another country. In a sense, the United States, UN, and OAS negotiated the return of Aristide, but by September 1994, the involvement looked more like humanitarian intervention than assisted negotiation. Akin to the U.S. role in ending the war in Bosnia at Dayton, this case is located at the far end of the spectrum with regard to the use of mediator leverage. This approach, in addition to the promise of a UN peacekeeping force, did produce negotiated settlements that established the basis for a transition back to Aristide's legitimate rule. But by acting so forcefully, the third parties, especially the United States, interfered with the accountability of Aristide to the Haitian people and decreased his incentives for reform and compromise that were necessary for stable democratic rule in Haiti.

Therefore, after the United States restored Aristide to power in 1994, he lacked sufficient accountability to the Haitian people and elites, and the U.S.-led intervention contributed in large part to that dearth in accountability. The United States clearly demonstrated its willingness to bear tremendous costs to keep the elected governments of Aristide and Préval in power. One reason for this was that, while in exile in the United States, Aristide had effectively managed to win over members of Congress and other elites.[26] Clinton also clearly came to have a vested interest in Aristide's remaining in power, given that the Clinton administration

---

24. For accounts of the CNP mission, see Pastor (1999); Carter (2007, 36–53); Troester (1996, 87). Note that, unlike Carter's mediation in the DPRK as a private citizen, CNP were authorized to officially represent U.S. interests.

25. See Rotberg (2003, 3, 9–10).

26. For various accounts of such affection for Aristide, see Pezzullo (2006, 88, 277).

took a great risk to restore his rule. Aristide additionally had considerable leverage over Washington due to his ability to make the refugee situation even worse (Pezzullo 2006, 276). Aristide could thus count on the United States to continue supporting the regime even in the midst of poor governance. In addition, the agreed arrangement that allowed the peaceful restoration of Aristide's power involved the exile of the military junta leaders, and one of the first reforms that Aristide took was to abolish the military. In this way, he removed a major institution that could check the power of the executive; this act is all the more significant because the legislature and courts were so weak. At the same time, the international peacekeeping presence was quickly reduced after Aristide returned to power even though both sides had insisted on a strong international presence during the transition.[27] Aristide thus faced scant institutionalized sources of accountability soon after his return.[28] As a final factor decreasing Aristide's domestic accountability, his natural charisma fostered a cult of personality in which populist pledges could for a time go unfulfilled without a significant mass backlash.

The lack of interdependence with domestic actors, for which the U.S.-led third-party involvement was in no small part responsible, contributed to major abuses of power, then strife, and ultimately Aristide's removal. Mediation had helped secure a temporary solution that, not surprisingly, faltered over time. In this case the third party (the United States) eventually scaled back its previously firm support so drastically that it actually intervened again to remove Aristide before the eruption of civil war—which became a possibility after a decade of perpetual mismanagement.

For Clinton, the risks of negotiating Aristide's return were worth taking, given the brutalities that occurred under the Cedras-led junta. In his memoirs, Clinton addresses the prescient reservations that CNP had about reinstating Aristide, whose commitment to representative democracy was already suspect, noting, "As subsequent events would prove, there was some merit to [CNP's] arguments. Haiti was deeply divided economically and politically and had little of the institutional capacity required to operate a modern state. Even if Aristide was returned without a hitch, he might not succeed. Still, he had been elected overwhelmingly, and Cedras and his crew were killing innocent people. We could at least stop that" (2004, 617).[29] The dilemma that Clinton faced in pursuing heavy-handed

---

27. See Rotberg (2003, 3, 9); Pezzullo (2006, 98). On the importance of the multinational force in the implementation of stable governance, see "Assessment Mission to Haiti" (1995).

28. Leandro Despouy, a UN diplomat overseeing the negotiations, lamented the fact that Arisistide had been returned on his own terms and had not been given sufficient incentives to compromise (Pezzullo 2006, 272).

29. On the skepticism of CNP, also see Pastor (1999, 515); Carter (2007, 39, 42). On the skepticism of other diplomats involved in the process, see Pezzullo (2006, 276).

involvement is thus clear: intervene and create perverse incentives for the re-stored regime to misbehave later, or do not intervene and allow the democratic experiment in Haiti to fail completely now. The excerpt from his memoirs also indicates that Clinton's primary interests were short-term ones. As it turns out, he did not have to personally deal with the ultimate failure of the Aristide regime because that task was left for the Bush administration. Rod Troester, a Carter bi-ographer, writing shortly after Aristide was reinstated, also astutely observed the tension between short-term and long-term U.S. objectives in Haiti: "In the long term, defusing the immediate conflict in Haiti and returning the democratically elected Aristide may prove to be an easier challenge than creating any sense of stability and prosperity for the Haitian people" (1996, 91).

Legitimacy and Spoilers: Oslo

A third issue that often arises in intrastate conflicts and that can generate an even starker mediation dilemma is the problem of addressing who has the right to speak for a particular group of people. This is an issue that is typically absent from interstate conflicts, in which the sovereigns or their plenipotentiaries ne-gotiate with little question of whether adequate authority exists for a deal to be made. In intrastate conflicts, questions of legitimate authority abound and can make mediation even more precarious in fostering stable peace than it otherwise might. When mediation occurs, there is often a recognition, usually implicit, that the parties at the negotiating table represent the interests of a particular group of people or polity and have the ability to speak on their behalf.[30] This can have at least three important ramifications for the post-mediation environment in civil conflicts.

First, by conferring legitimacy on a nonstate actor, mediation can compro-mise the authority of the state government. Allowing the leaders of a nonstate group to negotiate on behalf of a certain segment of the population is, at mini-mum, implicit recognition of overlapping layers of sovereignty in the polity and can even provide the explicit recognition of a fragmented sovereignty in which the government does not have control over portions of the state. This is an espe-cially important dynamic in secessionist conflicts, in which rebel leaders would like to convince their domestic and international audiences that they should be a viable independent government with sovereignty and a monopoly on the legiti-mate use of coercive force. When such combatants appear at the negotiating table

---

30. See Touval (2002); Melin and Svensson (2009, 5).

under the auspices of an international mediator, this can facilitate a perception of and precedent for self-rule. Decreasing the legitimacy of the government relative to that of an insurgency can, in turn, lead to greater instability in the long run because the rebels will demand more in the future if they continue to consolidate their legitimacy and hence gain bargaining power. The government will then also have a greater incentive to wage a massive preventive conflict to crush such competition to its sovereignty. In addition, credible commitment problems may be more difficult to resolve if the lines of authority and responsibility are blurred. Moreover, the weakening of the complete authority of the state could lead to more challenges from other nonstate actors that also want to be given legitimacy.[31]

Second, when there are multiple contenders for authority, the recognition of a select few can create incentives for the groups left out to spoil any resulting agreements.[32] Insurgencies are rarely monolithic movements in which there is one clear set of demands. Many intrastate conflicts involve multiple factions with different demands of the state. But to have any hope of progress in the short run, mediators often must limit the number of participants at the negotiating table. As a result, the excluded groups frequently become spoilers if they reject the authority of those claiming to represent their cause or if they are otherwise denied access to benefits in the peace agreement terms. The need for acquiescence from such groups thus presents a credible commitment problem for the actors that do participate in the negotiations and also increases the likelihood that there will be active attempts to disrupt implementation of any settlement that is reached. In this way, mediation that excludes certain actors competing for legitimacy increases the fragility of long-term peace.

Third, because mediation can confer legitimacy on nonstate actors, the attainment of that legitimacy through mediation in many cases becomes an end in itself. That is, mediation might be pursued insincerely for objectives other than peace, such as when the negotiators are really pursuing external recognition of their authority to speak for their own people. Once mediation is provided and legitimacy conferred, such newly legitimized leaders will lack incentives to implement a peace settlement, making the post-mediation peace less stable.

The Oslo peace process in the Middle East demonstrates how problems of legitimacy and spoilers often make long-term success using mediation especially difficult to attain in conflicts that involve non-state actors. The issue of who has the legitimate right to represent the Palestinian Arabs has plagued Middle East

---

31. For a related argument in which the potential for multiple challenges leads to conflict, see Walter (2006, 2009).

32. For an in-depth assessment of spoilers in civil-war peace processes, see Stedman (1997).

negotiations for decades. For example, Kissinger's attempt to broker a deal between Israel and Jordan regarding the West Bank faltered when the Arab League
recognized the PLO, and not the Kingdom of Jordan, as the sole representative of
the Palestinians in 1974.[33] Also, the participants in the 1978 Camp David peace
process did not make much progress in resolving the Palestinian question, in
part, because Egypt could not speak for the Palestinians and Israel refused to
negotiate with the PLO and thus recognize it as a viable political entity due to its
denial of the right of Israel to exist.

A new attempt to push for peace between Israel and the Palestinians renewed
in 1991 as part of the Madrid process when it became less clear to the Israeli
leadership that holding on to the occupied territories made Israel more secure.[34]
Moreover, Arafat's PLO became desperate for a breakthrough because it faced
major financial burdens. Its funding had dried up because it had supported the
Iraqi invasion of Kuwait and then witnessed its most important patron be defeated by a coalition that included other Arab states no longer wishing to donate
to the PLO cause.[35] The Madrid conference was the first time in which Palestinians participated in an Arab-Israeli peace process, but they were limited to merely
accompanying the Jordanian delegation. It took substantial pressure from U.S.
Secretary of State James Baker to allow even that to occur.[36] As difficult as it was
to achieve, such limited Palestinian representation made it very difficult to make
much substantive headway.[37]

The situation progressed further with the secretive Oslo talks, a continuation
of the Madrid process that in 1993 yielded the Declaration of Principles, also
known as the Oslo Accords. As part of this settlement, the PLO recognized the
right of Israel to exist and Israel recognized the PLO as the representative of the
Palestinian people. At the signing ceremony at the White House, Yitzak Rabin
and Yasser Arafat shook hands, further solidifying Arafat's place as leader of the
Palestinians. The Declaration of Principles also led directly to the formation of
the Palestinian Authority and established a framework for greater Palestinian
autonomy over a five-year period. Much of that framework was ultimately never

---

33. On the significance of the Rabat Declaration, see Stein (1999, 165–66).

34. For Rabin's justification for pushing for peace, see Clinton (2004, 545). See also Rabinovich
(2004, 43); Baker (1999).

35. See Behrendt (2007, 23–24).

36. James Baker notes, "One of the strongest points of leverage, with respect to all parties, was
the threat to, as I found myself saying all too often, lay the dead cat on their doorstep. No one wanted
to accept blame for scuttling the process. Some days this felt like the only leverage I had" (1999,
188). The United States also tied aid provisions to Israeli cooperation as another means of leverage
(Behrendt 2007, 14).

37. See Egeland (1999, 530).

implemented and failed to usher in a meaningful departure from the previous state of violent contestation.

It is arguable that on the White House lawn Arafat sought only recognition as an end in itself and never fully intended to take the difficult steps to reach a peaceful state of existence with Israel. After backing the wrong side in the Gulf War and being accused of being out of touch with local realities from his headquarters in Tunisia, Arafat was especially desperate for an affirmation of his leadership.[38] For this reason, his negotiators were insistent that the designation *PLO* replace all occurrences of *Palestinians* in the Declaration of Principles (Clinton 2004, 542; Egeland 1999, 537). That the Declaration of Principles was, in part, a myopic power grab that papered over the most difficult issues is at the root of Aaron David Miller's assessment that "For Arafat, Oslo was a trade-off: in exchange for recognizing him as the only Palestinian partner for Israel and America, he agreed to an interim process that deferred big issues like Jerusalem and refugees, and focused on mundane matters, such as actually governing what would become the Palestinian Authority" (2008, 60).

More starkly, some have claimed that Arafat was perniciously stalling for time to consolidate the power of the PLO and to wage a more effective campaign of terror in the years that followed. Shlomo Ben-Ami similarly argues that "Arafat's strategy was based on permanent negotiations," in the sense that his willingness to assent to the Declaration of Principles without assurances about Israeli settlements was really a "tactical plot aimed at sidelining the local leadership and gaining a foothold in the occupied territories from which he could move to the next stage in his wider strategy" (2005, 210). Others refute such claims, but we should at least note, even without evidence of a "smoking gun," that the use of a peace process for similar insincere motives is consistent with the expected risks of mediation in intrastate conflict.[39] This could certainly help explain why peace faltered after the significant breakthrough in the Declaration of Principles.

In addition to the potential problem of insincere motives, the Declaration of Principles also exacerbated the spoiler problem. By giving legitimacy to Arafat's leadership, the declaration generated stronger incentives for more radical groups, such as Hamas and Islamic Jihad, to disrupt the peace process and to assert their relevance in leading the cause for Palestinian rights and power. Shlomo Ben-Ami notes, "Hamas and Jihad lost no time in unleashing a campaign of terror in the hope that this would lead to the radicalisation of Israeli public

---

38. See Ross (2004, 709, 766–67); Ben-Ami (2005, 206–7).
39. For an overview of other such claims, as well as the rebuttals, see Rothstein (2006, 9–10); Rabinovich (2004, 305–6).

opinion and, consequently, to a shift to the right, which they expected would undermine and cripple Rabin's peace policies" (2005, 214).[40] The problem of spoilers was compounded by the fact that the bulk of the accords were crafted in secret with neither side making a concerted effort to sell them to a broad swath of their constituents. As a result, what was agreeable to the direct participants failed to filter down to the general public and appeared threatening to the elites left out of the conversation.[41] Speaking generally, Dennis Ross (2004, 762) similarly notes that extremists on both sides are frequently able to derail Middle East peace processes because Arab leaders tend to lack legitimacy—they are not democratically elected—and Israeli leaders preside over a very contentious landscape.

The importance of spoilers could be felt as the prospect of a full settlement steadily deteriorated after the signing of the Declaration of Principles, with increasing terrorist attacks that eventually culminated in an Israeli-Palestinian war of attrition, also called the Second Intifada, which erupted in 2000. Most notably, suicide bombings on February 25, 1996, left many Israelis questioning the peace process. Terrorist attacks by Hamas and Islamic Jihad incited Israel, especially since Arafat did not do enough to crack down on Palestinian extremists.[42] The February 1994 massacre of twenty-nine Palestinians in Hebron by an Israeli settler and the assassination of Rabin in 1995 by an Israeli extremist further demonstrate that extreme elements on the Israeli side, as well, felt threatened by the Oslo Accords and adopted violent measures to see that they would not be implemented.[43] Fractured Israeli politics contributed to a related spoiler problem, albeit a peaceful one, in the sense that Benjamin Netanyahu's premiership that began in 1996 put the brakes on implementing the Declaration of Principles (Pundak 2001, 33). The peace process had been struggling enough when Rabin was assassinated; the rise to power of an opposition leader who was not supportive of the Oslo process only compounded the problems.

The problems of legitimacy and spoilers, aggravated by the Oslo process, continued after Arafat's death when a war between Arafat's Fatah party and Hamas erupted. This intra-Palestinian conflict has not only directly increased violence in the region, but it has also indirectly made it more difficult to push for further agreements with Israel because Hamas will almost certainly not abide by any settlements made by Fatah. By attempting to co-opt the Palestinian leadership, in part through the Oslo process, Arafat and Fatah thus created greater incentives

---

40. See also Kemp and Pressman (1997, 74–79).

41. See Pundak (2001, 32); Egeland (1999, 541); Miller (2008, 381–83); Rothstein (2006, 7–8); Rabinovich (2004, 40, 57); Jones (1999, 138, 150).

42. On the effects of such attacks, see Kemp and Pressman (1997, 56); Pundak (2001, 33).

for other groups, such as Hamas, to overthrow the existing order, making sustainable peace unreachable.

Amid these threats to the long-term prospects for peace, it was thus all the more important for the international community to continue providing incentives for progress. Instead, the timeline for implementation was set at a mere five years. About this short time frame, Jan Egeland, one of the Norwegian diplomats instrumental in the peace process, writes, "Perhaps the biggest mistake made during the Oslo negotiations was to agree to judge the success of the peace process based on what could be achieved during a five-year period rather than over the course of a generation" (1999, 545).[44] Egeland's remarks speak directly to the struggle of mediation to enhance long-term peace. A self-sustaining peaceful relationship between Israel and the Palestinians could not be created, especially with assistance from third parties, in a five-year window. Although continued third-party engagement was needed, the Clinton administration, despite a number of follow-up conferences, was unable and unwilling to hold the parties sufficiently accountable and to cajole them into compliance. Dennis Ross, a key Clinton advisor on the peace process, admitted as much when he remarked, "I think [our] biggest mistake was letting a huge gap develop between the reality on the ground and the reality around the negotiating table. . . . From the beginning, we should have held both sides accountable for the commitments they made. We did not. And there are always good reasons, but once the commitments didn't have to be fulfilled, it created a mindset that commitments could be made but they didn't mean anything" (quoted in Enderlin 2002, 360–61).[45] As a result, peace faltered, leaving observers such as Avi Shlaim to lament that "the Oslo process actually worsened the situation in the occupied territories and confounded Palestinian aspirations for a state of their own" (2000, 530) because of the rise in extremism, drop in living standards in the territories from Israeli border closures, expansion of Israeli settlements, and Israeli retention of most of the scarce water resources. Charles Enderlin provides a rather scathing criticism of the Clinton administration for relying too heavily on the mere achievement of the signed accords when he writes, "The Clinton administration was unable to complete the political process that Yitzhak Rabin had begun without any American assistance. Because they did not understand that peace must first be made between nations and not solely between leaders, the peace team and the negotiators in both camps led the Middle East closer to hell" (2002, 361). Although such criticism belies

---

43. For details on the failure of the Oslo Accords, with particular emphasis on the importance of spoilers and domestic opposition, see Rabinovich (2004).

44. See also Rothstein (2006).

45. See also Pundak (2001, 40–41); Ross (2004, 770–71); Miller (2008, 260–68, 309–11).

the underlying difficulty of achieving peace in the Middle East, it does speak to the general tenor of my argument here that third-party involvement that tries to superficially patch up relations between antagonists will typically sow the seeds of renewed later conflict.

As a final note, the secret negotiations specifically in Norway did well to move the peace process forward with little risk of endangering long-term dynamics. Precisely because the talks were secret and not forced by a heavy-handed third party, these issues of legitimacy and insincere motives did not become factors until the negotiations were made public and the spectacle at the White House became possible. Indeed, the justification for the restricted Palestinian delegation at Madrid and the secretive talks in Oslo was to allow Palestinian representation while avoiding the issue of prematurely granting Arafat and the PLO the legitimacy that they sought.[46] The basic negotiation of the Declaration of Principles by low-level ministers carried less risk of these issues emerging, but Clinton's involvement in the ceremony and the handshake—motivated by the need to garner international support for the agreement and to give Arafat more of a stake in implementation—created the concerns about legitimacy and insincere motives.[47] In addition, the inability of the leaders to sell the accords to the wider domestic audiences after the peace process became public added to the perception that it was an agreement made by those in power imposed by fiat on those without. It might be argued that Arafat would never have consented to the signing of the Declaration of Principles without such a high-profile opportunity or with the requirement that he gain a broad coalition of support. If so, this further illustrates the nature of the dilemma that all the parties involved considered in 1993—that the pursuit of a landmark agreement would risk residual long-term struggles to attain a self-enforcing peace.

Insincere Motives: Sri Lanka

The potential for the disputants to have insincere motives for mediation is the final factor I consider here that is often stronger in intrastate conflict than in interstate conflict. This is not to say that actors in interstate conflicts do not exploit mediated peace processes to gain bargaining position—the DPRK example demonstrates such potential well. My argument is simply that the potential for

---

46. On the benefits of the secrecy of the talks, see Egeland (1999, 530, 538–39, 545); Egeland (2008, 166–67); Behrendt (2007, 27, 113).

47. For the motivation of the Clinton administration for the ceremony, see Ross (2004, 117–19).

mediation to be used for objectives other than peace is greater in civil wars, primarily because of the technologies of warfare. In interstate wars, the weapons of fighting are typically major industrial products, such as tanks, artillery, airplanes, bombs, and naval vessels. These take time and resources to produce, and opponents can typically decipher when the other side is building up its arms relatively easily. In addition, recruitment for military service is primarily done through official channels, and often there is a clear separation between civilians and soldiers. As a result, actors in interstate conflict find it difficult to mobilize discretely for renewed conflict, making it more difficult for them to exploit any period of cease-fire.

In contrast, actors in intrastate conflicts can more readily adopt the pretense of acquiescing while at the same time strengthening their positions and capacity to fight in the future. Insurgencies typically do not have the means to produce tanks, bombers, or battleships; instead, guerrilla armies primarily rely on small arms and improvised devices, which are easily concealed. They also recruit locally and in such a way that it is difficult to distinguish between rebel fighters and noncombatants. This is also true of paramilitary militias that often support the government but that remain separate from the official government forces.

Because mobilization can be more discrete in intrastate conflicts, peace processes and cease-fires are more prone to exploitation. Moreover, as we have seen in the discussion of the Madrid and Oslo processes, intrastate combatants often have the incentive to seek mediation primarily as a way to achieve recognition and not to actually resolve conflict. Given such potential for exploitation, mediated agreements often falter because the actors never intend to implement them but desire only a breather during which they can gain strength and legitimacy.

The 2002 Ceasefire Agreement (CFA) in Sri Lanka represents a classic case of a cease-fire reached in the midst of violent conflict that was not self-sustaining because of the insincere use of the mediated peace process. From 1983 until its defeat in 2009, the Liberation Tigers of Tamil Eelam (LTTE), led by Velupillai Prabhakaran, was a Sri Lankan insurgent group that attempted to create a separate state for the Tamil people. Norway mediated the CFA, which preserved relative peace until 2005.[48] Under that agreement, considerable autonomy was given to the LTTE, but the two sides returned to full-scale war in 2006 as violations of the cease-fire mounted and a more hard-line Sinhalese regime, led by President Percy Mahendra Rajapakse, took power. Rajapakse succeeded in reasserting government control over the entire island and ending the civil war.[49]

---

48. On the details of the peace process, see Höglund and Svensson (2002).

49. We should not presume that future Tamil groups will not again use violent struggle to demand greater autonomy, especially if the problem of displaced Tamils is not addressed.

We can make the case that both the LTTE and the Sri Lankan government benefited from a short-term cease-fire that allowed them to consolidate support among their constituents and rearm before returning to conflict in pursuit of ever-greater concessions. Although it is impossible to find definitive evidence that these were the primary motivating factors for their participation in the peace process, both sides exhibited a pattern of behavior consistent with their using mediation as a stalling tactic.

Let us start with the incentives of the LTTE, which had an interest in avoiding peace and saw in the mediated cease-fire an opportunity to maximize its profits from drawing out the conflict.[50] The LTTE justified its existence by the presence of struggle, and a permanent peace would have threatened its utility as a viable organization. Indeed, lucrative remittances declined during the more peaceful periods because interest in the conflict among the Sri Lankan Tamil diaspora waned (Human Rights Watch 2006). Prolonged spells of peace could in addition lead to the greater importance of business enterprises, the diaspora, and Jaffna elites, which would marginalize LTTE control.[51] The LTTE thus benefited from making insincere gestures of peace that actually lengthened conflict instead of shortening it.

The CFA also gave the LTTE space and time to gain strength through an aggressive recruiting campaign and the suppression of rival Tamil groups. This is perhaps best seen in its reliance on the conscription of child soldiers. A report from Human Rights Watch (2006) notes that the United Nations Children's Fund (UNICEF) documented 4,347 cases of child recruitment during 2002–2006, with over one-third of these cases involving children under the age of fifteen.[52] The report also estimates that there were around two hundred targeted killings from 2002 to 2006—during the cease-fire—in which the LTTE killed other Tamils from rival factions.

In addition to the illegal recruitment of child soldiers and the suppression of rival groups, the LTTE used the mediation initiative to gain international recognition as the only group to represent the Sri Lankan Tamils.[53] The LTTE has always insisted on bilateral talks with the Sinhalese government, excluding other Tamil groups from representation. Moreover, as part of the CFA conditions, the LTTE was able to secure not only protection for its own operations but

---

50. Bandarage (2009, 174) notes that the LTTE had a long history of using cease-fires to rearm, even before the CFA. See also Höglund and Svensson (2002, 2006).

51. The International Crisis Group (2006) has called this a "peace trap," in which the only way for the Tigers to get the more permanent terms of settlement that they demanded was to enter into a period of peace in which their own influence attenuated.

52. See also Bandarage (2009, 190–91).

53. See Bandarage (2009, 183).

also guarantees from the Sinhalese government to disband rival organizations.[54] Mediation was thus a way for the LTTE to legitimize its claim as representing the Tamil people. Indeed, Prabhakaran had reason to fear competing Tamil groups, as witnessed in how "Colonel Karuna" eventually led a split from the LTTE in 2004 and consolidated power in the east, making it easier for the government to pursue victory over the LTTE.

In this respect, one of the reasons that the CFA was so frustrating to many critics is that it actually enabled the LTTE to establish firmer control. The CFA helped weaken the potential for more of the Tamil population to be represented by other outlets and also turned a blind eye to the conscription of child soldiers and the imposition of illegal taxes on businesses.[55] Especially troublesome was the exclusion of Sri Lankan Monitoring Mission personnel from LTTE strongholds, where the Tigers could rearm and recruit with no oversight. The CFA also allowed aid to flow primarily through LTTE-controlled structures, such as through the Tamils Rehabilitation Organisation (TRO) in the aftermath of the 2004 tsunami, further enabling the Tigers to tap into new resources (Bandarage 2009, 184–96).

Finally, the LTTE had an additional incentive to seek mediation for insincere motives when it faced international pressure to move forward with the peace process. After September 11, 2001, the LTTE faced pressure to abandon its role in terrorism for fear of being implicated in the War on Terror (Höglund and Svensson 2002). Its going through the motions of a peace process was thus a way to avoid international scrutiny while settlement was not an objective.

Turning to the Sinhalese government, we see that its motivations to use mediation as a stalling tactic were twofold. First, the government faced mounting losses and a decrease in bargaining position in the lead-up to the CFA. The Norwegian mediation began after a very bloody period in 2000 and 2001, and the high levels of casualties led to the perception of substantial short-term costs of conflict.[56] Not only were the costs of conflict steep, but there had been noticeable setbacks for the government forces. In April 2000, the LTTE succeeded in overrunning the most fortified army base, and in July 2001 a small rebel team on a suicide mission destroyed half the air fleet at the Colombo airport. Moreover, the government was noticeably weakening, partly because of the strain of the conflict, as its GDP fell by 1.5 percent in 2001 (International Crisis Group

---

54. A report from the International Crisis Group (2006) similarly criticizes the CFA.

55. For more on these critiques, see International Crisis Group (2006); Bandarage (2009, 180–99).

56. On the perceived costs of the conflict, see Bandarage (2009, 168); Höglund and Svensson (2002).

2006). The Sinhalese government thus had strong incentives to seek a break in hostilities and to delay the negotiation process until it was better able to bargain from strength.

Second, domestic pressure against the war had increased such that it was politically convenient for the government to feign movement toward a peaceful settlement. Both dominant Sinhalese political parties, the United National Party (UNP) and the Sri Lanka Freedom Party (SLFP), had a history of cutting deals with the LTTE to secure greater representation and thus benefited from being able to use "ethnic outbidding" for minority votes (Bandarage 2009, 177). Playing along with a peace process provided an opportunity to woo Tamil votes, or at least to minimize mass Tamil support for the opposition party, after which the incumbent party intended to continue the struggle against the LTTE. Stalling also allowed the parties to create an image of seeking peace for a wider public increasingly discontent with the costs of endless war. The discontent concerning the government handling of the civil war was evident in the dramatic 2001 electoral victory of the UNP while running on a platform of moving toward a negotiated settlement.[57] Prior to its electoral losses in 2001, President Kumaratanga's SLFP had already invited Norway to broker talks in an effort to blunt criticism for its failed policies of aggression. It appears that there was thus a political motivation for beginning the mediation process in 2000. The mediation continued to be a political tool after the UNP came to power, in that the peace process allowed the UNP to present the image that it was the sole representative of the Sinhalese majority.

It is possible to argue that these characteristics of high conflict costs and domestic discontent should actually lead to *sincere* mediation. Although this is a possibility in general and should be considered, in the Sri Lankan case it does not appear that the government actually used the peace process and cease-fire to make lasting strides toward a peaceful resolution. The UNP, led by Ranil Wickremesinghe, excluded the opposition parties, mainly the SLFP and the Janatha Vimukthi Peramuna (JVP; People's Liberation Front), as well as the Muslim community from the peace process. Any meaningful long-term progress toward peace, however, would have required a multilateral approach because of the deep political divisions and the frequent power shifts between the UNP and SLFP. So, an ex post assessment of the Sinhalese government actions does not support the notion that it was sincerely seeking permanent conflict resolution at the time of the CFA.

---

57. See Höglund and Svensson (2002).

A Chance for Sustainable Peace?: Crisis Management Initiative in Aceh

Thus far, we have considered four factors—extreme vulnerability, the need for a social contract for effective governance, the problem of spoilers, and the potential for insincere motives—that are prominent in intrastate conflicts and that can make the long-term impact of mediation even riskier. I end on a more optimistic note and now consider a characteristic of many civil wars that can make them more amenable to successful mediation in both the short and long run—many intrastate conflicts, because they have endured for so long and involve combatants that are quite familiar with one another, do not have as much of an informational problem related to relative capabilities as interstate conflicts.[58] We can see this in the case of the 2005 Memorandum of Understanding (MoU), negotiated between the Free Aceh Movement (GAM) and the Indonesian government. This case additionally has the potential to yield a lasting peace because the other four problems considered in this chapter have been minimal.

Mediation in intrastate conflicts often operates in an environment that approximates a pure credible commitment problem, with relatively weaker informational barriers to settlement. Because civil wars typically last for many years among combatants that coexist within the same territory, informational problems have a greater opportunity to be resolved over time. So, to return to the discussion of vulnerability earlier in the chapter, credible commitment problems tend to dominate the difficulties of reaching a lasting settlement in a civil war because of the severe vulnerabilities that can accompany disarmament. The ideal role of the third party in these situations is to provide enough incentives for peace to prevent defection until the political and security relationships have been consolidated and the vulnerability decreases. With low uncertainty, the combatants should have a decent sense about what the ultimate mutually agreeable settlement looks like but simply need a means to get there without facing existential threats. Less uncertainty also allows the actors to renegotiate settlements more easily when needed. Mediators, if they are to provide meaningful long-term benefits, must serve as trustees—as bridges to more self-enforcing arrangements that should be relatively clear because of low levels of uncertainty. This requires care and patience on the part of the third party; we saw earlier in the case of Rwanda the disastrous consequences of promising such a bridge and luring the parties forward without sufficient follow through.

---

58. Fearon (2004) makes a similar point and focuses on commitment problems at the root of civil war.

The mediation by Martii Ahtisaari and his Crisis Management Initiative (CMI) in Aceh demonstrates third-party involvement providing such a bridge to a self-enforceable agreement. When Ahtisaari mediated between Indonesia and the breakaway Aceh province, the relative fighting capabilities of both sides were no longer in doubt after three decades of fighting and the 2004 tsunami that decimated GAM. Even before the tsunami, the GAM leadership had begun to realize that it could not achieve sufficient military success to justify its demands for independence and came to realize that autonomy without independence was preferable to ongoing conflict.[59] The devastation of the tsunami and the entice-ments of international aid increased the attractiveness of a peaceful settlement even more.[60] The tsunami contributed to a sense of desperation for peace that shifted domestic pressures on both sides toward making concessions instead of withholding them. Once the sides had a clear perception of what a durable solu-tion might look like, they had to get through the transition period in which GAM disarmed to become a purely political entity. After the 2004 tsunami, five rounds of talks were held in Helsinki, which produced the MoU on July 17, 2005. Un-like previous conflict resolution attempts, this one did receive widespread sup-port and was successfully implemented. Per the MoU, local elections were held in Aceh on December 11, 2006 for a new governor and a local parliament with increased autonomy. At present, it appears that a stable peace has been achieved. Through careful monitoring and other peacebuilding initiatives, Ahtisaari and CMI created an environment in which the transition to peace could proceed at acceptable levels of risk. In part for his role in this peace process, Ahtisaari was awarded the 2008 Nobel Peace Prize.

For the CMI mediation ultimately to produce a stable, self-enforcing peaceful relationship, it had to avoid the other factors endemic in intrastate conflicts that can worsen the interference of mediation with durable conflict resolution. First, although the international community became actively involved in the conflict management efforts, it did not pressure the parties into concessions that made them extremely vulnerable to defection. This was accomplished during both the negotiation and implementation stages. In the negotiation stage, CMI lacked sufficient leverage to pressure either GAM or the Indonesian government into concessions that were uncomfortable. In addition, Ahtisaari insisted on a com-prehensive settlement that helped avoid the timing issues that either side could exploit after agreement had been reached on a single beneficial piece.[61] In the

---

59. See Aspinall (2009, 222, 232).

60. On the importance of tsunami aid, see Aspinall (2009, 233); Feith (2007).

61. Ahtisaari insisted on the principle that "nothing is agreed until everything is agreed" (Aspi-nall 2009, 233, 236).

implementation phase, the deployment of the Aceh Monitoring Mission (AMM) was immediate, so that portions were already in place at the time of agreement. This greatly facilitated the ability for GAM to disarm and for the Indonesian military (Tentara Nasional Indonesia, TNI) to withdraw with less fear of being vulnerable to a major attack.[62] Whereas Rwanda is an example of the dangerous combination of strong international pressure and lackadaisical follow-through, Aceh is an example of gentle international engagement and committed effort to provide security guarantees. The timing of the peace process with regard to the reforms in Indonesian governance also contributed to there being less vulnerability. With democracy becoming stronger under President Susilo Bambang Yudhoyono and Vice President Jusuf Kalla, and reforms underway that brought TNI more under civilian control, the GAM leadership could feel more secure in its ability to retain power through legitimate political means and not be subjected to the brutal attacks from TNI or its agents that we observed in East Timor in 1999.[63]

Second, the CMI mediation did not have as great a risk of interfering with the social contract between ruler and ruled as, for example, the U.S. involvement in Haiti. Among the key points of agreement were that the Acehnese could be represented by local political parties and that elections would be held soon after agreement.[64] By doing this, the bonds of accountability and co-dependence dramatically *increased* after the agreement because the people now had a clear mechanism to express their voice. This accountability was a stark improvement over what had existed during the conflict, when much of the GAM leadership was in exile in Sweden and thus detached from the local population. With the local elections, GAM was able to transition from a military movement to a political movement.[65]

Third, the international involvement did not create the problem of prematurely legitimizing the GAM leadership's claims for independence. Although GAM sought such recognition, the international community responded coolly.[66] The potential for spoilers was also reduced through the emphasis on elections, which allowed the new leadership to emerge through a deliberative electoral process and not to be imposed by fiat. Even those not at the negotiating table thus had the opportunity to generate support for their candidacy and compete for leadership roles. Moreover, electoral losers could always lobby those in power

---

62. See Feith (2007).
63. On the importance of the Indonesian reforms, see Aspinall (2009, 15, 241); Feith (2007).
64. See Aspinall (2009, 237). Feith (2007) also describes the intentional efforts by the AMM to build local community consensus.
65. On this transition, see Aspinall (2009, 240).
66. See Aspinall (2009 227–29, 234).

and also try again in the future. That is, the mediation process and its promise of elections did not mute the voice of other constituencies absent from the negotiating table. In addition, AMM demobilization, disarmament, and reintegration (DDR) programs proved important in increasing the incentives for former combatants to buy into the system and not to try to spoil the peace process (Aspinall 2009, 243).

Finally, the CMI mediation did not have to contend with much potential for insincere motives. There were few opportunities for GAM to exploit. Unlike the LTTE, GAM did not receive much support from abroad and was more dependent on the people and thus less able and willing to recruit by force.[67] Moreover, even though there were major gas deposits present in the province, GAM did not have the capability to tap into them (Ross 2005). On the Indonesian side, the military had been sufficiently dominant in the years preceding the agreement that stalling would not have been advantageous.

Although it appears that the MoU has ushered in a durable peace in Aceh, we must of course remain cautious. As the previous analyses have revealed, the proclivity for a return to conflict after mediation sometimes takes a decade or so to materialize. There are four issues that follow from the CMI mediation that may yet prove destabilizing. First, the 2006 elections indicated a split in the former GAM leadership, between the elites in exile and those on the ground. The candidates preferred by the local elites won, which has potentially irked the exiled leadership and the general diaspora. It is not clear if the losers will attempt to spoil the new political dynamic to recapture influence. Another potential danger is a change in Indonesian leadership. The Yudhoyono regime has proven capable of abiding by its commitments and reining in the military, but the commitment of future administrations remains uncertain, especially given the shallow history of Indonesian democratic rule. An additional factor to consider is that the international support for the peace process that followed the 2004 tsunami is, of course, only temporary, and it remains to be seen how the incentives will shift as external aid diminishes. Moreover, the desperation for peace felt in the wake of the tsunami may also prove temporary, and there is a possibility that a resurgence in demands for independence will emerge as the Acehnese begin to prosper. It is reassuring, nonetheless, that the peace process would probably have proven successful even without the tsunami. Finally, the AMM is a delicate hybrid of EU and Association of Southeast Asian Nations (ASEAN) personnel, which could lead to coordination difficulties moving forward, even though the original mediation initiative involved a single international actor.

---

67. On the contrast between the LTTE and GAM, see Beardsley and McQuinn (2009).

In this chapter, I have examined through a number of illustrative case studies how the mediation dilemma might play out more strongly in civil wars. In the case of Rwanda, we observed that the greater vulnerability in intrastate conflicts, where former combatants must coexist, can make mediation particularly precarious in the long run. The Haiti case demonstrates that third parties have the potential to interfere with the mutual dependence between the governed and those governing that must exist in stable polities. We then considered the Oslo Middle East peace process, noting that third parties can affect the contest for legitimacy that often occurs in civil wars and can create the incentives for spoilers to emerge. The Sri Lankan conflict reveals that the nature of insurgency can generate incentives to use mediation for insincere motives and derail any post-mediation peace. Finally, we identified the mediation in Aceh as a potential example of a case in which the bargaining environment and the mediator techniques were conducive to reaching both a short- and long-term peace.

In the final chapter, I use these cases, along with the findings in the previous chapters, to understand when mediation is more worthwhile for conflict management and when mediation might be better if avoided, as well as how mediators can maximize their efficacy.

IMPLICATIONS, APPLICATIONS, AND CONCLUSIONS

All wars are follies, very expensive, and very mischievous ones. When will mankind be convinced of this, and agree to settle their differences by arbitration? Were they to do it, even by the cast of a dye, it would be better than by fighting and destroying each other.

—Benjamin Franklin, 1783

The quotation from Leo Tolstoy that begins this book laments the "impotency of human reason" to understand and avoid war. In the same letter, Tolstoy also writes that "Enlightened men cannot but know that occasions for war are always such as are not worth not only one human life, but not one-hundredth part of all that which is spent upon wars" (1904, 4). Like Benjamin Franklin, Tolstoy sees war as a wasteful enterprise that costs even the victors more than they gain. Scholars who treat war as a purely rational outcome of strategic behavior also understand it to be inefficient, in that war almost always ends in some settlement that was available prior to the loss of life and coin. Thus, one does not have to be a great moralist like Tolstoy to be convinced that war is folly from the standpoint of the common good. The challenge that lies before us is to use reason to understand better how political leaders can most effectively lead their people while minimizing the call to arms. As this book has shown, although third-party assistance in bargaining processes can certainly play an important role in this regard, it is by no means an antidote with only trivial side effects.

As we have learned, mediation, especially the heavy-handed variety, typically entails substantial long-term risks. At the same time, mediation is often necessary for conflict to give way to any semblance of peace. We have seen that mediation contributes to a number of short-term peaceful benefits including greater abilities for actors to achieve robust formal agreements, concessions, and lulls of peace. Third-party conflict management also offers the actors a chance to gamble on a different path toward resolution when their existing paths have proven fruitless. When actors become certain that the bilateral negotiations are going nowhere, they might take a flier on having a mediator inject new dynamics that, at least, may increase their chances of enjoying a peaceful lull and, at most, may lead to a much-needed breakthrough. That mediation more often leads to a decrease in long-term peace does not necessarily make it a bad bet. Even when outside involvement makes the long-term prospects for peace grim, which is certainly not always the case, mediation can be strictly better—to the disputing parties as well as to the international community—than the alternative of escalating hostilities. My argument and analysis in this book thus urge prudence, not pessimism, when considering mediation as a conflict management vehicle.

Oftentimes the short- and long-term trade-off is anticipated in advance, and from the standpoint of both the disputants and concerned observers, the potential benefits that mediation brings, even if only temporary or rare, can make the long-term risks worthwhile. Moreover, when mediation is judged to be worthwhile given the long-term risks, the participants can take steps—such as being more selective in the use of leverage and the inclusion of multiple third parties—to decrease the potential for external involvement to produce an unsustainable peace. That being said, mediation in some cases should be avoided, for example, if the downside of instability is likely to be great (e.g., when massive civilian fatalities are likely to result from conflict recurrence) or if the upside of short-term peace and a potential for breakthrough is not sufficiently substantial.

When considering case studies such as those in this book, it is natural to reflect on whether the third parties could have done better to minimize the trade-off between short-term peace and long-term stability. Often actors face a true dilemma, such that there is no ideal option to enhance both. Pursuing the option of mediation can be considered optimal compared to what would probably transpire without mediation or with mediation of a different type. In such situations, the third parties and combatants would choose the same course of action even if they could accurately assess the long-term consequences of their efforts. In other cases, we expect that reasonable combatants and third parties would choose differently if they could anticipate the stark trade-off correctly.

It is difficult, of course, to speculate about the wisdom of past conflict management choices because in hindsight we tend to take the outcomes as given even though at the time of decision they really had some probability distribution around their potential occurrence. That is, an action may have truly been a good idea, given the likelihood of events transpiring, but not turn out well because of misfortune. For example, if you can pay $1 to win $5 if you roll anything other than a six with a standard die, you should play that game. Even if you do roll a six, it was still a good idea to play. Similarly, when we assess the prudence of historical choices, whether the decision to launch a land war in Asia, to kick a field goal, or to participate in mediation, we must look beyond the actual outcome and instead consider the uncertainty involved at the time the decision was made.

So, taking up again the three cases of interstate conflict considered at length in this book, we can ask whether Henry Kissinger, Jimmy Carter, or Theodore Roosevelt, as well as the disputants in each case, could have adopted a different course of action to maximize the prospects of durable peace while achieving their objectives. With regard to the U.S. involvement in the Middle East between 1973 and 1979, we have observed that many of the decision makers anticipated and struggled with the dilemma and still resolved to push forward with the disengagement agreements, the Camp David Accords, and the Egyptian-Israeli Peace Treaty. A comprehensive peace, regardless of which conflict management strategies were chosen and regardless of whether Carter and future U.S. administrations could have sustained a high level of engagement, still faced significant hurdles. So, the parties involved found the risk of nailing down the interstate peace, even without strong linkages, worth taking in light of how much peaceful Egyptian-Israeli relations would mean to regional and global stability.

That being said, hindsight does suggest that perhaps both Kissinger and Carter missed two opportunities to make more progress on the comprehensive front. Given King Hussein's waning ability to speak for the Palestinian Arabs, Kissinger might have sought an agreement between Israel and Jordan much sooner, while regional tensions remained high in the wake of the October War and before the Arab League legitimized the PLO.[1] Although not a silver bullet that would have resolved the questions about Palestinian autonomy or statehood, this could have improved the chances of eventually reaching a comprehensive peace by beginning substantive discussions about possible autonomous Arab leadership in the West Bank (Judea and Samaria) and the status of the Israeli settlements much sooner than the early 1990s. Moreover, Carter would have done well not to have spent the first year of his presidency, when his political capital was at its zenith, on the vain pursuit of a return to Geneva. He would then have had more time to push for progress on the Framework for Peace before other concerns dominated his agenda. Both lessons point to how the timing of mediation can be an important element in determining how steep the trade-off between short-term success and long-term stability can be.[2] Just as some moments are better for de-escalation than others, some moments have a better constellation of actors and interests in place to improve the chances for the successful implementation of a

---

1. Isaacson (1992, 630–31) also considers this missed opportunity.

2. For an account of how timing matters in conflict abatement in the short term, see Regan and Stam (2000).

mediated agreement. Some ways in which these moments can be better identified are discussed later in the chapter.

With regards to the DPRK case, Carter's mediation yielded greater dividends for peace than originally expected, given his lack of tangible leverage and the well-demonstrated pattern of DPRK exploitation of peace processes. A strong case can be made that it was worth the effort because the DPRK nuclear arsenal would almost certainly be larger today without the eight-year nuclear freeze. The counterfactual argument that the nuclear crisis that has emerged since 2002 could have been avoided had Clinton gone ahead with sanctions and a potential military strike in 1994 rests on two specious assumptions: that the DPRK did not yet have enough reprocessed fissile material in 1994 to manufacture a device and that it would not have moved ahead with the uranium program in the absence of a nuclear freeze. The first assumption is not consistent with intelligence reports, and the second assumption does not seem plausible because a strike against the Yongbyon facility would only have increased the DPRK perception that it needed an uranium enrichment capability, which could be more easily hidden. The point here is that, even though an unmediated agreement probably would have been more stable than the Agreed Framework, it is doubtful that any agreement would have been reached absent Carter's mediation. That is, it is likely that the 1994 crisis would have morphed into the more recent one with no interlude. In hindsight, however, perhaps Carter could have drawn out the process and first gained strong ROK support, making the negotiation and implementation of the Agreed Framework smoother, or at least less easy for a perfidious DPRK regime to manipulate.

Turning to the Treaty of Portsmouth, we find that, because it was mainly a success story, there was not much that Roosevelt might have done differently to enhance both the short-term and long-term prospects for peace between Japan and Russia. Roosevelt did not employ much direct pressure to reach the agreement. We must recognize, however, that because the parties were more or less self-motivated in pursuing peace and because one of Roosevelt's main accomplishments was to simply get out of the way until he was needed, there is only a limited amount of advice that we can glean from this case. Roosevelt was fortunate to have such a favorable bargaining environment in 1905, and he also did not miss the opportunity to provide a few key nudges and suggestions along the way. Perhaps, however, an opportunity was missed to better pin down Japanese rights in Manchuria and commitments to keeping trade open in China because the vague formulations at Portsmouth were easy to manipulate ex post and contributed to later Chinese and U.S. animosity toward Japan. Side agreements with China and the United States could have decreased the rising tensions between Japan and these key players.

In each of the interstate cases, the risks of mediation were justified in terms of maximizing the objectives of those involved. The same cannot be said about some of the intrastate cases presented in chapter 6. The most obvious case of mediation misstep is the international pressure for agreement in Rwanda at Arusha, which created massive vulnerabilities after the third parties did not follow through with their peacekeeping commitments, resulting in genocide. And it is not as if such brutality was completely unforeseen—similar clashes between Hutus and Tutsis had plagued the region for decades. As destructive as the ongoing civil war in Rwanda would have been until a more natural settlement—or perhaps a RPF victory—was reached, the ability for the RPF to continue fighting would have most likely deterred and defended against the type of brutality that erupted in April 1994.

Similarly, the heavy-handed U.S. involvement in Haiti in hindsight appears extremely counterproductive in securing democratic governance and also did not generate sufficient short-term benefits to justify the insistence that Aristide be returned to power. Perhaps, for U.S. interests, the involvement of the United States was still worthwhile to secure democracy in the hemisphere by deterring future coups, but that is a benefit not apparently enjoyed by the Haitian people. That being said, the initiative by Carter, Nunn, and Powell, who, incidentally, anticipated the resulting governance problems, did well to avert hostilities and is not itself culpable for the difficulty in establishing effective governance in Haiti. Given that the United States was determined to restore Aristide, their efforts proved useful; it is that U.S. determination that is open to criticism here.

The U.S. involvement in the Oslo Middle East peace process and the Norwegian mediation in Sri Lanka resulted in clear trade-offs, but it is less clear whether third-party involvement in these cases made things worse than noninvolvement would have. In both cases, we might argue, the probability of settlement in these protracted conflicts was sufficiently small that, at worst, mediation could make things only more difficult at the margins. The risks of making hostilities much worse than they would otherwise be were considerably less in these cases than in Rwanda and Haiti. Yet the Sri Lankan civil war eventually resumed after the CFA was abandoned and ended with government victory, after massive costs of war and the displacement of hundreds of thousands of noncombatants. To be fair, Norway lacked leverage in Sri Lanka, so it is difficult to make the case that it forced an agreement that left the LTTE vulnerable to eventual absolute defeat in 2009, especially when we consider that the LTTE did its best to exploit the peace process and that much of the criticism directed at the Norwegian intermediaries was for supporting the LTTE too much. Similarly, the Israeli-Palestinian conflict resumed in full force after the Oslo process completely collapsed at Camp David in 2000, yielding to the Second Intifada. Here, too, we must consider that the likelihood of this complex and intractable conflict continuing on a similar course even without U.S. intervention was quite high. The chance to take some strides toward a comprehensive peace was arguably worth the costs and risks. Dennis Ross and David Makovsky echo this sentiment in their assessment of U.S. involvement in Israeli-Palestinian relations: "Whatever the limitations of engagement, there was one profound difference from disengagement: when Israelis and Palestinians are talking, they are less likely to be shooting. There may still be violence, but the scale is vastly different" (2009, 106). In fact, many lament that the Clinton administration squandered a crucial chance to be *more* engaged in the push for peace between the Israelis and the Palestinians because the environment following the Oslo Accords was particularly favorable to a path-breaking compromise.[3]

Beyond the question of whether the risks were worth taking, in both these cases hindsight suggests that an alternative *means* of mediation could have fared better. In both cases, the mediators provided legitimacy to leaders of nonstate actors by allowing them to operate explicitly as the sole representatives of their people. This reduced their incentives to continue compromising and increased the incentives of other factions to spoil the agreements.[4] In the Oslo process, and following the criticisms levied in chapter 6, the relevant question is not really whether the United States should have been involved in the Madrid and Oslo processes in the first place but, rather, whether mutual recognition between Israel and the PLO was worth pursuing directly and whether the United States could have better committed to more sustained engagement while continually holding Arafat and the Israelis accountable. Once the U.S. team decided on the course that gave Arafat the legitimacy that he sought, much more follow-through was required, particularly in regard to raising the incentives and capabilities for Arafat to self-police the more extreme Palestinian elements. The Sri Lankan case also reveals the potential for actors to exploit a mediated peace process in pursuit of consolidating power. By not providing clear guidelines for how to deal with noncompliant behavior or a strict timeline for further steps, the CFA allowed the parties to benefit from their insincere participation in the peace process. It is quite possible, however, that the Oslo Accords or the CFA would have never been signed if different approaches that withheld recognition had been used, which

---

3. See, for example, Miller (2008, 247–49).

4. It is interesting that, whereas the split between Arafat's Fatah party and the Hamas spoilers has made peace with Israel even more precarious, the split between the LTTE and Karuna actually made it possible for the Sri Lankan government forces to rout the LTTE and end the civil war. So, the unintended consequences of conferring legitimacy to nonstate actors in the case of the Oslo Accords made conflict even more intractable, but in Sri Lanka it helped lead to the possibility of peace through government victory.

brings us back to the mediation dilemma—the long-term risks to peace might have been necessary to make any immediate progress.

Policy-Relevant Recommendations

With these case studies in mind, seven recommendations are worth considering. *First, mediation should be used sparingly when there are major vulnerabilities to failed implementation.* We see this most prominently in the case of Rwanda, in which the mediators at Arusha promised a level of enforcement that could not be delivered and excluded key stakeholders. The resulting window of vulnerability became so destabilizing that it would have been wiser to limit the external peace-making efforts at Arusha. Third parties must be aware of the full implications of their involvement, and, although the risks are generally low in merely hosting talks, they need to holster their use of leverage when it is unlikely to foster an arrangement that will prove acceptable after the influence of the third party declines. Third parties should be especially cautious when mediating intrastate conflicts in which actors are already experiencing rather severe security dilemmas and related commitment problems. Creating a false sense of security can quickly degenerate into massive violence.

When the international community is unable to maintain its commitments, selective partitioning, as has occurred in the North-South Sudanese conflict, could be an option.[5] Even though it has not fully precluded conflict relapse, at the very least, the 2005 mediated agreement in Sudan did not generate massive vulnerabilities for genocide—as seen in Darfur—because the South remained well armed. In many cases, however, partitioning and autonomous agreements that leave the competing forces intact are not possible, as when rebel groups are fighting over the government and not for control of some region; in others, they are something that no government would allow unless forced to admit complete defeat. They can also worsen vulnerability concerns when the partitioning leaves ethnic enclaves unprotected. So, partition is not likely to be an attractive option typically available to most mediators.

Second, third parties need to be aware of issues related to legitimacy. This also relates principally to intrastate conflicts. By favoring those in power, third parties can weaken the mutual dependence domestically that is necessary for good governance; by recognizing the political standing of nonstate actors, third parties can undermine the legitimate authority of a state and exacerbate commitment

---

5. For a study finding that partitioning can provide a soluton to the commitment problem in civil wars, see Chapman and Roeder (2007).

problems; and by including only certain challengers, third parties can increase the incentives of spoiler groups to thwart the peace process. Of course, the recognition problem in particular is frequently unavoidable because a peace process without the key participants is not likely to accomplish much. One point here is that third parties would do well not to push for talks when one side is principally interested in recognition and will have no incentive to implement a compromise once the recognition is achieved.

Let us consider another example of the recognition problem. A difficult choice has arisen for NATO in trying to address the conflict between the Taliban and the Afghan government. Without talks between the Taliban and the government, peace will be impossible unless the Taliban is fully defeated—an outcome that, to date, appears remote. Nonetheless, involving the Taliban as an official negotiating partner—as is increasingly likely at time of writing—would provide recognition that the Afghan government and its allies cannot provide basic security and thereby help the Taliban gain support from segments of the population. That is, ignoring the Taliban will not make peace any more likely but negotiating directly with it could threaten the long-term viability of the government. A middle ground would be to encourage elements of the Taliban to evolve into a legitimate political force that operates within the legal bounds of the Afghan constitution. To do this, talks might be held with representatives or allies of the Taliban who are not themselves directly involved in the armed struggle—not unlike the role that Sinn Fein played in representing some of the (Provisional) Irish Republican Army (IRA) interests in Northern Ireland. Even this alternative course, however, has its difficulties. The 2010 incident in which the British intelligence service MI6 mediated between the Afghan government and an impostor claiming to be Akthar Mohammad Mansour, a Taliban leader—all the while the U.S. Central Intelligence Agency (CIA) lacked a White House directive to be involved in direct talks with the Taliban—demonstrates just how difficult it can be to foster such a peace process in practical terms.

Mediators can sometimes, as seen in Aceh, minimize problems of legitimacy by insisting that elections and other liberal institutional reforms follow a signed settlement; third-party support and recognition are less meaningful in establishing legitimacy when the people have the chance to define their representatives for themselves. But caution must also be used when an external actor supports liberalization; Roland Paris (2004) has demonstrated that liberalization before adequate institutional structures are in place can be another disaster awaiting former combatants in the post-conflict environment. Too often elections can provide the spark setting off violence, as the 2011 turmoil in Cote d'Ivoire exemplifies, when poll results are easily manipulated and firm processes for challenging the election results are not in place.

Third, outside actors should intervene more carefully when the disputants could benefit from using mediation for ends other than peace. In both the DPRK and Sri Lankan cases, insincere objectives help explain both the occurrences of mediation and the failures to reach lasting agreements. But the potential for such motives need not always deter third parties from trying to create a major breakthrough. Instead, they should be as careful as possible not to allow the disputants to exploit the peace processes. Specifically, cease-fires and temporary agreements should be permitted only when all parties can verify that their opponents are not regrouping and preparing for later aggression. For example, the United States was able to verify that the DPRK was not producing any plutonium while the Agreed Framework was in effect, making it difficult for the DPRK to exploit the arrangement. This stands in contrast to the rounds of six-party talks in which the DPRK was able to stall and extort aid, all the while building its nuclear arsenal. Similarly, cease-fires should be given a short deadline and clear benchmarks for compliance, so actors cannot get away with limitless stalling. In addition, third parties would do well to look for signs of stalling, as when leaders fail to prepare their publics for difficult compromises.[6]

This concern for insincere motives also applies to my second recommendation regarding legitimacy concerns in the presence of multiple stakeholders vying for recognition. Whether or not it could have been avoided, the fact remains that the Oslo process gave Arafat and his Fatah party the recognition that they sought as the legitimate representatives of the Palestinians, and, once achieved, this decreased their incentive to move forward in the peace initiative and exacerbated the spoiler problem. The more recent U.S.-led peace process that, to date, has included only Mahmoud Abbas to the exclusion of Hamas has further widened the schisms among the Palestinian Arabs and thereby made it more difficult for any self-sustaining settlement to be found. If it is impossible to have Israel sit down at the same table with Hamas because doing so would legitimize its denial of the right of Israel to exist and validate its refusal to denounce terrorism, then a crucial first step in the Middle East peace process would be reaching a stronger intra-Palestinian accord than what was reached in spring 2011. Only when that happens can representatives of the Palestinian people—not specifically Fatah or Hamas—enter into fruitful negotiations with Israel. As Aaron David Miller writes, "The Hamas problem to which there is no clear, quick, or easy solution boils down to this: without a unified Palestinian leadership that controls all the Palestinians, guns, and loyalties, no Israeli-Palestinian peace process will be possible" (2008, 381). Of course, third-party participation in such an endeavor entails

---

6. Dennis Ross (2004, 769) makes this point in the context of the Middle East.

having to deal directly with Hamas. Although some risk of legitimizing Hamas in intra-Palestinian talks is still present, it is much less than the risks arising from having Hamas and Israel actually at the same table.

Fourth, potential third parties should hesitate to become involved in a peace process when coordination on implementation is likely to prove difficult. The empirical findings in chapter 5 indicate that including multiple third parties or IGOs in mediation efforts provides two of the strongest detrimental effects on long-term peace. Having multiple decision points creates confusion and makes coordination in the post-conflict environment unwieldy. Similarly, actors in the international system should rely less on the UN and other collective bodies and more on individual states to provide mediation.[7] Collective bodies, without discounting their other benefits to international peace and security, are not well suited to producing self-enforcing arrangements between combatants. Relevant to contemporary events, the potential for renewed tension in the DRC after the massive peacekeeping force is eventually reduced is particularly worrisome because many actors have been involved as both peacemakers and peacekeepers and it is not readily evident which one would be most responsible for keeping the many state and nonstate stakeholders in the region accountable.

Although I do not examine it in the quantitative models, another policy-relevant implication is that states that experience frequent leadership turnover can struggle in credibly committing to long-term implementation assistance because the leaders who promise such assistance may not be the ones who are in office when it is time to follow through on that promise. Security guarantees from democracies are particularly concerning because foreign policy priorities are prone to shift from administration to administration. For example, as we observed, Reagan's commitment to a comprehensive Middle East peace paled in comparison to Carter's, making implementation of the Framework for Peace nearly impossible after 1981.

Fifth, the use of leverage itself is not actually a source of long-term instability; it is the attenuation over time of that leverage that increases the propensity for renegotiation. As the case of Egyptian-Israeli relations demonstrates, the constant application of leverage after a conflict can help sustain peace. Similarly, writing about the potential issues that arise when third parties try to rush through an agreement ending a civil war, Stephen John Stedman notes,

> On its face there is nothing wrong with an incomplete, expedient agreement, as long as it is mediated with an understanding that a flimsy

---

7. Touval (1994) makes this point more strongly.

> agreement signed under duress will likely demand much more forceful implementation than if the agreement is the product of lengthy, gradual relationship-building among adversaries. Expedient peace agreements only become problematic when coercive strategies are unavailable to the implementer. (2002, 11)

The point here is that third parties would do well to use substantial leverage in providing the incentives for conflict abatement only when they can sustain their level of involvement over time. If they cannot, then the combatants become more likely to return to conflict when the artificially imposed incentives from the third party disappear. Related to my recommendation four, this means that leverage should mostly be avoided when there are multiple third parties and co-ordination barriers. Even Richard Holbrooke (1998, 132, 232), who advocated "bombs for peace" while mediating in the Bosnian war, notes that heavy-handed third-party involvement can be effective only when there is a single actor in control of the peace process. Despite the relative success of securing a semblance of peace in Bosnia using heavy-handed tactics—in part because the international community remained involved for fear that renewed tensions in the Balkans could threaten greater European security—it is worth noting that Holbrooke (1998, 362) further posits that one of the flaws of the Dayton Accords was the setting of short and arbitrary time limits for the Implementation Force (IFOR) and Stabilisation Force (SFOR), which undermined the credibility of third-party involvement.

The prospect of security sector reform offers an alternative means by which strong third-party involvement can help facilitate stable post-conflict peace without the combatants' becoming dependent in the long run on sustained engagement. Monica Toft (2009) has found that security sector reform does much better at preventing conflict recurrence than third-party security guarantees. The logic is that security guarantees depend crucially on credible promises that are typically unsustainable in an anarchic world, but security sector reform, once implemented, changes the incentives of the game such that the combatants, on their own volition, have less incentive to defect. That is, security sector reform is a type of structural change that makes untrustworthy actors into trustworthy ones because they will no longer profit from exploiting cooperation. Security sector reform, which typically requires disarming large segments of the population and integrating the military with members of competing factions, does sometimes require heavy third-party monitoring and enforcement. The key is that, once the reforms are in place, the third parties should be able to leave and allow more natural deterrence mechanisms to keep the peace without key players being vulnerable to defection. In doing so, however, third parties need to make sure that the initial implemented reforms meet the needs of local actors and should avoid importing reform models from elsewhere.[8]

Externally imposed agreements should almost always be avoided. Not only do such agreements violate standards for fairness, but they are some of the least stable of all agreements because of the dependency on continual third-party influence. Yet many scholars and political leaders have claimed that the only way to solve the conflict in the Middle East is to impose a settlement. David Hirst, for example, writes while lamenting the Israeli unwillingness to compromise on the Palestinian question, "if Israel continues to kick against the pricks, any serious administration would need to resort to economic and diplomatic penalties of the kind that America has slapped on so many a miscreant down the years; and finally, if that does not work, impose a settlement with the aid of an international military force that will simultaneously guarantee the security of all the parties to it" (2010, 422). In light of the significant handicap to long-term peace that heavy-handed mediation brings, a better approach would be sustained and patient U.S. engagement that, however long it takes, urges and even gently leverages the actors to progress past this unsustainable status quo and toward peaceful arrangements that do not depend on outside coercion. As Dennis Ross states,

> An imposed solution will thus be no solution at all. Ultimately, the United States may make its greatest contribution to peace by standing against efforts to impose solutions and standing for the principle that regional leaders must finally exercise their responsibilities to confront history and mythology. Only when they are prepared to do that will the peace agreements endure. Only then will agreements be seen for what they are—authentic and legitimate reflections of what Israelis, Palestinians, and Arabs have decided. We can help them make these decisions, but we cannot substitute our will for theirs. (2004, 773)

Sixth, low-key involvement by a single mediator can work well in the long run. We have seen this demonstrated in the cases of Theodore Roosevelt at Portsmouth and of Martti Ahtisaari in Aceh. If third parties can direct the disputants toward an agreement without relying on carrots and sticks, then such agreements will have a stronger chance of surviving than those reached with the help of a heavy hand. In such cases of restrained involvement, the negotiating actors will depend less on outside influence and will therefore be less affected when the third party disengages. This means that leverage should be restrained when less intrusive tactics will probably do well in securing a cease-fire. The fact remains,

---

8. On this point, see Hendrickson and Karkoszka (2005).

however, that facilitation and formulation may not be sufficient in many situations to move the actors toward an initial agreement. Manipulative mediation may bring greater risks of crisis recurrence in the long term, but it also has the best chance of securing a short-term period of no conflict. That is, there can be a downside to avoiding leveraged mediation. Shlomo Ben-Ami notes this tension when he remarks about the Oslo process:

> Sometimes a small and unpretentious power like Norway can be better placed than a superpower to inspire confidence in the parties to a protracted conflict, and be effective in brokering an agreement between them. But the execution of the agreement could not be carried through without the guarantees of the superpower and its constant assistance and nursing. The American brokerage became a necessity if only because the Oslo process would immediately prove to be riddled with misunderstandings and ambiguities that bred crises and conflict almost from the first day. (2005, 213)

The key is that, when facilitative and formulative methods are sufficient, third parties should refrain from using leverage.

Dennis Ross and David Makovsky (2009) similarly advocate "engagement without illusions" in the Middle East, which is a middle course between U.S. disengagement, as espoused by neoconservatives, and external imposition of a settlement, as championed by some liberal realists. According to Ross and Makovsky, the United States must be a key element in moving the peace process ever forward but can also interfere with the ultimate settlement of the problems by ignoring Israeli interests and imposing its own blueprint for the region. Instead, the middle way is for the United States to engage the parties in helping to clarify the actions of both sides, in protecting and insulating against missteps, in mobilizing financial and political support for reconciliation, and in assuring the actors during each step. Aaron David Miller, a long-time adviser for the U.S. State Department on Middle East affairs, seeks a similar balance—although he sees U.S. leadership as even more essential than Ross and Makovsky do—when he writes, "We can't produce peace and reconciliation, but we can help to diminish conflict, defuse crises, and broker political agreements that might give Arabs and Israelis a chance to achieve these long-sought goals." He goes on to state in more dramatic terms that "The primary responsibility for peacemaking rests with the Arabs and Israelis, not with the Americans. The Middle East is their neighborhood, and its history and future is theirs. . . . But a region in ferment needs American leadership. . . . Even if the sun, moon, and stars are properly aligned, the chances for real and sustainable progress remain slight without a tough, forceful American role" (2008, 29). These views recognize the trade-off inherent in third-party peacemaking in that avoiding a difficult conflict like that between Israel and the Palestinians will miss crucial opportunities to improve the prospects for peace, but involvement that is overly heavy handed risks taking the onus of peace out of the hands of those whose responsibility it will be to preserve it.

Although the prospect of U.S. mediation following such a middle path sounds ideal in principle, it might be overly presumptuous to assume that the United States can actually adopt such a role. The importance of the Israeli-Palestinian conflict to broader regional peace, as well as the intricate ties to U.S. domestic politics, could make it prohibitively difficult to refrain from imposing a peace. That is, the political benefits of working toward a settlement, the desire to appear evenhanded to regional and global players, and the liability that the conflict poses to the U.S. War on Terror are likely to create sufficient incentives for the United States to be much more actively involved in the peace process than would be consistent with the middle path. If this is the case, then perhaps the United States can be useful only for short-term mediation gains in the Middle East and long-term mediation success should be relegated to some other actor, such as the European Union, with the capability to use leverage when absolutely necessary but to show restraint otherwise.

Seventh, mediation is worth the gamble when there is a large upside and not a substantial downside. With regards to the potential for a large upside, mediation is often worthwhile when the existing state of conflict is severe and unlikely to abate on its own. Carter's mediation in the DPRK is an example of this—the upside of securing a lasting framework that would lead to a denuclearized Korean peninsula would have been considerable. At the same time, it is doubtful that sanctions would have worked in getting the DPRK to come clean and probable that present-day tensions would be similar had Carter not paved the way for the Agreed Framework. In contrast, U.S. involvement in Haiti in 1994 seemed to have little upside for Haitian affairs, as feared by Carter, Nunn, and Powell—although there might have been some upside for other nascent democracies in the region. Cedras, the Haitian junta leader, in some respects appeared much more capable of effective governance than Aristide and at least gave lip service to the prospect of restoring power to civilian control. So the marginal benefit of (unrealized) democratic governance under Aristide compared to more of a protectorship under Cedras does not appear to be all that stark, and it was probably not worth the risk of injecting even more instability in domestic affairs.

When there is not a substantial downside, mediation is often worthwhile because the instability that it might cause is likely to be low level and/or easily calmed by further intervention. In other words, the downside of mediation may not be so troublesome in many cases when the potential resumption of conflict will not involve major violence and can again be met by assisted conflict management to keep tensions under control. For example, the 2002 mediation by U.S. Secretary of State Colin Powell between Spain and Morocco in their dispute over Parsley Island had very little chance of severely worsening the security environment even though it was also unlikely to fully resolve the competing territorial claims. In contrast to, say, the Rwanda case, the worst-case scenario of Powell's initiative would not have been much worse than the limited military engagements that had already occurred, especially because the actors could always try third-party conflict management again.

A few additional and quite practical implications follow from my analysis. To start, the third parties that are expected to be involved in implementation should also be either directly involved or frequently consulted in the mediation phase to avoid a fumbling of responsibilities when proceeding from negotiation to implementation. In this regard, Ban Ki-moon writes, "Experience has shown that peace agreements must meet certain criteria to withstand the stress of implementation. We have learned that, when the United Nations is expected to have an implementation role, it should be involved in brokering the agreement or, at the very least, have sufficient input into framing it to ensure that it is implementable" (2009, 13). Chester A. Crocker, Fen Osler Hampson, and Pamela Aall similarly advocate consistency in third parties across the mediation and implementation phases:

> Ideally, the party or parties that mediated the settlement should stay engaged in the peace process in the postsettlement or postimplementation phase. But this may not be possible because of restrictive third-party mandates, and changing personnel, or because other actors and institutions have the responsibility for implementation. In this case, coordination and properly timed handoffs are essential. Negotiation and implementation phases of the peace process are overlapping, intertwined, and mutually interdependent. Failure to recognize the interdependence of mediation roles and functions during the de-escalation phases may lead to an unraveling of the peace process as rival factions or "spoilers" attempt to undermine the settlement in question. (1999, 40)

It is also important to develop clear dispute resolution procedures in case the need for renegotiation arises. That is, even if the involvement of a mediator is likely to increase the need for renegotiation in the future, that mediator can take precautionary steps to decrease the propensity for conflict relapse by establishing a peaceful framework within which the renegotiations can transpire.[9] In this way,

---

9. Ban Ki-moon recommends that "Having a strong dispute resolution mechanism, as part of the structure that will monitor implementation and prevent or resolve crises, is critical to outcome" (2009, 13).

the efforts of the mediator to foster peace in the present might enable disputants to maintain that peace in the face of future challenges even if those challenges themselves cannot be prevented.

All this is to say that we will never be able to conjure up a precise formula of what is and what is not to be done in every peace process. The skilled practitioners that act where the proverbial rubber meets the road must continue to adapt and be creative in their approaches to some of the world's most nasty problems. The analysis here will help guide their efforts, especially when practitioners disagree on topics such as the effectiveness of leverage and when a professional bias creeps in that suggests peacemakers can do no wrong. To the extent that long-term conflict resolution is desirable, the intermediaries must find that delicate balance between providing needed assistance and letting the parties take ownership of the peace process.

QUANTITATIVE ANALYSES

The Data

One of the principal benefits of using the ICB and ICOW data is that neither data set requires that a significant amount of militarization be present for a conflict or dispute to be considered an observation. This means that the data sets catch a wide variety of mediation initiatives and not just those in the midst of massive bloodshed. The ICB data have the advantage over the ICOW data of complete global coverage. Published research on mediation that has used the ICB data includes Beardsley (2008, 2010), Beardsley et al. (2006), Quinn et al. (2006), and Wilkenfeld et al. (2003, 2005). The ICOW data have the advantage of containing much more information about the specific timing of third-party events. Published research on third-party conflict management that has used the ICOW data includes Gent and Shannon (2010), Hensel (2001), Mitchell (2002), Mitchell and Hensel (2007), and Mitchell, Kadera, and Crescenzi (2008).

According to Michael Brecher and Jonathan Wilkenfeld (2000), the original principal investigators who started the ICB data project, an international crisis has three necessary conditions that together are sufficient. First, there must be a threat that one state poses to the basic values of another. Second, there must be a finite time for states to respond to their threats. Third, the actors must perceive a heightened probability of military escalation. To find the set of cases to be included as crises for each year, Brecher and Wilkenfeld have surveyed international and regional experts about possible crises to consider. The ICB coders then use accounts of the candidate cases from periodicals, published scholarship, and memoirs to determine whether the three criteria are met. Once the set of crises has been determined, the coders use similar sources to record information at both the crisis level and the actor level. Each crisis is assigned to two coders, typically graduate students, who code the information independently and then form a consensus opinion with guidance from the principal investigators as necessary.

The following description of how the ICOW data were coded comes from the general codebook, written by Paul Hensel, accessible on the ICOW website.[1] An *issue claim* is defined as explicit contention between two or more states, in which explicit contention involves public statements in support of a claim by official representatives of the government. The ICOW data include information at the level of the overall claims and information at the level of the specific conflict management attempts. Peaceful settlement attempts cover a wide range of activity, from bilateral negotiations to binding adjudication, and, significantly, include each instance of third-party mediation. The ICOW data, funded in part by grants from the National Science Foundation, were primarily coded by graduate students and the principal investigators (Paul Hensel and Sara Mitchell). The data were coded in a two-step process, in which the coders, first, were assigned specific regions to identify the set of dyadic dispute claims and, then, recorded information about these claims.

Potential for Selection Effects in Mediation Data

A selection effects—or endogeneity bias—logic might play out differently across data sets with varying susceptibilities to biased inferences. For example, many quantitative studies of mediation use the ICOW data or Jacob Bercovitch's International Conflict Management (ICM) data, which have the conflict management attempt as the unit of analysis and have been used to directly compare mediated conflict management attempts to unmediated conflict management attempts.[2] Data sets of this type, with separate observations for each attempt, afford the analyst the opportunity to capture the many contours of often-complex peace processes. One drawback, however, to using such data for a direct comparison of mediated attempts to unmediated attempts is that there is a high potential for selection effects because unassisted negotiations will draw those periods in which the actors see few barriers to making progress toward peace.

Other data sets, such as the ICB, MID, or the UCDP/PRIO data, typically use the conflict or the dyad-year as the unit of analysis. Similarly, the SHERFACS data use the conflict phase as the unit of analysis. In contrast to the ICOW and ICM data, these data sets compare mediated periods to unmediated periods,

---

1. Issue Correlates of War website, http://www.icow.org.

2. For an overview of how different data sets on conflict management can be used to assess outcomes, see Gartner and Melin (2009).

which do not all include bilateral negotiations and, instead, are likely to involve fighting or stalemate in the absence of negotiations. As a result, the subset of nonmediated cases does not represent as cleanly a set of situations predisposed to bargaining success as in the ICOW or ICM data. This reduces the potential impact of the selection effects in those studies. With this in mind, we can better understand why studies using the ICOW or ICM data are less prone to finding that mediation, when compared to other negotiations, increases the likelihood of formal agreements or other peaceful outcomes.[3] As described later in this appendix, methods were used to account for potential selection effects in the models of mediation outcomes.

Mediation Incidence Analyses (Chapter 3)

The chapter 3 analyses with the ICB data were conducted as probit regression models with a dichotomous indicator of whether mediation occurred as the dependent variable. A Boolean probit model that distinguishes between the supply- and demand-side mechanisms was conducted as well to demonstrate robustness.[4] Although the ICB data have a variable that measures the occurrence of mediation, this variable is measured only at the crisis level. Because multiple crisis dyads can be part of a crisis with mediation, and mediation does not necessarily occur in every dyad, the existing mediation variable had to be recoded.[5]

The unit of analysis in these probit models is the crisis dyad, where the ICB dyads are defined by an updated version of Joseph Hewitt's (2003) data. I modify the ICB data by aggregating the intrawar crises—such that mediation and other crisis-level variables are coded as occurring in the aggregated war if they occurred during the component intrawar crises—and by omitting six crisis dyads that started before a previous one ended. It is likely that dyads within the same crisis will have correlated disturbance processes, so all the estimation generates standard errors that are robust to clustering on the crisis.

Starting with the measures of conflict severity and costs, *Violence level* is the most direct measure of the immediate costs experienced in the crisis. To measure

---

3. Specific to this discussion on the absence of a relationship between mediation and peaceful outcomes, see Bercovitch and Gartner (2006); Gartner and Bercovitch (2006); Gartner and Melin (2009); Hensel (2001).

4. For an overview of such a Boolean analysis, see Braumoeller (2003).

5. Using the same definition of mediation used in the ICB data, a new dyadic mediation variable was coded based on the ICB case summaries and historical accounts. Mediation occurred in a dyad only if there is documented evidence that a third party participated in negotiations with both sides of the dyad during the course of the crisis. I thank Nigel Lo for coding assistance.

violence, a four-point ICB variable is used, which varies from no violence to minor clashes to major clashes to full-scale war. Because ethnic conflicts are particularly protracted and costly, *Ethnic component* is a binary indicator of whether the crisis is motivated by secessionist or irredentist ethnic factors. *Crisis duration* is another measure of combatant desperation for a reprieve because it is assumed that longer crises are, ceteris paribus, costlier than shorter crises. There are direct costs related to the price of prolonged militarized engagement, as well as indirect opportunity costs related to the lost gains of mutual cooperation and the guns-butter trade-off. This variable is defined by taking the natural log of the length of a crisis in days.

Finally, an indicator of *Capability ratio* is used because the costs of conflict are related to the hurting stalemate concept in the existing literature.[6] We can anticipate greater expected conflict costs when there is relative power balance among the combatants. Seen another way, if the costs of conflict can be considered as a function of the capabilities of the opponent, then the mutual costs of conflict are relatively high when there is power parity. The independent variable that measures power balance is constructed by first taking the index of latent military power held by the stronger actor in the dyad and dividing by the index for the weaker actor. The natural log of that ratio is then taken to reduce the skew. The data on latent military power comes from the CINC scores in the National Military Capabilities data, version 4.0 (Singer, Bremer, and Stuckey 1972).

To measure leadership instability and its effect on shadow of the future, two variables are used. First, *Tenure* comes from the Archigos leadership data (Goemans, Gleditsch, and Chiozza 2007). I take the natural log of the number of days that the effective leader of each crisis actor has been in office. *Regime durability* is another measure that more directly accounts for domestic instability. It is measured as the number of years since a change in the Polity IV autocracy-democracy index score (Marshall and Jaggers 2002). Because there are multiple ways to produce dyadic measures of these variables, two different model specifications are used. The first uses simple averages, and the second uses the measures from the challenging state because that is the side most likely to need political cover for backing down or making concessions.[7] Because the ICB data do not identify challengers and targets, the second approach is used only with the ICOW data. To test whether these measures of political instability have stronger effects in the presence of democratic institutions, when the leaders are more account-

---

6. See, for example, Zartman (1985); Touval and Zartman (1985); Kriesberg (1991); Rubin (1991); Mooradian and Druckman (1999).

7. In calculating the averages, if tenure or durability information is missing for only one of the actors, the value for the other actor is used.

able, these variables are included in an analysis of just democratic dyads (or just democratic challengers), defined as whether the actors have more than a 6 on the Polity IV democracy-autocracy index.

Turning to supply-side factors, the *Number of neighbors* variable is a sum of the number of contiguous countries each side in a dyad has. The reasoning here is that negative externalities will be most strongly felt in contiguous countries. More contiguous countries to a crisis entails more interested third parties in containing the crisis. Similarly, if crisis actors in democratic neighborhoods are more likely to be pressured to involve a third party in mediation, then the summed *Number of democratic neighbors* is useful to capture that relationship. Finally, a five-point variable from the ICB data of *Geostrategic salience* measures the level of interests that other actors in the international system are likely to have for the outcome of the crisis in question. This variable ranges from 1, in which the crisis is relevant only to a single subregion, to 5, in which the crisis has consequences for the entire international system.

The models run with the ICB data also control for the number of previous mediation attempts between the actors in each dyad. Dyads with a frequent history of mediation are likely to have different levels of conflict intensity than others and are also more likely to have a higher proclivity for mediation in the current crisis.

The analyses with the ICOW data are conducted as duration models with time until third-party conflict management as the outcome of interest. Note that both mediation and legal dispute resolution are included as parts of third-party conflict management in the ICOW data. Similar logic used to explain the incidence of mediation can apply to general third-party consensual involvement. Separating mediation from other types of third-party involvement in a duration context would require a competing risk model. While results are robust to such a setup, the simpler specification was chosen for ease of interpretation. Only substantive instances of third-party conflict management are considered as outcomes here because procedural or functional attempts presumably follow different logics than those that actually have a bearing on the resolution of the key issues.

The ICOW data are structured such that a dyad enters the data on the first day of a claim and exits after the claim has been resolved or on December 31, 2001. Observations are taken at the beginning of each dyad year and at each conflict management event, whether it involves a third party or not. In this way, the models can employ time-varying covariates. Because many claims involve multiple conflict management attempts, the models are run as the time until each third-party conflict management attempt. Cox models are used to avoid overly restrictive assumptions on the shape of the hazard function. An elapsed-time specification is used, such that the "clock" does not reset after each conflict management attempt. Elapsed time was chosen because the conflict management attempts are likely to develop simultaneously—multiple third parties can become involved at the same time in separate events or be considered conflict managers at the same time (Box-Steffensmeier and Jones 2004). Because the occurrence of previous third-party conflict management events can influence the occurrence of subsequent ones, I generate robust standard errors clustered on each claim dyad to account for the potential for correlated errors across repeated events. In addition, the models stratify on a variable that counts the number of previous third-party conflict management attempts, as a means of accounting for the possibility that the time until a mediation attempt is conditional on how many previous mediation attempts have already occurred.

The first measure of severity and conflict costs with the ICOW data is the number of MIDs that have occurred in that year of the contentious claim. Although this variable picks up the immediate costs of conflict, I also include another variable that counts the number of MIDs that have occurred between the disputants in the previous five years. This captures the cumulative costs of conflict that the actors have had to bear recently. In addition, I include *Capability ratio* (log transformed), *Tenure* (log transformed), and *Regime durability*, which are measured the same way as in the analyses with the ICB data. On the supply side, the number of neighbors and the number of democratic neighbors are also included and calculated in the same way.

The analyses with the ICOW data control for whether the issue type is territorial because conflict over territorial claims are likely to be distinct from those over river or maritime claims. They also control for the salience of the dispute to the actors involved because salience is likely to shape both conflict intensities and the choices over conflict management.

Table 3.1 presents the results of three models using the ICB data. Model 1 is the basic probit model that informs most of the results discussed in the chapter body. Model 2 only uses the set of democratic dyads to demonstrate that measures of institutional instability matter much more, and in the hypothesized directions, in democracies. Note that the other covariates are dropped in this model because of estimation problems with such a low number of observations. These results should thus be interpreted with some caution. Model 3 presents the Boolean probit results, produced by simultaneously estimating an equation in which the demand-side factors are the covariates and an equation in which the supply-side factors are the covariates. The Boolean estimation is set up such that either equation could lead to the occurrence of mediation. The point here is that the demand- and supply-side factors might not have an additive linear effect on the proclivity for mediation, as a basic probit model assumes. If either high levels of demand or high levels of supply are sufficient for mediation to occur,

TABLE 3.1 Mediation occurrence, ICB data

	1	2	3
	BASE	**DEMOCRACIES**	**BOOLEAN**
Demand-side factors			
Violence level	0.172*		0.197*
	(0.0783)		(0.0985)
Ethnic component	0.765**		1.418**
	(0.189)		(0.241)
ln(Crisis duration)	0.134**		0.232**
	(0.0498)		(0.0666)
ln(Capability ratio)	−0.189**		−0.237**
	(0.0461)		(0.0860)
ln(Average tenure)	0.0396	−1.471**	0.0653
	(0.0635)	(0.627)	(0.106)
Regime durability, average	0.00531*	−0.119**	0.00573
	(0.00257)	(0.0472)	(0.00398)
Democratic dyad	−0.0745		0.244
	(0.313)		(0.614)
Supply-side factors			
Number of neighbors	−0.0309*		−0.0447*
	(0.0184)		(0.0235)
Number of democratic neighbors	0.0394		0.0337
	(0.0299)		(0.0343)
Geostrategic salience	−0.291**		−0.392**
	(0.0689)		(0.131)
Previous mediation	0.117		0.190**
	(0.0745)		(0.0697)
Constant	−1.259**	8.991**	−3.572**
	(0.514)	(3.800)	(0.979)
Constant (2nd equation)			−0.0549
			(0.289)
Observations	696	27	696

Notes: ** indicates significance at $p < 0.01$ and * indicates significance at $p < 0.05$ in a one-tailed test. Standard errors appear in parentheses.

TABLE 3.2 Third-party conflict management occurrence, ICOW data

	4	5	6	7
	BASE (DYAD)	BASE (CHALLENGER)	DEMOCRATIC DYADS	DEMOCRATIC CHALLENGERS
Demand-side factors				
Fatal MIDs, current year	1.149**	0.961**		
	(0.333)	(0.362)		
Fatal MIDs, past 5 years	0.386**	0.402**	0.0672	0.425
	(0.124)	(0.120)	(0.452)	(0.312)
ln(Capability ratio)	−0.00248	−0.0174	−0.186*	0.0680
	(0.0501)	(0.0525)	(0.106)	(0.0711)
ln(Average tenure)	−0.106		−0.561**	
	(0.0755)		(0.128)	
ln(Challenger tenure)		−0.0591		−0.179**
		(0.0591)		(0.0690)
Regime durability, average	−0.0111**		−0.0140*	
	(0.00404)		(0.00680)	
Regime durability, challenger		−0.00682**		−0.00984**
		(0.00194)		(0.00252)
Democratic dyad	−0.118	−0.117		
	(0.172)	(0.181)		
Supply-side factors				
Number of neighbors	0.000222	0.00704	−0.0629	−0.0330
	(0.0206)	(0.0222)	(0.0500)	(0.0286)
Number of democratic neighbors	0.0458*	0.0376	0.0893*	0.0790*
	(0.0260)	(0.0296)	(0.0538)	(0.0389)
Territorial issue	−0.540**	−0.534**	−0.511*	−0.532**
	(0.186)	(0.188)	(0.271)	(0.210)
Salience, joint	0.0337		0.112*	
	(0.0377)		(0.0678)	
Salience, challenger		0.0445		0.0222
		(0.0673)		(0.0940)
Observations	10,061	9,600	2,610	3,972

Notes: ** indicates significance at $p < 0.01$ and * indicates significance at $p < 0.05$ in a one-tailed test. Values are coefficient estimates. Standard errors appear in parentheses. MIDs, militarized interstate disputes.

then a probit model could produce misleading results. The Boolean probit demonstrates the robustness of the findings when a more complex causal mechanism is considered.

Table A3.2 presents the results using the ICOW data. Models 4 and 5 produce results from the basic model with all dyads; Model 6 produces results restricted to the joint democracies and Model 7 produces results restricted to democratic challengers.[8]

The results demonstrate that outside involvement is more likely when there are high costs of conflict. The capability ratio measure, however, is statistically insignificant in some of the ICOW models. With regard to the political instability measures, we see that the effects of tenure and regime durability on the proclivity for outside involvement are conditional on the presence of democratic institutions that enable the leaders to be accountable to their publics. Regime durability has a consistently negative and significant effect in the ICOW models that is even stronger in the restricted samples. On the supply side, we do see the importance of democratic communities in the ICOW data in that third-party conflict management becomes more likely as the number of neighboring democracies increases.

Short-Term Benefits Analyses (Chapter 4)

As in the chapter 3 analyses, I use both the ICB and ICOW data where possible to evaluate the hypotheses. With the ICB data, the principal dependent variable used to test the formal agreement hypothesis is a dichotomous measure of whether a *voluntary* formal agreement ended the crisis. The ICB data code this as true if the crisis ended with a treaty, armistice, or cease-fire agreement. Using the ICB case summaries, as well as data from Fortna (2004c) and Lo, Hashimoto, and Reiter (2008), I recoded this variable at the dyadic level.

To assess whether mediation affects the strength of the agreements reached, I also generated a dichotomous variable of whether a robust formal agreement was reached and an ordinal variable of agreement strength that ranges from no agreement to nonrobust formal agreement to robust agreement to strongly robust agreement. This typology considers whether the formal agreements contain provisions for peacekeeping, confidence-building measures, arms control, or further conflict resolution of the most contentious issues. These categories simplify similar indicators of agreement strength that Fortna (2004c) uses. From her measures, I collapse the different types of peacekeeping into one category,

---

8. The current-year fatal MIDs variable is omitted from Models 6 and 7 because of estimation issues given the infrequency of violent conflict in democratic dyads.

I consider demilitarized zones and internal control of rogue activity as part of arms control, and I do not take into account the length in words of the formal agreements (longer agreements do not necessarily indicate stronger ones). Non-robust formal agreements are those that do not contain these additional proto-cols and are merely formalized intents to withdraw from combat areas. At the other extreme, I coded for agreements that contained multiple such provisions for peacebuilding initiatives. For example, the strongly robust agreement that terminated the war between Ethiopia and Eritrea in 2000 was signed by UN Sec-retary General Kofi Annan and U.S. Secretary of State Madeleine Albright, and it called for 4,200 UN peacekeepers and post-conflict progress toward such ar-rangements as a demilitarized border, prisoner exchange, and compensation. Of the 172 formal agreements in the data, I code 19 as nonrobust agreements, 107 as robust, and 46 as strongly robust.

The ICOW data, used in other analyses in chapter 4 to validate the theoreti-cal linkage between mediation and short-term benefits, are not well suited for examining the impact of mediation on the attainment of formal agreements even though they do contain rich information about the conflict management processes in each dispute. One problem is that the data do not allow media-tion episodes to be compared to analogous episodes in which there is no conflict management. The ICOW data are set up such that there is one observation per conflict management attempt, so there is no information about the time peri-ods in which there is not a conflict management attempt; mediation can thus be compared only to binding third-party involvement and bilateral settlement attempts.[9] The theoretical framework, however, is chiefly about the benefits of mediation over continuing the dispute and does not rule out that other types of conflict management have their own merits. We want to know whether the com-batants improve their prospects for short-term peace by turning to mediation, but we cannot get traction on this question if we do not know what the prospects are when the disputants do not turn to explicit conflict management attempts. Note that this is not a criticism of the ICOW data but, rather, a statement about how the question being asked does not neatly amend itself so that the ICOW data can be used.

Another problem is that there is not an appropriate unit of analysis that would allow for like comparisons of situations in which a formal agreement is possible. Comparing conflict management attempts to one another, in terms of which ones resulted in formal agreements and which ones did not, is actually not a

---

9. Periods of militarized conflict can also be compared, but we would still be missing all the times in which the actors are simply staying with the status quo level of dispute and not deescalating or escalating the hostilities.

suitable comparison of like units. There is extreme heterogeneity in what a conflict management attempt entails. In using the ICOW data, the average conflict management attempt is between five and six months, with many lasting less than a month. Yet the standard deviation is nearly fifteen months, with a maximum length over twenty years. It would be a stretch to think that comparing a conflict management attempt that lasts a few days to an attempt that lasts over two decades should yield meaningful results.[10]

To allow for comparisons of like units in the analyses of concessions and short-term peace lulls, the models using the ICOW data are only conducted on the set of conflict management attempts that reached a formal agreement. In this way, we can compare formal agreements achieved with mediation to those without. The results remain robust when using a Heckman-type selection model to account for the nonrandom selection of formal agreements that define the sample. In the selection model setup, the natural log of the capability ratio, number of failed conflict management attempts in the previous five years, and number of successful conflict management attempts in the previous five years are used in the equation that explains the presence of an agreement but not in the outcome equations. In each model, the correlation between the selection and outcome equations is not statistically significant.

So, analyses of concessions and of short-term lulls in peace are possible using both the ICB and the ICOW data. For the ICB data, concessions are defined directly from the ICB actor-level data and the variable is true whenever either actor in the dyad compromised or was defeated. These are the types of outcomes from which leaders tend to need political cover. Note here that defeat is not in terms of complete collapse, but only the inability to achieve any of the objectives of the actor. The ICOW data code whether the challenger made concessions and, more generally, whether major or minor concessions were made in the dyad. Each of these categories of concessions is used as a dichotomous dependent variable. With regard to short-term lulls in hostilities, the ICB data code whether tensions have noticeably been reduced in the five-year period after a crisis. Similarly, the ICOW data code whether the claim has been settled in the two-year period following an agreement.[11]

---

10. Duration analyses using the ICOW data, akin to those in chapter 3, are not as problematic because the comparisons are effectively duration processes across and within disputes. Although it would be interesting to see how mediation shapes the time until a formal agreement in a duration analysis, the ICOW data do not provide information on the timing of the formal agreements within the conflict management attempts.

11. The ICOW data do contain a variable that captures whether a MID occurred within five years of agreement. This variable, however, does not capture the same information as the reduction of tensions variable in the ICB data because it does not account for the initial level of tensions in the dispute and does not capture nonmilitary tensions.

Because all but one of the dependent variables are dichotomous, the estimation uses a probit specification. Ordered probit is used for the model with the ordered strength of agreement as the dependent variable. For the ICB data, the control variables in the empirical models correspond to those found to affect formal agreement strength by Fortna (2004c). First, the number of previous crises in the past ten years, as a measure of the conflict history of a crisis dyad, is a crucial control variable because it provides information about rivalries.[12] Second, violence level captures the severity and costs of conflict, and it is coded from the existing ICB data as a four-point variable from no violence to minor clashes to major clashes to full-scale war. Third, I include the natural log of the length of each crisis (in days) as an indicator of the potential for a mutually hurting stalemate to have been reached. Fourth, a joint democracy variable captures the role of domestic institutions and is coded as true if both sides of the conflict dyad are a democracy—both states have at least a 6 value on the Polity IV democracy-autocracy index.[13] Fifth, the nature of the crisis outcome—victory for one side or a tie—should provide a key indicator of the willingness of the actors to bargain, the extent to which the conflict relationship has been clarified by fighting, and whether a mutually hurting stalemate has been reached. *Victory* is coded in the ICB data as whether a state has achieved all its crisis goals. There is one change in the control variables for the ICB models of concessions, which is that the victory variable is removed because the coding of the victory variable comes from the same ICB variable used to code the occurrence of concessions.

The control variables for the analyses using the ICOW data are similar. Conflict history is captured by the number of fatal MIDs in the past five years and by the number of previous third-party conflict management attempts. The severity of the conflict is measured by the number of fatal MIDs in the current year. The claim duration is also included,[14] akin to the crisis duration variable, as is a measure of joint democracy. I also include as control variables the ICOW salience index and whether it is a territorial dispute because there is substantial heterogeneity in dispute types within the ICOW data. Victory is not included because

---

12. Diehl and Goertz (2000) and Goertz, Jones, and Diehl (2005) stress rivalries as important to conflict behavior. Greig (2005) finds that rivalry history matters to mediation occurrence.

13. This variable does not appear in Fortna (2004c), but it is included because of the oft-studied role of domestic institutions in shaping conflict propensities, the bargaining environment, and third-party conflict management.

14. Patrick Regan and Allan Stam (2000) show that the timing of a conflict is an important determinant of mediation success. This variable helps control for the timing of intervention. Moreover, when the natural log of claim duration is included, following Regan and Stam (2000), the results remain robust.

the observations in the ICOW data are taken from within each dispute and thus make it impossible for victory to have been achieved yet.

There is a strong potential for selection effects (endogeneity bias) to confound accurate inferences of the true impact of mediation on these outcomes. If mediation occurs when certain outcomes are more predisposed than others are, it will be difficult to isolate the mediation process effect from the selection effect (Gartner and Bercovitch 2006). The environment in which mediation occurs is typically not the same as the environment in which it does not occur. It is possible that mediation is actually not causally related to formal agreements but only reflects some underlying dynamics of the bargaining environment that drive both mediation incidence and formal agreements. Although the regression models use control variables to account for variation in the observed bargaining environments between the mediated and unmediated cases, and previous work argues that the more difficult cases tend to get mediation,[15] it is conceivable that unobserved factors may yet confound the inferences. To address this potential for inferential bias, a bivariate probit model, also known as a recursive seemingly unrelated probit model, is used for the ICB data. This simultaneously estimates an equation of the mediation selection process and an equation of the outcome processes while accounting for the correlation in disturbances across the two equations. The mediation equation is specified based on the key factors found to affect mediation incidence in chapter 3. By controlling for the correlation in the errors between the two equations, this approach captures the unobserved factors that drive both processes. In most cases, the correlation in errors between the two equations is not statistically significant, which means that the simultaneous-equations approach is not necessary. When the correlation in the errors is statistically significant, the results are robust with regard to mediation, the key explanatory variable.

Table 4.1 presents the results of the models using the ICB data. Model 1 has any formal agreement as the dependent variable, Model 2 has robust formal agreements as the dependent variable, and Model 3 uses the four-point agreement type variable. Model 4 has concessions as the dependent variable. And Model 5 presents the results with short-term tension reduction as the dependent variable. Model 3 is estimated using an ordered probit, whereas the other four are estimated using regular probit. In all the models, mediation has a positive and statistically significant relationship with the outcome of interest.

Finally, table 4.2 presents the results of the models using the ICOW data. Model 6 uses challenger concessions as the dependent variable, Model 7 uses the attainment of low-level concessions and Model 8 uses the attainment of

---

15. See, for example, Gartner and Bercovitch (2006); Svensson (2008). See also Beber (2010a).

TABLE 4.1 Mediation and short-term outcomes, ICB data

	1	2	3	4	5
	FORMAL AGREEMENT	ROBUST AGREEMENT	AGREEMENT STRENGTH	CONCESSIONS	TENSION REDUCTION
Mediation	0.790**	0.738**	0.630**	0.310*	0.706**
	(0.209)	(0.224)	(0.210)	(0.177)	(0.180)
Number of previous crises (in 10 years)	−0.0150	0.0178	−0.0382	−0.0262	−0.0289
	(0.0672)	(0.0695)	(0.0589)	(0.0563)	(0.0631)
Violence level	−0.00958	−0.00401	0.0497	0.0223	−0.293**
	(0.0956)	(0.100)	(0.0918)	(0.0904)	(0.0883)
ln(Crisis duration)	0.319**	0.376**	0.387**	−0.0397	−0.0822*
	(0.0707)	(0.0781)	(0.0787)	(0.0479)	(0.0499)
Democratic dyad	−0.623*	−0.754*	−0.492	0.276	0.318
	(0.344)	(0.397)	(0.350)	(0.277)	(0.303)
Victory	−0.242	−0.258	−0.231		0.310*
	(0.176)	(0.189)	(0.183)		(0.151)
Constant	−2.244**	−2.646**		0.0450	0.530*
	(0.346)	(0.388)		(0.247)	(0.303)
Cut 1			2.667		
			(0.390)		
Cut 2			2.776		
			(0.385)		
Cut 3			3.716		
			(0.351)		
Observations	729	729	729	729	720

Notes: ** indicates significance at $p < 0.01$ and * indicates significance at $p < 0.05$ in a one-tailed test. Standard errors appear in parentheses.

TABLE 4.2 Mediation and short-term outcomes, ICOW data

	6	7	8	9
	CHALLENGER CONCESSIONS	**MINOR CONCESSIONS**	**MAJOR CONCESSIONS**	**CLAIM ENDS WITHIN 2 YEARS**
Mediation	0.543**	0.428*	−0.323	0.367*
	(0.223)	(0.206)	(0.292)	(0.224)
Arbitration/adjudication	1.183**	0.574**	1.050**	1.180**
	(0.186)	(0.176)	(0.184)	(0.197)
Fatal MIDs, current year	−0.233	−0.0821	0.655	0.506*
	(0.486)	(0.338)	(0.408)	(0.308)
Salience, joint		−0.00615	−0.0249	−0.0387
		(0.0241)	(0.0313)	(0.0258)
Salience, challenger	−0.0607			
	(0.0529)			
Democratic dyad	−0.0378	−0.167	0.0663	0.0176
	(0.150)	(0.130)	(0.183)	(0.141)
Fatal MIDs, previous 5 years	0.402*	−0.260	0.898**	0.939**
	(0.184)	(0.171)	(0.194)	(0.176)
Territorial issue	−0.223	−0.00723	−0.124	−0.0423
	(0.167)	(0.135)	(0.201)	(0.132)
Claim duration	−4.32e-06	−2.38e-05**	−2.58e-06	−2.06e-05**
	(7.15e-06)	(5.26e-06)	(7.70e-06)	(5.19e-06)
Previous third-party attempts	−0.106**	0.0401	−0.142**	−0.0272
	(0.0355)	(0.0386)	(0.0608)	(0.0428)
Constant	−0.745**	−0.437**	−0.972**	−0.246
	(0.230)	(0.183)	(0.245)	(0.198)
Observations	918	918	918	888

Notes: ** indicates significance at $p \leq 0.01$, * indicates significance at $p \leq 0.05$ in a one-tailed test. Standard errors appear in parentheses. MIDs, militarized interstate disputes.

high-level concessions. The outcome variable in Model 9 is the end of the claim within two years after the agreement. We see that mediation is positively and significantly related to the achievement of challenger concessions, low-level concessions, and the end of the claim within two years.[16] Mediation does not have a statistically significant effect on the attainment of high-level concessions.

Long-Term Benefits Analyses (Chapter 5)

The models of crisis recurrence with the ICB data use event-history methods. Essentially, I use a Cox semi-parametric specification with time-varying covariates and with the proportional-hazards assumption relaxed. When data such as these have units (dyads) that can fail repeatedly, Janet Box-Steffensmeier and Bradford Jones (2004) advocate using a stratified event-history model, in which the repeated events are treated as conditional on there being a previous failure. I thus define the strata as how many crises a dyad has been in since entering the data set and run the Cox models using the conditional gap-time specification.[17] Robust standard errors are generated clustered on each dyad.

The unit of analysis remains the crisis dyad. The dyads enter the data on the first day of their first crisis and exit the last day possible for the analysis—either the last day that the dyad exists or on December 31, 2006. The dyads are observed at the start of each year and at the onset of a new crisis, with time since the previous crisis measured in days. Event history analyses of international conflicts often use too long a time frame in which recurrence can occur.[18] For example, in 1919, Britain and Afghanistan engaged in a crisis during the Third Afghan War. These two countries did not participate on opposing sides in a crisis again until 2001, after an eighty-two-year pause. Conventional event history models of recurring conflict would treat the 2001 crisis as a repeat of the 1919 one, even though the two crises are so far removed from and have nothing to do with one another. As a result, the analysis uses a ten-year temporal domain in which

---

16. Note that the *p* value for the mediation coefficient in the claim-ending model is just slightly greater than 0.05 ($p \leq 0.05$ when rounding down) in a one-tailed test.

17. Relatively few dyads experienced more than five repeated events, so, to ensure sufficient observations in each stratum, I set the stratification variable equal to 5 for the cases that have repeated more than five times. We might suspect additional unobserved heterogeneity from unique characteristics of each dyad. In such a situation, Box-Steffensmeier and Jones (2004) and Box-Steffensmeier, De Boef, and Joyce (2007) recommend using a frailty model. When a frailty model is estimated, however, the observed variance of the random effect, which reveals the potential for unobserved heterogeneity, is not statistically significant.

18. See Goertz, Jones, and Diehl (2005).

failure can occur.[19] That is, all observations between the ten-year cutoff and the next crisis are omitted, and a dyad reenters the data when a subsequent crisis terminates.

The key independent variables are indicators of whether mediation occurred in the previous crisis and also the characteristics of those mediation attempts. Their interactions with elapsed time are also important explanatory variables because they allow us to examine how the impact of mediation changes as the time since crisis termination increases. The models include as controls the same variables used in the analyses in chapter 4. In addition, I control for contiguity because of the strong role it plays in the opportunity for interstate actors to be in dispute and renew hostilities. The interaction of time with these controls is also included to relax the assumption of proportional hazards.[20]

With the ICOW data, the analyses use the occurrence of a MID within ten years of agreement as the dependent variable. As mentioned previously, the low-level nature of the ICOW disputes and the finality of the claim terminations do not allow an analysis of time until dispute recurrence. The occurrence of a MID within ten years of an agreement, however, provides a useful basis for analysis of the long-term stability or fragility of a mediated peace. Probit models are used, and the sample is again restricted to the set of conflict management attempts that achieved agreement.[21] The control variables are also the same as in the chapter 4 analyses.

Selection effects are again a concern in these analyses because mediation might not be randomly distributed with respect to the underlying propensity for conflict recurrence or the general post-conflict stability of peace. I again use bivariate probit models, after transforming the ICB data to a discrete-time dyad-year format, to estimate simultaneously the mediation selection and the outcome processes while accounting for the correlation in the errors between the two equations. In all cases, we cannot reject the null hypothesis of no relationship between the mediation and recurrence equations, so it appears that selection effects are not plaguing the results.

The curves in figure 5.1 (see chap. 5) come from a probit model on the ICB data, transferred into a dyad-year setup that includes the elapsed time and its interaction with mediation. I use the probit model to facilitate manipulation of the interactive term for the graphical display. Box-Steffensmeier and Jones (2004) similarly advocate using models such as probit on grouped duration data when substantive

---

19. Diehl, Reifschneider, and Hensel (1996) use the same period.
20. See Box-Steffensmeier, Reiter, and Zorn (2003).
21. The results are also robust when using a Heckman-type censored probit model to account for selection bias.

TABLE 5.1 Mediation and crisis recurrence, ICB data

	1	2	3
	BASE	MANIPULATION	LOW SEVERITY
Mediation	−0.913**		−1.084*
	(0.264)		(0.558)
Mediation × time	0.000539**		0.000313
	(0.000212)		(0.000360)
Manipulation		−1.432**	
		(0.469)	
Manipulation × time		0.000770**	
		(0.000313)	
Other mediation		−0.613*	
		(0.328)	
Other mediation × time		0.000397	
		(0.000254)	
Previous crises	0.419**	0.437**	0.853**
	(0.127)	(0.132)	(0.258)
Previous crises × time	−0.000328**	−0.000329**	−0.000698**
	(0.000105)	(0.000105)	(0.000199)
Violence level	0.232*	0.237*	
	(0.136)	(0.137)	
Violence level × time	−0.000368**	−0.000368**	
	(0.000102)	(0.000103)	
Crisis duration	0.302**	0.298**	
	(0.0857)	(0.0851)	
Crisis duration × time	−0.000337**	−0.000334**	
	(6.32e-05)	(6.27e-05)	
Democratic dyad	−0.605	−0.516	−0.477
	(0.626)	(0.646)	(0.590)
Democratic dyad × time	−4.61e-05	−8.59e-05	0.000124
	(0.000406)	(0.000428)	(0.000429)
Victory	0.607**	0.577**	0.719*
	(0.209)	(0.208)	(0.321)
Victory × time	−0.000543**	−0.000529**	−0.000463*
	(0.000152)	(0.000152)	(0.000238)
Contiguity	1.237**	1.245**	1.847**
	(0.342)	(0.340)	(0.618)
Contiguity × time	−0.000589**	−0.000595**	−0.00102**
	(0.000197)	(0.000197)	(0.000348)
Observations	5,128	5,128	1,516

Notes: ** indicates significance at $p < 0.01$ and * indicates significance at $p < 0.05$ in a one-tailed test. Values are coefficient estimates. Standard errors appear in parentheses.

interpretations of duration dependency are required. To account for duration dependence in this probit model, I follow David Carter and Curtis Signorino (2010) and include the squared and cubed elapsed times as covariates as well. This approach allows for more flexibility in how the baseline hazard rates vary and greater ability to track how recurrence proclivity changes with the elapsed time.

Model 1 in table 5.1 presents the results of the base Cox model with mediation and its interaction with time as the key variables. The primary finding is that mediation reduces the hazard rate of recurrence only when the elapsed time (in days) is small. The interaction between the mediation variable and event time indicates that as the time since crisis termination increases, mediation eventually has a positive effect on the rate of recurrence.

The remaining analyses explore the factors that condition this trade-off. Model 2 presents the results of a model that disaggregates mediation into situations that involve the use of manipulative tactics and situations in which only facilitative and formulative tactics are used. As evident, the trade-off is starker with manipulation, and it appears that the interactions of time with facilitation and formulation are not statistically significant. This means that nonmanipulative mediation tends not to disrupt sustainable peace. But note also that the short-term effect of manipulation is much larger than that for nonmanipulative mediation, indicating that pursuing only facilitation or formulation does trade some short-term success for better long-term success. Model 3 assesses the impact of mediation on the subsample of crises with low severity, as defined by the absence of major violent clashes and a less-than-average crisis length. On this subsample, we see that mediation does not have a significant attenuating effect over time, which means that mediation in such cases can have a lasting influence on decreasing the hazard rate of recurrence.

Table 5.2 (Model 4) disaggregates the types of third parties identified as the principal mediators in a crisis. Global IGO mediators primarily include the League of Nations and the United Nations, whereas regional governmental organization (RGO) mediators are typically regional security organizations. *Concert* mediators include instances in which a third party is a cohesive coalition of representatives from multiple states, such as the Contadora group that was active in Central America. Whereas RGO and concert mediators do not have much of a pacifying effect, IGO mediators produce the trade-off between short-term peace and long-term peace. Other mediators do quite well in producing a lasting peace; the constitutive term is negative and statistically significant, whereas the interaction term is not significant.

The results of the analysis that separates mediators into single and multiple third parties are presented in Model 5 of table 5.3. When mediation involves only one third party, we observe a decrease in the hazard rate that persists because the

TABLE 5.2 Mediator types and crisis recurrence, ICB data

	4
	TYPES
Global IGO	−1.137*
	(0.532)
Global IGO × time	0.00106**
	(0.000380)
RGO	−0.679
	(0.517)
RGO × time	0.000472
	(0.000380)
Concert	−0.922
	(0.609)
Concert × time	0.000146
	(0.000445)
Other mediation	−0.941*
	(0.420)
Other mediation × time	0.000514
	(0.000319)
Previous crises	0.455**
	(0.127)
Previous crises × time	−0.000376**
	(0.000104)
Violence level	0.223
	(0.137)
Violence level × time	−0.000359**
	(0.000103)
Crisis duration	0.312**
	(0.0868)
Crisis duration × time	−0.000354**
	(6.50e-05)
Democratic dyad	−0.605
	(0.641)
Democratic dyad × time	−2.59e-05
	(0.000375)
Victory	0.613**
	(0.211)
Victory × time	−0.000568**
	(0.000157)

TABLE 5.2   Mediator types and crisis recurrence, ICB data (*Continued*)

	4
	TYPES
Contiguity	1.211**
	(0.337)
Contiguity × time	−0.000555**
	(0.000199)
Observations	5128

Notes: ** indicates significance at $p < 0.01$ and * indicates significance at $p < 0.05$ in a one-tailed test. Values are coefficient estimates. Standard errors appear in parentheses. IGO, intergovernmental organization; RGO, regional governmental organization.

interaction with time is statistically insignificant. The *Other mediation* category in this model implies the presence of multiple mediators, which are associated with the typical short- and long-term trade-off.

The final model using the ICB data is Model 6, which assesses the conditioning effect of peacekeeping on mediation. Peacekeeping forces are defined using the International Military Intervention (IMI) data—including information on all forceful interventions across state lines from 1946—assembled by Jeffrey Pickering and Emizet Kisangani (2009). For the purposes of this analysis, *peacekeeping* is defined as the deployment of military personnel to a foreign state by the UN, a regional security organization, or a coalition of states.[22] The purpose of the force also must be for observing, patrolling, monitoring, disarming, intimidating, or combating. Because this definition could also include collective security actions that clearly are not peacekeeping, I have excluded such interventions as the U.S.-led UN force in the Korean War. The peacekeeping variable is coded as true if a peacekeeping force has been deployed to at least one of the actors in the post-crisis dyad. Peacekeeping is still coded as having occurred if peacekeepers had been present at one point since the previous crisis but had departed by the time of the observation. The results are robust if, instead, we look at only the ongoing deployments. The results indicate that the short- and long-term trade-off of mediation exists with and without peacekeepers.

---

22. Only missions that fall under the purview of the UN, regional security organizations, or coalitions are considered as peacekeeping missions because the designation of forces from single states, such as the Russian "peacekeepers" in South Ossetia and Abkhazia, as really being intended for peace is often dubious.

TABLE 5.3 Additional mediation characteristics and crisis recurrence, ICB data

	5	6
	MULTIPLE MEDIATORS	**PEACEKEEPING**
Solo mediation	−0.879**	
	(0.363)	
Solo mediation × time	0.000394	
	(0.000275)	
Other mediation	−1.053**	
	(0.362)	
Other mediation × time	0.000834**	
	(0.000247)	
Mediation with PKO		−0.906*
		(0.415)
Mediation with PKO × time		0.000619*
		(0.000297)
Mediation without PKO		−0.871**
		(0.319)
Mediation without PKO × time		0.000483*
		(0.000256)
Previous crises	0.426**	0.499**
	(0.129)	(0.141)
Previous crises × time	−0.000333**	−0.000331**
	(0.000106)	(0.000109)
Violence level	0.240*	0.182
	(0.134)	(0.149)
Violence level × time	−0.000385**	−0.000318**
	(0.000101)	(0.000111)
Crisis duration	0.301**	0.446**
	(0.0848)	(0.0937)
Crisis duration × time	−0.000334**	−0.000378**
	(6.14e-05)	(6.89e-05)
Democratic dyad	−0.617	−1.043*
	(0.628)	(0.613)
Democratic dyad × time	−3.59e-05	0.000241
	(0.000390)	(0.000308)
Victory	0.623**	0.642**
	(0.208)	(0.265)
Victory × time	−0.000577**	−0.000484**
	(0.000153)	(0.000172)
Contiguity	1.228**	1.160**
	(0.340)	(0.377)
Contiguity × time	−0.000583**	−0.000559**
	(0.000196)	(0.000216)
Observations	5128	4200

Notes: ** indicates significance at $p < 0.01$ and * indicates significance at $p < 0.05$ in a one-tailed test. Values are coefficient estimates. Standard errors in parentheses. PKO, peacekeeping organization.

Finally, table 5.4 presents the probit results using the ICOW data. Model 7 examines all the formal agreements for a relationship between mediation and the occurrence of a MID within ten years. No relationship exists for mediation, and arbitration and adjudication also do not have a strong long-term pacifying effect. Models 8 and 9 restrict the sample further to only the mediated agreements to assess which factors can make mediation more effective in the long run. From Model 8, both IGOs and RGOs have a negative relationship with the long-term effectiveness of mediation, and the coefficient for RGOs is statistically significant. In Model 9, we again see that having single third parties can actually increase the long-term effectiveness of mediation.

TABLE 5.4   Mediation characteristics and MID occurrence within ten years, ICOW data

	7	8	9
	MEDIATION	IOs	SOLO
Mediation	0.205		
	(0.248)		
Global IGO		−0.176	
		(0.756)	
RGO		−1.191*	
		(0.530)	
Solo			1.179**
			(0.471)
Arbitration/adjudication	0.319		
	(0.206)		
Fatal MIDs, current year	−1.130**		
	(0.356)		
Salience, joint	−0.137**	−0.301*	−0.257*
	(0.0438)	(0.159)	(0.148)
Democratic dyad	0.424*		
	(0.247)		
Fatal MIDs, previous 5 years	−0.317*	−1.127**	−0.947*
	(0.177)	(0.352)	(0.467)
Territorial issue	0.209	−1.803*	−1.367
	(0.203)	(0.995)	(0.863)
Claim duration	−02.87e-05**	4.24e-07	−2.33e-05
	(5.89e-06)	(1.87e-05)	(1.85e-05)
Previous third-party attempts	0.104*	0.458**	0.611**
	(0.0586)	(0.168)	(0.167)
Constant	1.765**	4.270**	2.858*
	(0.356)	(1.833)	(1.601)
Observations	774	50	50

Notes: ** indicates significance at $p \leq 0.01$ and * indicates significance at $p \leq 0.05$ in a one-tailed test. Standard errors appear in parentheses. IGO, intergovernmental organization; IOs, international organizations; MIDs, militarized interstate disputes; RGO, regional governmental organization.

References

Allee, Todd L., and Paul K. Huth. 2006. "Legitimizing Dispute Settlement: International Legal Rulings as Domestic Political Cover." *American Political Science Review* 100(2): 219–34.

Aspinall, Edward. 2009. *Islam and Nation.* Stanford: Stanford University Press.

"Assessment Mission to Haiti." 1995. Report from the Carter Center. January, www.cartercenter.org/documents/642.pdf.

Auslin, Michael. 2005. "Japanese Strategy, Geopolitics and the Origins of the War, 1792–1895." In *The Russo-Japanese War in Global Perspective: World War Zero,* ed. John W. Steinberg, Bruce W. Menning, David Schimmelpenninck van der Oye, David Wolff, and Shinji Yokote, 3–22. Boston: Brill.

Baker, James A., III. 1999. "The Road to Madrid." In *Herding Cats: Multiparty Mediation in a Complex World,* ed. Chester A. Crocker, Fen Osler Hampson, and Pamela Aall, 183–206. Washington, D.C.: United States Institute of Peace.

Baker, Raymond William. 1978. *Egypt's Uncertain Revolution under Nasser and Sadat.* Cambridge, Mass.: Harvard University Press.

Ban, Ki-moon. 2009. "Report of the Secretary-General on Enhancing Mediation and Its Support Activities." United Nations Security Council document S/2009/189, New York.

Bandarage, Asoka. 2009. *The Separatist Conflict in Sri Lanka.* New York: Routledge.

Barnett, Michael. 2002. *Eyewitness to a Genocide: The United Nations and Rwanda.* Ithaca: Cornell University Press.

Beardsley, Kyle. 2008. "Agreement without Peace?: International Mediation and Time Inconsistency Problems." *American Journal of Political Science* 52(4): 723–40.

———. 2009. "Intervention without Leverage: The Political Determinants of Weak Mediation." *International Interactions* 35(3): 272–97.

———. 2010. "Pain, Pressure, and Political Cover: Explaining Mediation Selection." *Journal of Peace Research* 47(4): 395–406.

Beardsley, Kyle, and Brian McQuinn. 2009. "Rebel Groups as Predatory Organizations: The Political Effects of the 2004 Tsunami in Indonesia and Sri Lanka." *Journal of Conflict Resolution* 53(4): 624–45.

Beardsley, Kyle, David Quinn, Bidisha Biswas, and Jonathan Wilkenfeld. 2006. "Mediation Style and Crisis Outcomes." *Journal of Conflict Resolution* 50(1): 58–86.

Beber, Bernd. 2010a. "The Effect of International Mediation on War Settlement: An Instrumental Variables Approach." Working paper, New York University and University of Oxford, http://homepages.nyu.edu/~bb89/files/Beber_MediationIV.pdf.

———. 2010b. "The (Non-)Efficacy of Multi-Party Mediation in Wars since 1990." Paper presented at the Annual Meeting of the American Political Science Association, Washington, D.C.

Behrendt, Sven. 2007. *The Secret Israeli-Palestinian Negotiations in Oslo.* London: Routledge.

Ben-Ami, Shlomo. 2005. *Scars of War, Wounds of Peace: The Israeli-Arab Tragedy.* London: Weidenfeld and Nicolson.

Bercovitch, Jacob. 1986. "International Mediation: A Study of Incidence, Strategies, and Conditions of Successful Outcomes." *Cooperation and Conflict* 21(3): 155–68.

——. 1996. "Understanding Mediation's Role in Preventive Diplomacy." *Negotiation Journal* 12(3): 241–58.

——. 1997. "Mediation in International Conflict: An Overview of Theory, a Review of Practice." In *Peacemaking in International Conflict: Methods and Techniques*, ed. I. William Zartman and J. Lewis Rasmussen, 125–53. Washington, D.C.: United States Institute of Peace.

Bercovitch, Jacob, J. Theodore Anagnoson, and Donnette L. Wille. 1991. "Some Conceptual Issues and Empirical Trends in the Study of Successful Mediation in International Relations." *Journal of Peace Research* 28(1): 7–17.

Bercovitch, Jacob, and Scott Sigmund Gartner. 2006. "Is There Method in the Madness of Mediation?: Some Lessons for Mediators from Quantitative Studies of Mediation." *International Interactions* 32: 329–54.

Bercovitch, Jacob, and Allison Houston. 1996. "The Study of International Mediation: Theoretical Issues and Empirical Evidence." In *Resolving International Conflicts: The Theory and Practice of Mediation*, ed. Jacob Bercovitch, 11–35. Boulder: Lynne Rienner.

Bercovitch, Jacob, and Richard Jackson. 2001. "Negotiation or Mediation?: An Exploration of Factors Affecting the Choice of Conflict Management in International Conflict." *Negotiation Journal* 17(1): 59–77.

Bercovitch, Jacob, and Jeffrey Langley. 1993. "The Nature of the Dispute and the Effectiveness of International Mediation." *Journal of Conflict Resolution* 37(4): 670–91.

Bercovitch, Jacob, and Gerald Schneider. 2000. "Who Mediates?: The Political Economy of International Conflict Management." *Journal of Peace Research* 37(2): 145–65.

Berton, Peter. 2007. "From Enemies to Allies: The War and Russo-Japanese Relations." In *The Impact of the Russo-Japanese War*, ed. Rotem Kowner, 78–87. London: Routledge.

Betts, Richard K. 1994. "The Delusion of Impartial Intervention." *Foreign Affairs* 73(6): 20–33.

Betts, Wendy. 1999. "Third Party Mediation: An Obstacle to Peace in Nagorno Karabakh." *SAIS Review* 19(2): 161–83.

Blainey, Geoffrey. 1973. *The Causes of War.* New York: Free Press.

Bobrow, Davis B., and Mark A. Boyer. 1997. "Maintaining System Stability: Contributions to Peacekeeping Operations." *Journal of Conflict Resolution* 41(6): 723–48.

Böhmelt, Tobias. 2009. "International Mediation and Social Networks: The Importance of Indirect Ties." *International Interactions* 35(3): 298–319.

——. 2010a. "The Impact of Trade on International Mediation." *Journal of Conflict Resolution* 54(4): 566–92.

——. 2010b. "Why Many Cooks If They Can Spoil the Broth?: The Determinants of Multi-Party Mediation." Paper presented at the Annual Meeting of the American Political Science Association, Washington, D.C.

Box-Steffensmeier, Janet, Suzanna De Boef, and Kyle A. Joyce. 2007. "Event Dependence and Heterogeneity in Duration Models: The Conditional Frailty Model." *Political Analysis* 15(3): 237–56.

Box-Steffensmeier, Janet, and Bradford S. Jones. 2004. *Event History Modeling: A Guide for Social Scientists.* New York: Cambridge University Press.

Box-Steffensmeier, Janet, Dan Reiter, and Christopher Zorn. 2003. "Nonproportional Hazards and Even History Analysis in International Relations." *Journal of Conflict Resolution* 47(1): 33–53.

Bradley, James. 2009. *Imperial Cruise.* New York: Little, Brown and Co.

Braumoeller, Bear F. 2003. "Causal Complexity and the Study of Politics." *Political Analysis* 11(3): 209–33.

Brecher, Michael, and Jonathan Wilkenfeld. 2000. *A Study of Crisis.* 2nd ed. Ann Arbor: University of Michigan Press [with CD-ROM].

Brzezinski, Zbigniew. 1985. *Power and Principle.* Rev. ed. New York: Farrar, Straus, Giroux.

Bueno de Mesquita, Bruce, and Randolph M. Siverson. 1995. "War and the Survival of Political Leaders: A Comparative Study of Regime Types and Political Accountability." *American Political Science Review* 89(4): 841–55.

Bueno de Mesquita, Bruce, Randolph M. Siverson, and Gary Woller. 1992. "War and the Fate of Regimes: A Comparative Analysis." *American Political Science Review* 86(3): 638-46.

Bueno de Mesquita, Bruce, Alastair Smith, Randolph M. Siverson, and James D. Morrow. 2003. *The Logic of Political Survival.* Cambridge, Mass.: MIT Press.

Buhaug, Halvard, and Kristian S. Gleditsch. 2008. "Contagion or Confusion?: Why Conflicts Cluster in Space." *International Studies Quarterly* 52(2): 215–33.

Carnevale, Peter J. D. 1986. "Strategic Choice in Mediation." *Negotiation Journal* 2(1): 41–56.

Carnevale, Peter J. D., and Richard Pegnetter. 1985. "The Selection of Mediation Tactics in Public-Sector Disputes: A Contingency Analysis." *Journal of Social Issues* 41(2): 65–81.

Carnevale, Peter J. D., and Dean G. Pruitt. 1992. "Negotiation and Mediation." *Annual Review of Psychology* 43: 561–62.

Carter, David B., and Curtis S. Signorino. 2010. "Back to the Future: Modeling Time Dependency in Binary Data." *Political Analysis* 18(3): 271–92.

Carter, Jimmy. 1982. *Keeping Faith: Memoirs of a President.* New York: Bantam Books.

——. 1984. *Negotiation: The Alternative to Hostility.* Macon, Ga.: Mercer University Press.

——. 2007. *Beyond the White House: Waging Peace, Fighting Disease, Building Hope.* New York: Simon and Schuster.

Chapman, Terrence L. 2007. "International Security Institutions, Domestic Politics, and Institutional Legitimacy." *Journal of Conflict Resolution* 51(1): 134–66.

Chapman, Terrence L., and Dan Reiter. 2004. "The United Nations Security Council and the Rally 'Round the Flag Effect." *Journal of Conflict Resolution* 48(6): 886–909.

Chapman, Thomas, and Philip G. Roeder. 2007. "Partition as a Solution to Wars of Nationalism: The Importance of Institutions." *American Political Science Review* 101(04): 677–91.

Chastelain, John de. 1999. "The Good Friday Agreement in Northern Ireland." In *Herding Cats: Multiparty Mediation in a Complex World,* ed. Chester A. Crocker, Fen Osler Hampson, and Pamela Aall, 435–68. Washington, D.C.: United States Institute of Peace.

Chiozza, Giacomo, and Ajin Choi. 2003. "Guess Who Did What: Political Leaders and the Management of Territorial Disputes, 1950–1990." *Journal of Conflict Resolution* 47(3): 251–78.

Chiozza, Giacomo, and H. E. Goemans. 2003. "Peace through Insecurity: Tenure and International Conflict." *Journal of Conflict Resolution* 47(4): 443–67.

——. 2004a. "Avoiding Diversionary Targets." *Journal of Peace Research* 41(4): 423–43.

——. 2004b. "International Conflict and the Tenure of Leaders: Is War Still Ex Post Inefficient?" *American Journal of Political Science* 48(3): 604–19.

Christopher, Warren. 1985. *American Hostages in Iran: The Conduct of a Crisis.* New Haven: Yale University Press.

Clausewitz, Carl von. 1832 [1968]. *On War.* New and rev. ed. Trans. J. J. Graham. Harmondsworth: Penguin.

Clinton, William Jefferson. 2004. *My Life.* New York: Alfred A. Knopf.

Cohen, Raymond. 1996. "Culture Aspects of International Mediation." In *Resolving International Conflicts,* ed. Jacob Bercovitch, 107–28. Boulder: Lynne Rienner.

Creekmore, Marion V. 2006. *A Moment of Crisis: Jimmy Carter, the Power of a Peacemaker, and North Korea's Nuclear Ambitions.* New York: Public Affairs.

Crescenzi, Mark J. C., Kelly M. Kadera, and Sara McLaughlin Mitchell. 2007. "A Supply Side Theory of Third-Party Conflict Management." Unpublished manuscript, University of Iowa.

Crocker, Chester A. 1999. "Peacemaking in Southern Africa." In *Herding Cats: Multiparty Mediation in a Complex World,* ed. Chester A. Crocker, Fen Osler Hampson, and Pamela Aall, 211–44. Washington, D.C.: United States Institute of Peace.

Crocker, Chester A., Fen Osler Hampson, and Pamela Aall. 1999. "Multiparty Mediation and the Conflict Cycle." In *Herding Cats: Multiparty Mediation in a Complex World,* ed. Chester A. Crocker, Fen Osler Hampson, and Pamela Aall, 19–45. Washington, D.C.: United States Institute of Peace.

——. 2001. "Is More Better?: The Pros and Cons of Multiparty Mediation." In *Turbulent Peace: The Challenges of Managing International Conflict,* ed. Chester A. Crocker, Fen Osler Hampson, and Pamela Aall, 497–513. Washington, D.C.: United States Institute of Peace.

Cronin, Richard P. 1994. "North Korea: U.S. Policy and Negotiations to Halt Its Nuclear Weapons Program; an Annotated Chronology and Analysis." Congressional Research Service Report for Congress, Washington, D.C.

Cunningham, David E. 2006. "Veto Players and Civil War Duration." *American Journal of Political Science* 50(4): 875–92.

Dallek, Robert. 2007. *Nixon and Kissinger.* New York: Harper Collins.

Davenport, Christian, and Allan C. Stam. 2009. "What Really Happened in Rwanda." Miller-McCune, October 6, 2009, www.miller-mccune.com/politics/what-really-happened-in-rwanda-3432/.

Dayan, Moshe. 1981. *Breakthrough.* London: Weidenfeld and Nicolson.

Del Pero, Mario. 2006. *The Eccentric Realist: Henry Kissinger and the Shaping of American Foreign Policy.* Ithaca: Cornell University Press.

Dennett, Tyler. 1959. *Roosevelt and the Russo-Japanese War.* Gloucester, Mass.: Doubleday.

Diehl, Paul. 1994. *International Peacekeeping.* Baltimore: Johns Hopkins University Press.

Diehl, Paul, and Gary Goertz. 2000. *War and Peace in International Rivalry.* Ann Arbor: University of Michigan.

Diehl, Paul, Jennifer Reifschneider, and Paul R. Hensel. 1996. "United Nations Intervention and Recurring Conflict." *International Organization* 50(4): 683–700.

Dixon, William J. 1996. "Third-Party Techniques for Preventing Conflict Escalation and Promoting Peaceful Settlement." *International Organization* 50(4): 653–81.

Downs, George W., David M. Rocke, and Peter N. Barsoom. 1996. "Is the Good News about Compliance Good News about Cooperation?" *International Organization* 50(3): 379–406.

Doyle, Michael W., and Nicholas Sambanis. 2000. "International Peacebuilding: A Theoretical and Quantitative Analysis." *American Political Science Review* 94(4): 779–801.

——. 2006. *Making War and Building Peace: United Nations Peace Operations.* Princeton: Princeton University.

Druckman, Daniel. 1973. *Human Factors in International Negotiations: Social-Psychological Aspects of International Conflict.* Beverly Hills: Sage.

Egeland, Jan. 1999. "The Oslo Accord: Multiparty Facilitation through the Norwegian Channel." In *Herding Cats: Multiparty Mediation in a Complex World,* ed. Chester A. Crocker, Fen Osler Hampson, and Pamela Aall, 527–46. Washington, D.C.: United States Institute of Peace.

——. 2008. *A Billion Lives.* New York: Simon and Schuster.

Enderlin, Charles. 2002. *Shattered Dreams: The Failure of the Peace Process in the Middle East, 1995–2002.* New York: Other Press.

Esthus, Raymond A. 1988. *Double Eagle and Rising Sun: The Russians and Japanese at Portsmouth in 1905.* Durham: Duke University Press.

Favretto, Katja. 2009. "Should Peacemakers Take Sides?: Major Power Mediation, Coercion, and Bias." *American Political Science Review* 103(02): 248–63.

Fearon, James D. 1994. "Domestic Political Audiences and the Escalation of International Disputes." *American Political Science Review* 88(3): 577–92.

——. 1995. "Rationalist Explanations for War." *International Organization* 49(3): 379–414.

——. 1998. "Bargaining, Enforcement, and International Cooperation." *International Organization* 52(2): 269–305.

——. 2004. "Why Do Some Civil Wars Last So Much Longer than Others?" *Journal of Peace Research* 41(3): 275–301.

Feith, Pieter. 2007. "The Aceh Peace Process: Nothing Less than Success." Special Report 184. United States Institute of Peace, Washington D.C.

Fey, Mark, and Kristopher W. Ramsay. 2010. "When Is Shuttle Diplomacy Worth the Commute? Information Sharing through Mediation." *World Politics* 62(4): 529–60.

Filson, Darren, and Suzanne Werner. 2002. "A Bargaining Model of War and Peace: Anticipating the Onset, Duration, and Outcome of War." *American Journal of Political Science* 46(4): 819–37.

Fisher, Roger, and William Ury. 1981. *Getting to Yes: Negotiating Agreement without Giving In.* New York: Penguin.

Fortna, Virginia Page. 2004a. "Does Peacekeeping Keep Peace?: International Intervention and the Duration of Peace after Civil War." *International Studies Quarterly* 48(2): 269–92.

——. 2004b. "Interstate Peacekeeping: Causal Mechanisms and Empirical Effects." *World Politics* 56: 481–519.

——. 2004c. *Peace Time: Cease-Fire Agreements and the Durability of Peace.* Princeton: Princeton University.

——. 2008. *Does Peacekeeping Work?: Shaping Belligerents' Choices after Civil War.* Princeton: Princeton University Press.

——. 2009. "Where Have All the Victories Gone?: Peacekeeping and War Outcomes." Paper presented at the American Political Science Association 2009 meeting, Toronto, http://papers.ssrn.com/sol3/papers.cfm?abstract_id=1450558.

Frazier, Derrick V., and William J. Dixon. 2006. "Third-Party Intermediaries and Negotiated Settlements, 1946–2000." *International Interactions* 32: 385–408.

Funabashi, Yoichi. 2007. *The Peninsula Question: A Chronicle of the Second Korean Nuclear Crisis.* Washington, D.C.: Brookings Institution.

Gartner, Scott S., and Jacob Bercovitch. 2006. "Overcoming Obstacles to Peace: The Contribution of Mediation to Short-Lived Conflict Settlements." *International Studies Quarterly* 50(4): 819–40.

Gartner, Scott S., and Molly M. Melin. 2009. "Assessing Outcomes: Conflict Management and the Durability of Peace." In *Sage Handbook on Conflict Resolution,* ed. Jacob Bercovitch, Victor Kremenyuk, and I. William Zartman, 564–79. Thousand Oaks: Sage.

Gelpi, Christopher, and Joseph M. Grieco. 2001. "Attracting Trouble: Democracy, Leadership Tenure, and the Targeting of Militarized Challenges, 1918–1992." *Journal of Conflict Resolution* 45(6): 794–817.

Gelpi, Christopher F., and Michael Griesdorf. 2001. "Winners and Losers? Democracies in International Crisis, 1918—94." *American Political Science Review* 95(3): 633–47.

Gent, Stephen E., and Megan Shannon. 2010. "The Effectiveness of International Arbitration and Adjudication: Getting into a Bind." *Journal of Politics* 72(2): 366–80.

Gilligan, Michael, and Ernest J. Sergenti. 2008. "Do UN Interventions Cause Peace?: Using Matching to Improve Causal Inference." *Quarterly Journal of Political Science* 3(2): 89–122.

Gilligan, Michael, and Stephen John Stedman. 2003. "Where Do the Peacekeepers Go?" *International Studies Review* 5(4): 37–54.

Gleditsch, Kristian. 2002. *All International Politics Is Local: The Diffusion of Conflict.* Ann Arbor: University of Michigan Press.

——. 2007. "Transnational Dimensions of Civil War." *Journal of Peace Research* 44(3): 293–309.

Gleditsch, Kristian, Idean Salehyan, and Kenneth Schultz. 2008. "Fighting at Home, Fighting Abroad: How Civil Wars Lead to International Disputes." *Journal of Conflict Resolution* 52(4): 479–506.

Gleditsch, Kristian, and Michael D. Ward. 2000. "War and Peace in Space and Time: The Role of Democratization." *International Studies Quarterly* 44(1): 1–29.

Gleditsch, Nils Petter, Peter Wallensteen, Mikael Eriksson, Margareta Sollenberg, and Havard Strand. 2002. "Armed Conflict 1946–2001: A New Dataset." *Journal of Peace Research* 39: 615–37.

Goemans, H.E. 2000. *War and Punishment: The Causes of War Termination and the First World War.* Princeton: Princeton University Press.

——. 2009. "Risky but Rational: War as an Institutionally Induced Gamble." *Journal of Politics* 71(1): 35–54.

Goemans, H.E., Kristian Gleditsch, and Giacomo Chiozza. 2007. "Archigos: A Data Set of Leaders 1875–2004." April 2007, http://mail.rochester.edu/ hgoemans/ CaseDescriptionApril2007.pdf.

Goertz, Gary, Bradford Jones, and Paul F. Diehl. 2005. "Maintenance Processes in International Rivalries." *Journal of Conflict Resolution* 49(5): 742–69.

Gourevitch, Philip. 1998. *We Wish to Inform You That Tomorrow We Will Be Killed with Our Families.* New York: Picador USA.

Gowan, Richard. 2009. "The Future of Peacekeeping Operations: Fighting Political Fatigue and Overstretch." FES Briefing Paper no. 3. Friedrich Ebert Stiftung, New York, library.fes.de/pdf-files/iez/global/06238–20090331.pdf.

Greig, J. Michael. 2001. "Moments of Opportunity: Recognizing Conditions of Ripeness for International Mediation between Enduring Rivals." *Journal of Conflict Resolution* 45(6): 691–718.

——. 2005. "Stepping into the Fray: When Do Mediators Mediate?" *American Journal of Political Science* 49(2): 249–66.

Greig, J. Michael, and Paul F. Diehl. 2005. "The Peacekeeping-Peacemaking Dilemma." *International Studies Quarterly* 49: 621–45.

——. 2006. "Softening Up: Making Conflicts More Amenable to Diplomacy." *International Interactions* 32: 355–84.

Greig, J. Michael, and Patrick M. Regan. 2008. "When Do They Say Yes?: An Analysis of the Willingness to Offer and Accept Mediation in Civil Wars." *International Studies Quarterly* 52(4): 759–82.

Gurses, Mehmet, Nicolas Rost, and Patrick McLeod. 2008. "Mediating Civil War Settlements and the Duration of Peace." *International Interactions* 34(2): 129–55.

Haas, Richard. 1991. "Ripeness, De-escalation, and Arms Control." In *Timing the De-escalation of International Conflicts,* ed. Louis Kriesberg and Stuart J. Thorson, 83–96. Syracuse: Syracuse University Press.

Harel, Amos, and Avi Issacharoff. 2008. *34 Days: Israel, Hezbollah, and the War in Lebanon.* New York: Palgrave.

Hendrickson, Dylan, and Andrzej Karkoszka. 2005. "Security Sector Reform and Post-Conflict Peacebuilding." In *Security Sector Reform and Post-Conflict Peacebuilding,* ed. Albrecht Schnabel and Hans-Georg Ehrhart, 19–44. New York: UN University Press.

Hensel, Paul. 2001. "Contentious Issues and World Politics: The Management of Territorial Claims in the Americas, 1816–1992." *International Studies Quarterly* 45(1): 81–109.

Hewitt, Joseph. 2003. "Dyadic Processes and International Crises." *Journal of Conflict Resolution* 47(5): 669–92.

——. 2009. "Trends in Global Conflict, 1946–2007." In *Peace and Conflict 2010,* ed. J. Joseph Hewitt, Jonathan Wilkenfeld, and Ted Robert Gurr. Boulder: Paradigm.

Hirakawa, Sachiko. 2007. "Portsmouth Denied: The Chinese Attempt to Attend." In *The Russo-Japanese War in Global Perspective: World War Zero,* Vol. 2, ed. David Wolff, Steven G. Marks, Bruce W. Menning, David Schimmelpenninck van der Oye, John W. Steinberg, and Yokote Shinji, 531–49. Boston: Brill.

Hirst, David. 2010. *Beware of Small States: Lebanon, Battleground of the Middle East.* New York: Nation Books.

Höglund, Kristine, and Isak Svensson. 2002. "The Peace Process in Sri Lanka." *Civil Wars* 5(4): 103–18.

——. 2006. "'Sticking One's Neck Out': Reducing Mistrust in Sri Lanka's Peace Negotiations." *Negotiation Journal* 22(4): 367–87.

Holbrooke, Richard. 1998. *To End A War.* New York: Random House.

Hopmann, P. Terrence. 2001. "Bargaining and Problem Solving: Two Perspectives on International Negotiation." In *Turbulent Peace: The Challenges of Managing International Conflict,* ed. Chester A. Crocker, Fen Osler Hampson, and Pamela Aall. Washington, D.C.: United States Institute of Peace.

Horne, Alistair. 2009. *Kissinger: 1973, the Crucial Year.* New York: Simon and Schuster.

Human Rights Watch (HRW). 2006. *Funding the 'Final War': LTTE Intimidation and Extortion in the Tamil Diaspora.* Chicago: Human Rights Watch.

Iklé, Fred Charles. 1971 [2005]. *Every War Must End.* 2nd rev. ed. New York: Columbia University Press.

International Crisis Group (ICG). 2006. *Sri Lanka: The Failure of the Peace Process.* Asia Report no. 124. Colombo/Brussels: International Crisis Group.

Isaacson, Walter. 1992. *Kissinger: A Biography.* New York: Simon and Schuster.

Jarque, Xavier, Clara Ponsati, and Jozsef Sakovics. 2003. "Mediation: Incomplete Information Bargaining with Filtered Communication." *Journal of Mathematical Economics* 39(7): 803–30.

Jervis, Robert. 1976. *Perception and Misperception in International Politics.* Princeton: Princeton University Press.

Jones, Deiniol. 1999. *Cosmopolitan Mediation?: Conflict Resolution and the Oslo Accords.* New York: Manchester University Press.

Kathman, Jacob D. 2010. "Civil War Contagion and Neighboring Interventions." *International Studies Quarterly* 54: 989–1012.

Kemp, Geoffrey, and Jeremy Pressman. 1997. *Point of No Return: The Deadly Struggle for Middle East Peace.* Washington, D.C.: Carnegie Endowment for International Peace.

Khadiagala, Gilbert M. 2002. "Implementing the Arusha Peace Agreement on Rwanda." In *Ending Civil Wars: The Implementation of Peace Agreements,* ed. Stephen John Stedman, Donald Rothchild, and Elizabeth M. Cousens, 463–98. Boulder: Lynne Rienner.

Kipling, Rudyard. 1903. "Kipling on the Japanese: An Unpublished Letter Written at the Time of the Russo-Japanese War to William Joshua Harding R. N. 2 September 1903." Houghton Library, Cambridge, Mass.

Kissinger, Henry. 1982. *Years of Upheaval.* Boston: Little, Brown, and Co.

Kleiboer, Marieke. 1994. "Ripeness of Conflict: A Fruitful Notion?" *Journal of Peace Research* 31: 109–16.

Kressel, Kenneth. 1972. *Labor Mediation: An Exploratory Survey.* New York: Association of Labor Mediation Agencies.

Kriesberg, Louis. 1991. "Introduction: Timing Conditions, Strategies, and Errors." In *Timing the De-Escalation of International Conflicts,* ed. Louis Kriesberg and Stuart J. Thorson, 1–24. Syracuse: Syracuse University Press.

Kuperman, Alan J. 1996. "The Other Lesson of Rwanda: Mediators Sometimes Do More Damage than Good." *SAIS Review* 16(1): 221–40.

——. 2001. *The Limits of Humanitarian Intervention.* Washington, D.C.: Brookings Institution.

——. 2008. "The Moral Hazard of Humanitarian Intervention: Lessons from the Balkans." *International Studies Quarterly* 52(1): 49–80.

Kydd, Andrew. 2003. "Which Side Are You On?: Bias, Credibility and Mediation." *American Journal of Political Science* 47(4): 597–611.

——. 2005. *Trust and Mistrust in International Relations.* Princeton: Princeton University Press.

——. 2006. "When Can Mediators Build Trust?" *American Political Science Review* 100(3): 449–62.

Lake, David A. 1992. "Powerful Pacifists: Democratic States and War." *American Political Science Review* 86(1): 24–37.

——. 2003. "International Relations Theory and Internal Conflict: Insights from the Interstices." *International Studies Review* 5(4): 81–90.

——. 2009. *Hierarchy in International Relations.* Ithaca: Cornell University Press.

Lake, David A., and Donald Rothchild. 1996. "Containing Fear: The Origins and Management of Ethnic Conflict." *International Security* 21(2): 41–75.

Licklider, Roy. 1995. "The Consequences of Negotiated Settlements in Civil Wars, 1945–1993." *American Political Science Review* 89(3): 681–90.

Lo, Nigel, Barry Hashimoto, and Dan Reiter. 2008. "Ensuring Peace: Foreign-Imposed Regime Change and Postwar Peace Duration, 1914–2001." *International Organization* 62(4): 717–36.

Lukoianov, Igor Vladimirovich. 2008. "The Portsmouth Peace." In *The Treaty of Portsmouth and Its Legacies,* ed. Steven Ericson and Allen Hockley, 41–61. Hanover, N.H.: Dartmouth College Press.

Luttwak, Edward N. 1999. "Give War a Chance." *Foreign Affairs* 78(4): 36–44.

——. 2001. "The Curse of Inclusive Intervention." In *Turbulent Peace: The Challenges of Managing International Conflict,* ed. Chester A. Crocker, Fen Osler Hampson, and Pamela Aall, 265–272. Washington, D.C.: United States Institute of Peace.

Mack, Andrew. 1994. *North Korea's Nuclear Program: The Options Are Shrinking.* Canberra: Australian National University.

Marshall, Monty, and Keith Jaggers. 2002. *Polity IV Project: Political Regime Characteristics and Transitions 1800–2002; Dataset User's Manual. University of Maryland.* http://www.cidcm.umd.edu/polity/.

Mattes, Michaela, and Burcu Savun. 2009. "Fostering Peace after Civil War: Commitment Problems and Agreement Design." *International Studies Quarterly* 53(3): 737–59.

Mearsheimer, John J., and Stephen M. Walt. 2007. *The Israel Lobby and US Foreign Policy.* New York: Farrar, Straus and Giroux.

Melin, Molly M., and Isak Svensson. 2009. "Incentives for Talking: Accepting Mediation in International and Civil Wars." *International Interactions* 35(3): 249–71.

Miller, Aaron David. 2008. *The Much Too Promised Land: America's Elusive Search for Arab-Israeli Peace.* New York: Bantam.

Mills, Greg, and Terence McNamee. 2009. "Mission Improbable: International Interventions, the United Nations, and the Challenge of Conflict Resolution." In *ConUNdrum: The Limits of the United Nations and the Search for Alternatives,* ed. Brett D. Schaefer, 57–93. Lanham: Rowman and Littlefield.

Mitchell, Sara McLaughlin. 2002. "A Kantian System?: Democracy and Third-Party Conflict Resolution." *American Journal of Political Science* 46(4): 749–59.

Mitchell, Sara McLaughlin, and Paul R. Hensel. 2007. "International Institutions and Compliance with Agreements." *American Journal of Political Science* 51(4): 721–37.

Mitchell, Sara McLaughlin, Kelly M. Kadera, and Mark J.C. Crescenzi. 2008. "Practicing Democratic Community Norms: Third Party Conflict Management and Successful Settlements." In *International Conflict Mediation: New Approaches and Findings,* ed. Jacob Bercovitch and Scott Gartner. New York: Routledge.

Mitusch, Kay, and Roland Strausz. 2000. "Mediation in Situations of Conflict." www.econometricsociety.org/meetings/wc00/pdf/0361.pdf.

Mooradian, Moorad, and Daniel Druckman. 1999. "Hurting Stalemate or Mediation?: The Conflict over Nagorno-Karabakh, 1990–95." *Journal of Peace Research* 36(6): 709–27.

Moore, Christopher W. 1986. *The Mediation Process: Practical Strategies for Resolving Conflict.* San Francisco: Jossey-Bass.

Most, Benjamin A., and Harvey Starr. 1980. "Diffusion, Reinforcement, Geopolitics, and the Spread of War." *American Political Science Review* 74(4): 932–46.

North, Douglas C., and Barry R. Weingast. 1989. "Constitutions and Commitment: The Evolution of Institutional Governing Public Choice in Seventeenth-Century England." *Journal of Economic History* 49(4): 803–32.

Northedge, Frederick Samuel, and Michael Donelan. 1971. *International Disputes: The Political Aspects.* London: Europa.

Olson, Mancur, Jr., and Richard Zeckhauser. 1966. "An Economic Theory of Alliances." *Review of Economics and Statistics* 48(3): 266–79.

Ott, Marvin C. 1972. "Mediation as a Method of Conflict Resolution: Two Cases." *International Organization* 26: 595–618.

Papers Relating to the Foreign Relations of the United States. 1906. Washington, D.C.: U.S. Government Printing Office.

Paris, Roland. 2004. *At War's End: Building Peace after Civil Conflict.* New York: Cambridge University Press.

Pastor, Robert A. 1999. "More and Less than It Seemed: The Carter-Nunn-Powell Mediation in Haiti, 1994." In *Herding Cats: Multiparty Mediation in a Complex World,* ed. Chester A. Crocker, Fen Osler Hampson, and Pamela Aall, 505–28. Washington, D.C.: United States Institute of Peace.

Pezzullo, Ralph. 2006. *Plunging into Haiti.* Jackson: Mississippi University Press.

Pickering, Jeffrey, and Emizet F. Kisangani. 2009. "The International Military Intervention Dataset: An Updated Resource for Conflict Scholars." *Journal of Peace Research* 46(4): 589–99.

Pillar, Paul R. 1983. *Negotiating Peace: War Termination as a Bargaining Process.* Princeton: Princeton University Press.

Powell, Robert. 1999. *In the Shadow of Power: States and Strategies in International Politics.* Princeton: Princeton University Press.

——. 2004a. "Bargaining and Learning while Fighting." *American Journal of Political Science* 48(2): 344–61.

——. 2004b. "The Inefficient Use of Power: Costly Conflict with Complete Information." *American Political Science Review* 98(2): 231–41.

——. 2006. "War as a Commitment Problem." *International Organization* 60: 169–203.

Pressman, Jeremy. 2008. *Warring Friends: Alliance Restraint in International Politics.* Ithaca: Cornell University Press.

Princen, Thomas. 1992. *Intermediaries in International Conflict.* Princeton: Princeton University Press.

Pruitt, Dean G. 1981a. "Kissinger as a Traditional Mediator with Power." In *Dynamics of Third Party Intervention: Kissinger in the Middle East,* ed. Jeffrey Z. Rubin, 136–47. New York: Praeger.

——. 1981b. *Negotiation Behavior.* New York: Academic Press.

Pruitt, Dean G., and Douglas G. Johnson. 1970. "Mediation as an Aid to Face Saving in Negotiation." *Journal of Personality and Social Psychology* 14(3): 239–46.

Pundak, Ron. 2001. "From Oslo to Taba: What Went Wrong." *Survival* 43(3): 31–45.

Putnam, Robert D. 1988. "Diplomacy and Domestic Politics: The Logic of Two-Level Games." *International Organization* 42(3): 427–60.

Quandt, William B. 1986. *Camp David: Peacemaking and Politics.* Washington, D.C.: Brookings Institution.

——. 2001. *Peace Process: American Diplomacy and the Arab-Israeli Conflict since 1967.* Washington, D.C.: Brookings Institution and University of California Press.

Quinn, David, Jonathan Wilkenfeld, Kathleen Smarick, and Victor Asal. 2006. "Power Play: Mediation in Symmetric and Asymmetric International Crises." *International Interactions* 32(4): 441–70.

Rabin, Yitzhak. 1979. *The Rabin Memoirs.* Boston: Little, Brown and Co.

Rabinovich, Itamar. 2004. *Waging Peace: Israel and the Arabs, 1948–2003.* Princeton: Princeton University Press.

Randall, Peter E. 1985. *There Are No Victors Here: A Local Perspective on the Treaty of Portsmouth*. Portsmouth, N.H.: Portsmouth Marine Society.

Rauchhaus, Robert. 2006. "Asymmetric Information, Mediation and Conflict Management." *World Politics* 58(2): 207–41.

———. 2009. "Principal-Agent Problems in Humanitarian Intervention: Moral Hazard, Adverse Selection, and the Commitment Dilemma." *International Studies Quarterly* 53(4): 871–84.

———. 2011. "International Conflict Management: Using Power and Information to Resolve Disputes." Unpublished manuscript.

Regan, Patrick, and Aysegul Aydin. 2006. "Diplomacy and Other Forms of Intervention in Civil Wars." *Journal of Conflict Resolution* 50(5): 736–56.

Regan, Patrick, and Allan C. Stam. 2000. "In the Nick of Time: Conflict Management, Mediation Timing, and the Duration of Interstate Disputes." *International Studies Quarterly* 44: 239–60.

Reiter, Dan. 1995. "Exploding the Powder Keg Myth: Preemptive Wars almost never Happen." *International Security* 20(2): 5–34.

———. 2003. "Exploring the Bargaining Model of War." *Perspectives on Politics* 1(1): 27–43.

———. 2009. *How Wars End*. Princeton: Princeton University.

Reiter, Dan, and Allan C. Stam. 1998. "Democracy, War Initiation, and Victory." *American Political Science Review* 92(2): 377–89.

Richmond, Oliver. 1998. "Devious Objectives and the Disputants' View of International Mediation: A Theoretical Framework." *Journal of Peace Research* 35(6): 707–22.

Ritscher, Allison. 2005. "A More Effective Role for SFOR." In *Security Sector Reform and Post-Conflict Peacebuilding*, ed. Albrecht Schnable and Hans-Georg Ehrhart, 114–32. New York: UN University Press.

Roeder, Philip G., and Donald Rothchild. 2005. *Sustainable Peace: Power and Democracy after Civil Wars*. Ithaca: Cornell University Press.

Ross, Dennis. 2004. *The Missing Peace*. New York: Farrar, Straus and Giroux.

Ross, Dennis, and David Makovsky. 2009. *Myths, Illusions, and Peace: Finding a New Direction for America in the Middle East*. New York: Viking.

Ross, Michael L. 2005. "Resources and Rebellion in Aceh, Indonesia." In *Understanding Civil War*, Vol. 2, ed. Paul Collier and Nicholas Sambanis, 35–58. Washington, D.C.: World Bank.

Rotberg, Robert I. 2003. *Haiti's Turmoil: Politics and Policy under Aristide and Clinton*. Cambridge, Mass.: World Peace Foundation.

Rothstein, Robert L. 2006. *How Not to Make Peace: "Conflict Syndrome" and the Demise of the Oslo Accords*. Washington, D.C.: United States Institute of Peace.

Rubin, Jeffrey Z. 1981. "Introduction." In *Dynamics of Third Party Intervention: Kissinger in the Middle East*, ed. Jeffrey Z. Rubin, 3–43. New York: Praeger.

———. 1991. "The Timing of Ripeness and the Ripeness of Timing." In *Timing the De-escalation of International Conflicts*, ed. Louis Kriesberg and Stuart J. Thorson, 237–46. Syracuse: Syracuse University Press.

Sadat, Anwar. 1984. *Those I Have Known*. New York: Continuum.

Sambanis, Nicholas. 2007. "Short-Term and Long-Term Effects of United Nations Peace Operations." World Bank Policy Research Working Paper no. 4207. Post-Conflict Transitions Working Paper no. 11. World Bank, Washington, D.C.

Sandler, Todd. 1977. "The Impurity of Defense: An Application to the Economics of Alliances." *Kyklos* 30(3): 443–60.

Saul, Norman. 2005. "The Kittery Peace." In *The Russo-Japanese War in Global Perspective: World War Zero*, ed. John W. Steinberg, Bruce W. Menning, David

Schimmelpenninck van der Oye, David Wolff, and Shinji Yokote, 485–508. Boston: Brill.

Savun, Burcu. 2008. "Information, Bias, and Mediation Success." *International Studies Quarterly* 52(1): 25–47.

Schimmelpenninck van der Oye, David. 2005. "The Immediate Origins of War." In *The Russo-Japanese War in Global Perspective: World War Zero,* ed. John W. Steinberg, Bruce W. Menning, David Schimmelpenninck van der Oye, David Wolff, and Shinji Yokote, 23–44. Boston: Brill.

——. 2008. "Russia's Relations with Japan before and after the War: An Episode in the Diplomacy of Imperialism." In *The Treaty of Portsmouth and Its Legacies,* ed. Steven Ericson and Allen Hockley, 11–23. Hanover: Dartmouth College Press.

Schmidt, Holger. 2004. "Biased for Peace?: Commitment Problems, Impartiality, and the Effectiveness of Third-Party Guarantees." Paper presented at the annual meeting of the American Political Science Association, Chicago.

Schrodt, Philip A., and Deborah J. Gerner. 2004. "An Event Data Analysis of Third-Party Mediation in the Middle East and Balkans." *Journal of Conflict Resolution* 48(3): 310–30.

Schroeter, Kirsten, and Jana Vyrastekova. 2003. "Does It Take Three to Make Two Happy?: An Experimental Study on Bargaining with Mediation." Discussion paper no. 2003–60. Tilburg University, Center for Economic Research.

Shlaim, Avi. 2000. *The Iron Wall: Israel and the Arab World.* New York: W. W. Norton.

Sick, Gary. 1985. "The Partial Negotiator: Algeria and the US Hostages in Iran." In *International Mediation in Theory and Practice,* ed. Saadia Touval and I. William Zartman, 21–66. Boulder: Westview Press.

Simmons, Beth A. 2002. "Capacity, Commitment, and Compliance: International Institutions and Territorial Disputes." *Journal of Conflict Resolution* 46(6): 829–56.

Singer, J. David, Stuart Bremer, and John Stuckey. 1972. "Capability Distribution, Uncertainty, and Major Power War." In *Peace, War, and Numbers,* ed. Bruce M. Russett, 19–48. Beverly Hills: Sage.

Sisk, Timothy D. 2008. *International Mediation in Civil Wars: Bargaining with Bullets.* New York: Routledge.

Siverson, Randolph M., and Harvey Starr. 1990. "Opportunity, Willingness, and the Diffusion of War." *American Political Science Review* 84(1): 47–67.

——. 1991. *The Diffusion of War.* Ann Arbor: University of Michigan Press.

Slantchev, Branislav. 2003. "The Principle of Convergence in Wartime Negotiations." *American Political Science Review* 97(4): 621–32.

——. 2004. "How Initiators End Their Wars: The Duration of Warfare and the Terms of Peace." *American Journal of Political Science* 48(4): 813–29.

Smith, Alastair, and Allan Stam. 2003. "Mediation and Peacekeeping in a Random Walk Model of Civil and Interstate War." *International Studies Review* 5(4): 115–35.

Snyder, Glenn H. 1984. "The Security Dilemma in Alliance Politics." *World Politics* 36(4): 461–95.

Snyder, Glenn H., and Paul Diesing. 1977. *Conflict among Nations.* Princeton: Princeton University.

Snyder, Jack. 1984. "Civil-Military Relations and the Cult of the Offensive, 1914 and 1984." *International Security* 9: 108–46

Snyder, Jack, and Robert Jervis. 1999. "Civil War and the Security Dilemma." In *Civil Wars, Insecurity, and Intervention,* ed. Barbara F. Walter and Jack Snyder. New York: Columbia University Press.

Solingen, Etel. 2007. *Nuclear Logics: Contrasting Paths in East Asia and the Middle East.* Princeton: Princeton University Press.

Stam, Allan. 2008. "Understanding the 1994 Rwandan Genocide." Presentation at Emory University, Department of Political Science, November 11.

Starr, Harvey, and Benjamin A. Most. 1983. "Contagion and Border Effects on Contemporary African Conflict." *Comparative Political Studies* 16(1): 92–117.

Stedman, Stephen John. 1997. "Spoiler Problems in Peace Processes." *International Security* 22(2): 5–53.

——. 2002. "Introduction." In *Ending Civil Wars*, ed. Stephen John Stedman, Donald Rothchild, and Elizabeth M. Cousens. Boulder: Lynne Rienner.

Stedman, Stephen John, and Donald Rothchild. 1996. "Peace Operations: From Short-Term to Long-Term Commitment." *International Peacekeeping* 3(2): 17–35.

Stein, Kenneth W. 1999. *Heroic Diplomacy: Sadat, Kissinger, Carter, Begin, and the Quest for Arab-Israeli Peace.* New York: Routledge.

Stein, Kenneth W., and Samuel W. Lewis. 1991. *Making Peace among Arabs and Israelis.* Washington, D.C.: United States Institute of Peace.

Steinberg, John W. 2005. "The Operational Overview." In *The Russo-Japanese War in Global Perspective: World War Zero,* ed. John W. Steinberg, Bruce W. Menning, David Schimmelpenninck van der Oye, David Wolff, and Shinji Yokote, 105–28. Boston: Brill.

Stettenheim, Joel. 2002. "The Arusha Accords and the Failure of International Intervention in Rwanda." In *Words over War: Mediation and Arbitration to Prevent Deadly Conflict,* ed. Melanie C. Greenberg, John H. Barton, and Margaret E. McGuinness. New York: Rowman and Littlefield.

Susskind, Lawrence, and Jeffrey Cruikshank. 1987. *Breaking the Impasse: Consensual Approaches to Resolving Public Disputes.* New York: Basic Books.

Svensson, Isak. 2007a. "Bargaining, Bias and Peace Brokers: How Rebels Commit to Peace." *Journal of Peace Research* 44(2): 177–94.

——. 2007b. "Mediation with Muscles or Minds?: Exploring Power Mediators and Pure Mediators in Civil Wars." *International Negotiation* 12: 229–48.

——. 2008. "Do Mediators Go Where They Are Needed Most?: Mediation Selection in Civil Wars." Unpublished manuscript. B University, Sweden.

Tarar, Ahmer. 2005. "Constituencies and Preferences in International Bargaining." *Journal of Conflict Resolution* 49(3): 383–407.

——. 2006. "Diversionary Incentives and the Bargaining Approach to War." *International Studies Quarterly* 50(1): 169–88.

Tarar, Ahmer, and Bahar Leventoglu. 2009. "Public Commitment in Crisis Bargaining." *International Studies Quarterly* 53(3): 817–39.

Telhami, Shibley. 1990. *Power and Leadership in International Bargaining: The Path to the Camp David Accords.* New York: Columbia University Press.

Teramoto, Yasutoshi. 2008. "Japanese Diplomacy before and after the War: The Turning Point on the Road to the Pacific War." In *The Treaty of Portsmouth and Its Legacies,* ed. Steven Ericson and Allen Hockley, 24–40. Hanover: Dartmouth College Press.

Terris, Lesley G., and Zeev Maoz. 2005. "Rational Mediation: A Theory and a Test." *Journal of Peace Research* 42(5): 563–83.

Toft, Monica D. 2009. *Securing the Peace: The Durable Settlement of Civil Wars.* Princeton: Princeton University Press.

Togo, Kazuhiko. 2008. "The Contemporary Implications of the Russo-Japanese War: A Japanese Perspective." In *The Treaty of Portsmouth and Its Legacies,* ed. Steven Ericson and Allen Hockley, 157–82. Hanover: Dartmouth College Press.

Tolstoy, Leo. 1904. *Tolstoy's Letter on the Russo-Japanese War.* Boston: The American Peace Society.

Touval, Saadia. 1975. "Biased Intermediaries: Theoretical and Historical Considerations." *Jerusalem Journal of International Relations* 1: 51–69.

——. 1982. *The Peace Brokers: Mediation in the Arab-Israeli Conflict, 1948–1979.* Princeton: Princeton University Press.

——. 1994. "Why the UN Fails." *Foreign Affairs* 73(5): 44–57.

——. 2002. *Mediation in the Yugoslav Wars: The Critical Years, 1990–1995.* New York: Palgrave.

Touval, Saadia, and I. William Zartman. 1985. "Introduction: Mediation in Theory." In *International Mediation in Theory and Practice,* ed. Saadia Touval and I. William Zartman, 7–18. Boulder: Westview Press.

Trani, Eugene P. 1969. *The Treaty of Portsmouth: An Adventure in American Diplomacy.* Lexington: University of Kentucky Press.

Troester, Rod. 1996. *Jimmy Carter as Peacemaker: A Post-Presidential Biography.* Westport, Conn.: Praeger.

Uvin, Peter. 1998. *Aiding Violence: The Development Enterprise in Rwanda.* West Hartford, Conn.: Kumarian Press.

Vance, Cyrus. 1983. *Hard Choices: Critical Years in America's Foreign Policy.* New York: Simon and Schuster.

Wall, James A., Daniel Druckman, and Paul Diehl. 2002. "Mediation by International Peacekeepers." In *Studies in International Mediation,* ed. Jacob Bercovitch, 141–63. New York: Palgrave Macmillan.

Walt, Stephen M. 1987. *The Origins of Alliances.* Ithaca: Cornell University Press.

Walter, Barbara F. 1997. "The Critical Barrier to Civil War Settlement." *International Organization* 51(3): 335–64.

——. 2002. *Committing to Peace: The Successful Settlement of Civil Wars.* Princeton: Princeton University Press.

——. 2006. "Building Reputation: Why Governments Fight Some Separatists but Not Others." *American Journal of Political Science* 50(2): 335–64.

——. 2009. *Reputation and Civil War: Why Separatist Conflicts Are So Violent.* New York: Cambridge University Press.

Ward, Michael D., and Kristian Skrede Gleditsch. 2002. "Location, Location, Location: An MCMC Approach to Modeling the Spatial Context of War and Peace." *Political Analysis* 10(3): 244–60.

Weizman, Ezer. 1981. *The Battle for Peace.* New York: Bantam Books.

Werner, Suzanne. 1999a. "Choosing Demands Strategically: The Distribution of Power, the Distribution of Benefits, and the Risk of Conflict." *Journal of Conflict Resolution* 43(6): 705–26.

——. 1999b. "The Precarious Nature of Peace: Resolving the Issues, Enforcing the Settlement, and Renegotiating the Terms." *American Journal of Political Science* 43(3): 912–34.

Werner, Suzanne, and Amy Yuen. 2005. "Making and Keeping Peace." *International Organization* 59(2): 261–92.

White, John Albert. 1964. *The Diplomacy of the Russo-Japanese War.* Princeton: Princeton University Press.

Wilkenfeld, Jonathan, Kathleen Young, Victor Asal, and David Quinn. 2003. "Mediating International Crises: Cross-National and Experimental Perspectives." *Journal of Conflict Resolution* 47(3): 279–301.

Wilkenfeld, Jonathan, Kathleen J. Young, David M. Quinn, and Victor Asal. 2005. *Mediating International Crises.* New York: Routledge.

Wit, Joel S., Daniel B. Poneman, and Robert L. Gallucci. 2004. *Going Critical: The First North Korean Nuclear Crisis*. Washington, D.C.: Brookings Institution.

Wolff, David. 2008. "Riding Rough: Portsmouth, Regionalism, and the Birth of Anti-Americanism in Northeast Asia." In *The Treaty of Portsmouth and Its Legacies*, ed. Steven Ericson and Allen Hockley, 125–41. Hanover: Dartmouth College Press.

Wolford, Scott. 2007. "The Turnover Trap: New Leaders, Reputation, and International Conflict." *American Journal of Political Science* 51: 772–88.

Woodward, Susan. 1999. "Bosnia and Herzegovina: How Not to End Civil War." In *Civil Wars, Insecurity, and Intervention*, ed. Barbara F. Walter and Jack Snyder, 73–115. New York: Columbia University Press.

Yokote, Shinji. 2008. "Political Legacies of the Portsmouth Treaty." In *The Treaty of Portsmouth and Its Legacies*, ed. Steven Ericson and Allen Hockley, 106–22. Hanover: Dartmouth College Press.

Young, Oran R. 1967. *The Intermediaries: Third Parties in International Crises*. Princeton: Princeton University Press.

——. 1972. "Intermediaries: Additional Thoughts on Third Parties." *Journal of Conflict Resolution* 16(1): 51–65.

Zartman, I. William. 1985. *Ripe for Resolution: Conflict and Intervention in Africa*. New York: Oxford University Press.

Zartman, I. William, and Saadia Touval. 1985. "International Mediation: Conflict Resolution and Power Politics." *Journal of Social Issues* 41(2): 27–45.

Zimmerman, Warren. 1996. Origins of a Catastrophe: Yugoslavia and Its Destroyers. New York: Times Books.

Index

Note: Page numbers followed by *f* or *t* indicate figures and tables.